D0290728

FEMALE INTELLIGENCE

TAMMY M. PROCTOR

FEMALE INTELLIGENCE

Women and Espionage in the First World War

New York University Press • *New York and London*

NEW YORK UNIVERSITY PRESS
New York and London

© 2003 by New York University

Library of Congress Cataloging-in-Publication Data
Proctor, Tammy M., 1968-
Female intelligence : women and espionage
in the First World War / Tammy M. Proctor
p. cm.
Includes bibliographical references and index.
ISBN 0-8147-6693-5 (cloth : alk. paper)
1. World War, 1914-1918—Secret service—
Great Britain.   2. Women spies—Great Britain—
History—20th century.   I. Title.
D639.S7P76   2003
940.4'8641'082—dc21   2003000908

New York University Press books are printed on acid-free paper,
and their binding materials are chosen for strength and durability.

Manufactured in the United States of America

10 9 8 7 6 5 4 3 2 1

Contents

	Preface	vii
	List of Illustrations	xi
	List of Abbreviations	xiii
	Timeline	xv
	Introduction	1
1	Intelligence before the Great War	7
2	DORA's Women and the Enemy within Britain	29
3	Women behind the Scenes	53
4	Soldiers without Uniforms	75
5	Spies Who Knew How to Die	99
6	Intimate Traffic with the Enemy	123
	Conclusion: "Perpetual Concubinage to Your King and Country"	145
	Notes	151
	Bibliography	183
	Index	199
	About the Author	205

Preface

Female intelligence workers of the First World War might seem an odd topic for a social historian of British youth to discover, but, in fact, I was led to women spies by my study of Britain's Girl Guides. In 1997, as I was finishing my manuscript on the history of guiding and scouting in interwar Britain, I ran across some interesting descriptions of Girl Guides that had been employed at the British War Office. I knew that Girl Guides had done war work, but I was astounded to find that adolescent girls had been entrusted with reports and secret memoranda at Military Intelligence 5, Counterespionage (MI5) headquarters in London, one of the major secret offices in the British government. What began as an interesting idea for an article on girls' employment at MI5 became a book-length study of women's significant contributions to the development and history of British intelligence during the World War I.

Historians rely not only on voices from the past but also rely on good counsel and assistance from those around them. The librarians and experts in their fields who shared their knowledge with me were especially helpful with this project, including Scott Taylor at the Russell Bowen Collection, Lauinger Library at Georgetown University, Mitch Yockelson and Rick Peuser at the National Archives and Records Administration (NARA), Andrew Perry at the Post Office Heritage Centre (Consignia), Paul Moynihan at the Scout Association, and Emmanuel Debruyne at Centre d'Etudes et de Documentation Guerre et Sociétés contemporaines (CEGES). In addition, I am grateful to the staffs of the Bibliothèque Marguerite Durand, the British Library, the Churchill College Archives in Cambridge, the Department of Documents at the Imperial War Museum, the Library of Congress, the Ohio State University Library, the Public Library of Cincinnati, the Public Record Office at Kew Gardens, the Salle Ulysse Capitaine at the Central Library in Liège, the Salon des Documents at the Archives Générales du Royaume in

Brussels, and the Service historique de l'armée de terre, Château de Vincennes in Paris. Closer to home, I would like to thank those at Wittenberg University's Thomas Library who helped with interlibrary loans, reference inquiries, and strange requests. Thanks to Gina Entorf, Ken Irwin, Lori Judy, Alisa Mizikar, and Suzanne Smailes.

I would also like to thank everyone who has discussed the book with me, read chapters, or provided necessary information, including Jim Beach, Emmanuel Debruyne, Vince DiGirolamo, Leen Engelen, Malia Formes, Susan Grayzel, Beatrix Hoffman, Ben Lammers, April Masten, Scott Sandage, Susanne Terwey, and Molly Wood. Thanks to the Wittenberg University Works in Progress Group, especially David Barry, Marcia Frost, Jim Huffman, Linda Lewis, Amy Livingstone, Miguel Martinez-Saenz, Nancy McHugh, Rochelle Millen, Rebecca Plante, Don Reed, and Robert Smith. Also, my gratitude goes to VICKI-Spice: Carol Engelhardt, Barry Milligan, Chris Oldstone-Moore, and Elizabeth Teare. Special gratitude goes to Jenny Macleod and Pierre Purseigle for their organization of an outstanding conference on the First World War in Lyon in September 2001. Also, New York University Press has been supportive from the beginning of the project: thanks to Niko Pfund, Eric Zinner, and Emily Park.

Financial support from Wittenberg University and Lakeland College helped me complete the research for this project between 1997 and 2002; I appreciate the generosity of those institutions in supporting European research. In addition to monetary support, the history faculty at both Wittenberg and Lakeland have provided emotional and intellectual support for my research and teaching. Thanks to Tony Peffer and Rich Wixon, as well as Charles Chatfield, Bob Cutler, Margaret DeButy, Dar Brooks Hedstrom, Joe O'Connor, Dick Ortquist, Scott Rosenberg, and Tom Taylor. Students at these institutions have also contributed to the development of this book, and I would like to thank all those who have provided feedback, newspaper clippings, and ideas over the years. In particular, my gratitude goes to Matt Kull and Shobi Landes for reading chapters, and to my long-suffering and excellent faculty aide, Jessie Zawacki. Jessie translated some German passages, compiled bibliographic research, searched through several years of *New York Times* issues, took notes, and read chapters over the course of two years. I would also like to thank Maureen Fry, director of the Wittenberg Writing Workshop, for reading and making editorial suggestions on the whole manuscript.

In the end, my most profound debt of gratitude is to my family for reading sections of the book, asking about its progress, forgiving my long gaps without visiting, and supporting my work with kind words and interest. Thanks to Eleanor Proctor, Carole and Rex McGuire, Gayla and Rob Rich, Dennis and Anne Proctor, Don and Suzy Proctor, Charlie Greninger, and all my nieces and nephews. Also, my gratitude goes to the Shirley clan: Brenda, Johnnie, Terry, Karen, Rachael, Jonathan, Lisa, and Mike. To Todd Shirley, who endured countless war memorials, tiny Belgian towns, and possible head rebaking in Eeklo, I will just say thanks.

List of Illustrations

Cartoon from *Punch* (2 September 1914), 202.   36

Cartoon from *Punch* (21 October 1914), 343.   37

MI5 cartoon (1919)—Girl Guides   58

MI5 cartoon (1919)—"Kill That File"   65

Map showing extent of *La Dame Blanche* network   80

Chart showing ages of Battalion III, *La Dame Blanche*   82

Chart showing occupations of Battalion III, *La Dame Blanche*   83

Photograph of Gabrielle de Monge   88

Photograph of *La Dame Blanche* memorial in Liège   97

Edith Cavell propaganda postcard   103

Edith Cavell monument, London   108

Edith Cavell monument, Norwich   109

Stavelot Monument   114

Gabrielle Petit portrait   117

Gabrielle Petit monument, Brussels   118

Mata Hari as a dancer before the war   128

Mata Hari in 1917 before her execution   129

List of Abbreviations

AEF American Expeditionary Force

ARA Aliens Restrictions Act (Great Britain)

BEF British Expeditionary Force

BEM British Empire Medal

BNSA British Nationality and Status of Aliens Act

CBE Commander of the British Empire

CIA Central Intelligence Agency (United States)

CID Criminal Investigation Department (Great Britain)

CRB Commission for Relief in Belgium

DMI Director of Military Intelligence (Great Britain)

DMO Director of Military Operations (Great Britain)

DORA Defence of the Realm Acts (Great Britain)

FIC Foreign Intelligence Committee (Great Britain)

GHQ General Headquarters (British Army)

IB Intelligence Branch (Great Britain)

ID Intelligence Department (Great Britain)

KGB Komitet Gosudarstvennoi Bezopasnoti
(Soviet State Security Committee)

MBE Member of the British Empire

MI1B Military Intelligence, Enemy Wireless (Great Britain)

MI1C   Military Intelligence, Foreign Secret Service (Great Britain)

MI5   Military Intelligence, Counterespionage (Great Britain)

MI7   Military Intelligence, Press Control (Great Britain)

MI9   Military Intelligence, Postal Censorship Branch (Great Britain)

MO5   Military Intelligence, Counterespionage (Great Britain)

NID   Naval Intelligence Department (Great Britain)

OBE   Officer of the British Empire

OSS   Office of Strategic Services (United States)

SIS   Secret Intelligence Service (Great Britain)

T&S   Topographical and Statistical Department (Great Britain)

WAAC   Women's Army Auxiliary Corps (Great Britain)

WAAF   Women's Auxiliary Air Force (Great Britain)

WPS   Women's Police Service (Great Britain)

Timeline

PREWAR Erkstine Childers's *Riddle of the Sands* published (1903)

Aliens Act (1905)

William Le Queux's *The Invasion of 1910* published (1906)

Creation of the British Secret Service Bureau (1909)

Official Secrets Act (1911)

1914 Germans invade Belgium (August 3)

United Kingdom declares war on Germany (August 4)

Aliens Restriction Act (August 5)

Defence of the Realm Act (August 5)

The first enemy aliens interned in United Kingdom (August)

Postal Censorship Branch (MI9) hires women workers (September)

Creation of the Commission for Relief in Belgium (October)

MI5 Registry staffed entirely by women (November)

Edith Cavell hides her first two soldiers (November)

1915 Louise de Bettignies hired by the British (February)

Sinking of the *Lusitania* (May 7)

Major anti-alien riots in England (May)

Internment of all enemy alien males in Britain (May)

Edith Cavell executed in Belgium (October)

1916 Military Service Act (January)

Creation of the Directorate of Military Intelligence (January)

Battle of Verdun begins (February)

Gabrielle Petit executed in Belgium (April)

Battle of the Somme begins (July)

1917 United States enters WWI (April)

La Dame Blanche formally affiliates with the British (July)

Elise Grandprez shot in Belgium (July)

Leonie Rameloo and Emilie Schattemann shot in Belgium (September)

Mata Hari executed in France (October)

British government begins rationing sugar (December)

1918 German Spring Offensive (March)

Billing libel trial opens in London (May)

Louise de Bettignies dies in Germany (September)

Women prisoners at Siegburg released by revolutionaries (October)

Armistice (November)

1919 Demobilization of women war workers and soldiers begins in Europe

Introduction

I was a Secret Service agent, not a ridiculous young girl.
—Marthe McKenna, *I Was a Spy* (1932)

BETWEEN THE FORMAL CREATION of the permanent British Secret Service Bureau in 1909 and the war demobilization of 1919, more than six thousand women served in either civil or military occupations as members of the British intelligence community. These women performed a variety of tasks, and they represented an astonishing diversity of nationality, age, and class. From sixteen-year-old English Girl Guides to octogenarian Belgian grandmothers, women enabled the government to develop a modern, professional intelligence service. In fact, the operation of large-scale intelligence during the war was absolutely dependent on the availability of women workers, yet these women were in a paradoxical position. Barred from voting and holding political office, women in Britain could not even hold a permanent civil service job if they were married; however, these same women were being entrusted with state secrets and national security as employees of intelligence organizations.

This book examines both the powerful cultural images of the woman spy and the realities of women's intelligence work during the period of the British Secret Service's expansion and professionalization—the First World War.

Both men and women had been involved in information gathering prior to World War I, but intelligence did not assume its modern form until it had been shaped by the events of 1914 to 1918. Despite the historic use of women for information gathering and espionage purposes, as long as state intelligence remained intermittent, underfunded, and amateur, women existed only behind the scenes and on the fringes of

1

espionage activity. Women had been used as informants and spies prior to 1914, but only in small-scale operations and on a rather informal basis. Their activities were useful, but not central to the intelligence gathering of the state until the advent of the massive information-gathering bureaucracies that accompanied the development of mechanized mass warfare of the First World War. Only after civilian involvement in war increased and the investigation of its citizenry expanded did the British government seek the work of more women.

The women sought as necessary workers were not above suspicion, especially because government officials defined espionage as an internal threat that was tied to sexual perversion and moral corruption—both problems that were associated with women. Targeted as part of this construction of the enemy within, women still staffed the surveillance operations that the government used to track such subversive activity. When across Europe war was declared in 1914 and again in 1939, and with the advent of a perpetual militarized state during the Cold War, the rapidly ballooning bureaucracies of the secret state needed women's labor power. In short, without the exploitation of cheaper female labor, the British government could not have created the vast networks of surveillance that yielded hundreds of thousands of pages detailing the activities of enemy aliens, domestic dissidents, and suspected spies between 1914 and 1918. The modern system of counterespionage and secrecy in Britain was built and organized partly through the labor of the women employed during the Great War.[1] But why was this secret information gathering necessary?

During the war, the British government's anxiety grew over the movement of information and people within Britain and across its borders. Port controls were transformed into interrogation centers, passports were issued for the first time after 1915, and civilians were limited in their access to coasts and military installations. The British government instituted much of this curtailing of its citizens' freedoms through the Defence of the Realm Act of 1914 (DORA) and its later amendments. DORA allowed the government to regulate the lives of its citizenry in unprecedented ways, ranging from shortened pub business hours to curfews for married women. People accepted the invasion of their privacy in the interest of safety and national security.[2] The environment of secrecy and the fears regarding enemies of the state created and sustained by DORA also sparked the development of special wartime offices to catch spies and traitors. These offices included the cable, press, and postal censorship divisions of the civil service as well as the code/cipher offices for listening to enemy transmissions. Women were hired in large numbers to staff these organizations, and they proved essential to their successful operation, especially given the discrepancies between the size of the bureaucracies' tasks and the rudimentary technology they had available.

The war not only witnessed the entry of women into formal intelligence work, but also brought about the birth of some of the most powerful twentieth-century cultural images of female spies and male intelligence officers, with Mata Hari as one of its most famous icons. In creating a professional and permanent intelligence industry between 1909 and 1919, the British government emphasized that the professional agent was male, cool under pressure, and a loyal soldier for the state. Many of the early secret service chiefs were former military officers, and these men hired like-minded men as their subordinates. Against this model of the new intelligence agent, the foreign, sexualized, female spy became a useful foil in media, fiction, and popular imagination. Sexy female spy-prostitutes and cocky, but professional, male operatives have proven to be enduring images of spies and still pervade film and fiction about espionage in the twenty-first century. Even the International Spy Museum in Washington, D.C. features an exhibit on women spies that has at its center a boudoir with a phantom Mata Hari's face speaking from a mirror. The explicitly gendered vision of intelligence that emerged during the First World War has served to erase the crucial role of women in shaping and staffing the emerging intelligence industry. Their real roles as intelligence officers, field agents, clerical workers, and supervisors have been lost as popular culture has celebrated the mostly mythical female "vamp."

As both a labor history of espionage and intelligence workers and as a cultural examination of the gendering of espionage during World War I, this book restores female intelligence to the history of World War I.[3] Using personal accounts and letters, official documents, and newspaper reports, in the following pages I will challenge different and apparently contradictory understandings of gender in the competing spheres of espionage activity. By fusing traditional studies of intelligence networks with social and cultural history sources, it is possible to examine the invisible functioning of the secret service in wartime. Often, histories of intelligence, military strategy, societies, and women have not overlapped. Past histories of British intelligence would best be

4

described as intellectual and diplomatic studies of policy.[4] Using government records and correspondence, scholars have delved into the intricate world of official secrets and high diplomacy, while histories of women spies have tended to focus specifically on individual biographies and cultural representations.[5] Scholars of World War I sometimes mention intelligence and espionage, but usually as footnotes to discussions of military campaigns or in the context of spy panics.[6]

This book fills gaps in the field of the history of espionage by approaching the study of intelligence in three new ways. First, espionage has often been portrayed as a male-dominated profession, while the women who have worked and died in the intelligence business have been largely ignored. Utilizing government and private records, I ask new questions regarding women's and men's actual experiences and the gendered perceptions of their utility for the state. Second, my story focuses on a period that has been given little attention by other scholars of intelligence: pre–Cold War Britain. By examining the formative years of military intelligence and the impact of the First World War on this system, I can document the professionalization of this new intelligence activity and its acceptance by the public as a necessary function in wartime and peace. Last, by using records from several nations, this book reconstructs the cross- cultural workings of the British intelligence network during wartime. Human intelligence gathering relied on the labor of men and women from a variety of language, class, and national backgrounds, and this study seeks to capture the nature of this collaboration. Sources in Britain, France, Belgium, and the United States demonstrate that women were involved in most areas of the wartime intelligence networks, working for both the British civil government and branches of the military. In addition to the labor of British women on the home front, women of other nationalities were recruited to work as everything from field couriers to cryptographers to clerks. Newspapers, posters, films, and popular fiction provide insight into the cultural constructions and gendered nature of espionage during and after World War I.

Scholars of women and the civilian experience in war have recently begun to examine women spies and their cultural meaning by studying individual female spies.[7] These works provide balanced views of the realities of women's lives while simultaneously examining the powerful cultural images their names evoke. Although these scholars interrogate and expose the archetypal women spies of popular imagination, some of these authors unintentionally feed the popular notion that only a few glamorous or exceptional women became involved in wartime intelligence, and that they were virtually alone in this pursuit. This view of a few "great" women in espionage, oddly enough, reinforces sensational studies of women spies published in the 1930s and 1950s.[8] Such romantic visions of seductive women spies abound in popular fiction and films, but many of the women who assumed dangerous jobs in the field worked as soldiers not seductresses. The British Army and civil intelligence authorities hired women of many nationalities to carry messages, gather information, and smuggle men throughout occupied Belgium, France, and other theatres of war. Individual women such as Louise de Bettignies and Gabrielle Petit died and were celebrated for their participation in these activities, but hundreds of other women quietly pursued their work as agents until the armistice.

Although women were quickly released from their wartime occupations in intelligence networks after the war ended in 1919, many were awarded civilian and military war medals and some even received pensions. Women's participation in World War I intelligence organizations set a precedent for their later work in WWII and established their important roles in espionage. Only a few women remained working in government intelligence departments during the interwar period, but women were hired immediately in even greater numbers for service in World War II, suggesting that women's participation in intelligence between 1914 and 1918 had a lasting effect. Women spies of the Great War both enabled the creation of the modern intelligence industry and gave the twentieth century its popular and enduring images of female secret service agents—cultural icons that still inform our visions of gender, secrecy, and sexuality today.

I

Intelligence before the Great War

Women have many good qualifications for spying and would doubt-
less be again used in war time as they have been the past, and as they
still are in peace time. But they have weak points, and they can seldom
disguise their cleverness. . . .

—Robert Baden-Powell,
Aids to Scouting for N.C.O.s and Men (1914)

OFTEN DESCRIBED BY HISTORIANS as the world's "second oldest profession," espionage holds a fascination for scholars and audiences alike. Historically, female spies have been categorized either as self-sacrificing patriots bent on saving their countries or as whores with an inherent character weakness driving them to treason and betrayal for the sake of money or fame. In the popular imagination, women, seen in the Western tradition as having natural skills for duplicity, disguised their cleverness and used their sexuality to gain knowledge. Women, foreigners, the poor, and the patriotic (albeit men willing to sacrifice their virtue) became the spies of choice in popular culture. In short, professional spies were seen as villainous characters, part of an "ignominious tribe" with suspect morals and motives.[1]

The use and popular understanding of spies changed in the twentieth century, however. Those men and women who had earlier been seen as shady characters increasingly gained "professional" status as agents and clerks for the emerging intelligence community. As Thomas Fergusson points out, by 1914 the British "had acquired (or [were] in the process of acquiring) many of the characteristics commonly associated with 'modern' intelligence organizations."[2] Such characteristics included state-funded information gathering, storage and analysis of intelligence, investigation of internal security threats, and use of technology for surveillance.[3] Modern intelligence, both overt and covert, evolved as politicians, soldiers, and the general public sought to shape its meaning and structure. As this established system of intelligence emerged, an image of the sexual division of labor arose of those employed for secrets work. An explicitly male, "cool under pressure," professional intelligence operative functioned in opposition to the sexualized "mata-hariesque" female spy. *Female Intelligence* explores the emergence of this cultural image and its implications for women in intelligence work.

To begin that examination I will provide a background for the study of World War I by looking at how espionage and information gathering functioned prior to 1914 in Britain. In particular, I will examine the broad outlines of British secret service work from the Elizabethan period to the Victorian period and the coming of age of intelligence after the Anglo-Boer War, as well as focus specifically on the role women played in these early organizations. Finally, I will explore the creation of the professional British Secret Service in 1909 and its fundamental need for educated labor, leading to its reliance on women during the Great War. From World War I to the present, women have maintained a formal presence in modern intelligence organizations both in Britain and around the world—but their participation has been far from easy.

THE "IGNOMINIOUS TRIBE" PRIOR TO 1909

There were few professional spies before World War I because Britain's intelligence gathering prior to the twentieth century, like that of many other European nations, was disorganized and intermittent. European monarchs used diplomatic posts to gather information from the early Middle Ages and before, but overseas paid spy networks were uncommon until the later Middle Ages and remained erratic.[4] Intelligence networks flourished most during civil conflicts and foreign wars—springing up out of military necessity—but informants and messengers were only temporary employees of Britain and its enemies. Armies needing reconnaissance in the field during the late Middle Ages developed a network of scout-spies directed by a scoutmaster. These military scouts often obtained information on the enemy from voluntary informants, but the amount of information was difficult to sift and use in a timely fashion.[5] Later, the Tudors developed some excellent intelligence networks during periods of conflict, most notably under Elizabeth I's spy-master, Sir Francis Walsingham,[6] but the existence of these organizations waxed and waned according to perceived threats from within Britain and abroad. In fact, intelligence gathering was not regularized in any way until the seventeenth century when Oliver Cromwell used state funds to develop a massive network of spies and informers.[7]

Government interest in small, permanent intelligence organizations only gained prominence in the seventeenth century as states centralized and developed new bureaucratic mechanisms. Most European nations began to develop "black chambers" for the examination of normal and ciphered messages and mail, and some political leaders also began to regularize their use of diplomatic spies. From the long-term use of spy-diplomats and members of the intelligentsia such as Samuel Pepys, Aphra Behn, and Daniel Defoe, to the use of paid police agents, governments tried to insure their control of domestic and foreign policy.[8] The European interest in formal intelligence was initially expressed in England through two connected practices: the scrutiny of the Royal Mail and the use of paid informants.

Beginning in the 1600s, the Royal Mail was opened and read by a "secret man" in order to gain intelligence regarding seditious or treasonous activities before being resealed and sent. The office went so far as to manufacture counterfeit wax seals to cover evidence of tampering. What started with a single person opening mail became two organized offices that by the eighteenth century routinely examined foreign and domestic correspondence even in times of peace.[9] The post office's secret surveillance also included rudimentary code breaking and deciphering of messages. Clerks were hired for this task, and one expert cryptographer, Oxford mathematician Dr. John Wallis worked as a freelance code breaker for the government from the 1640s to the 1670s.[10] This surveillance of mail through what later became known as the post office's "Secret Office" was an important seventeenth-century intelligence tool that has remained viable today, especially in times of war.

The seventeenth century intelligence practice of using paid informants involved the operation of networks of couriers and spies both within Britain and on the European continent. This work was directed from the Office of the Secretaries of State, but responsibility for intelligence was often broader. Many agents who worked for the state were ex-soldiers, but the mix of spies seemed to be remarkably diverse and included people of different social classes, sexes, occupations, and nationalities. Some were professionals, but amateur spies often volunteered as well.[11] But even these networks were typically small-scale and inefficient; historian Alan Marshall estimates that the total number of agents working during the Restoration period averaged about eighteen to twenty per year.[12]

The real precursors to the establishment of modern intelligence seems to have been the French Revolution and the Napoleonic Wars. With the rise of revolutionary ferment in the American colonies in the 1770s and especially in France after 1789, the British government decided to halt domestic subversion and promote the restoration of the monarchy in France. War and the fear of war spurred the growth of intelligence and surveillance institutions, setting a precedent for later generations of Britons to turn to these devices when war threatened again in 1899, 1914, and 1939. In the eighteenth century, a series of parliamentary acts led to civil surveillance and the creation of a foreign secret service by the mid-1790s. Three specific actions by Parliament were crucial in the development of surveillance organizations in Britain and provided a model for later generations of government officials who enacted similar restrictions during World War I.

First, the Police Act of June 1792 allowed for the creation of "stipendiary magistrates" to infiltrate political gatherings and to report seditious or treasonous activities. These secret police, whose job was mainly to prevent revolution, were drawn from the urban intelligentsia and reported to the King not to Parliament. Their work involved listening at political gatherings, frequenting taverns known to host debating societies, and generally maintaining "civil law and order."[13] Widely mistrusted by the populace, the public saw these spy-police as sneaks.[14] This perception proved true in 1793 after the police arrested leading radicals from the Society for Constitutional Information on flimsy evidence from planted informers who had infiltrated the society. Eventually, the police were able to rely less on spy-police informers by persuading Parliament to suspend some suspects' rights.[15]

The suspension of the Habeas Corpus Act, the second important Parliamentary action, in May of 1793 removed the right of subjects of the King to be free from illegal imprisonment. King Louis XVI had been executed in January 1793 leaving France entirely in the hands of republicans and at war with Britain by late spring of that year. Fueling the fears of elites in Britain that revolution could spread across the English Channel, Prime Minister William Pitt reported to the House of Commons on May 16 the arrest of prominent republicans in Britain. He followed his announcement with a request for action to stop the "total subversion of the Constitution, the annihilation of Parliament, and the destruction of the King himself."[16] It took only two days for the legislation suspending *habeas corpus* to pass, making it possible to imprison suspects without trial and mounting a significant attack on the Constitution.

The third and last major Parliamentary action in establishing a rudimentary wartime intelligence system was the passage of the Alien Act on January 8, 1793. Modeled on similar French legislation, the procedure mandating the registration of foreigners was new to Britain but quickly became acceptable in time of war. Under the Alien Act's provisions, all foreign residents or visitors had to register with the government at a police office or port, and all *habeas corpus* rights for foreigners were forfeited.[17]

The establishment of civil magistrates, suspension of basic *habeas corpus* rights, and mandated registration of foreigners heralded a new era in Britain. The suspension of civil rights and the government's ability to control and watch its population became crucial tools for the budding intelligence establishments of the late 1700s, reappearing in later conflicts. Although many officials worried about the impact of this legislation on individual rights and constitutional guarantees, they fretted more about the devastating effects of a possible revolution, infrequently voicing their qualms. Other governmental legislation focused on the danger from reformers and revolutionaries specifically, such as the Seditious Meetings Bill (1795) and the acts of 1799 and 1800 banning certain political and labor organizations.[18] The passing of these parliamentary acts and the ongoing practice of opening mail in the Secret Office are British intelligence practices in their embryonic stages.

In addition to legislative measures at home, the government protected its interests abroad by putting into place a network of couriers and informants in Britain, France, and Switzerland as well as in other continental nations. The intentions behind the informant network were to undermine revolutionary ideas and to support royalist activities. During the Peninsular Wars, commander of the British forces the Duke of Wellington, extended this system by paying informants and sending out disguised officers for reconnaissance. Many historians have noted the ways in which the operations side of European and British army organization was fundamentally changed by the Napoleonic conflicts, but the art of intelligence was also transformed during the years of continental warfare from 1793 to 1815.[19]

The Congress of Vienna in 1815 marked the end of the wartime state, and government surveillance gradually relaxed. Most security branches of government continued to use informers but focused instead on the more immediate domestic threat of anti-industrial agitators. In particular, the British police tried to expose the Luddites, whose destruction of machines and factories between 1811 and 1813 caused fear and financial woes for middle-class industrialists. After the Luddite threat had passed, government agents infiltrated other subversive groups such as labor agitators, Irish nationalists, and anarchists.[20] As the century progressed, however, the mechanisms of state intelligence and surveillance were dismantled or reformed, not to be reinstituted until World War I. The Post Office's mail censorship was abolished after a diplomatic incident in the 1840s, and the Alien Act—although not formally repealed until 1872—was no longer necessary.[21] Intelligence collection had receded so far into the background of government concerns by the 1850s that at the outset of the Crimean War (1854–1856) intelligence witnessed some terrible blunders. The intelligence failures can be explained by the state being unaware of the uses of intelligence as well as the dismal performance and state of unpreparedness of the army.[22] The 1857 Indian Mutiny-Rebellion that led to the highly- publicized deaths of men, women, and children civilians also pointed to weaknesses in British information gathering on local politics and sentiments in the British colonies.[23]

The Crimean War and the Indian Mutiny-Rebellion, often depicted as blights on British military traditions, led to a rapid reorganization of intelligence and information-gathering groups. Out of the melee came the Topographical and Statistical Department (T&S), an intelligence organization developed in 1855 in the midst of the Crimean conflict.[24] After the war, T&S, which was designed to collect maps and statistics about foreign countries, produced excellent domestic ordnance survey maps but gathered virtually no information on foreign armies. T&S stumbled along until the early 1870s when the department was again reorganized to expand its duties and the Intelligence Branch (IB, later renamed ID) was created. It was not until 1887 that the position of Director of Military Intelligence was created.[25] Additionally, the first formal Criminal Investigation Department (CID) for domestic policing was founded in 1877, followed by the creation of the Special Branch of the London Metropolitan Police in 1887. Both of these offices remained small, and the Special Branch concerned itself mostly with Irish agitation.[26] The British Admiralty followed the Army in developing the small Foreign Intelligence Committee (FIC) in 1883 and the larger Naval Intelligence Department (NID) in 1886.[27] These Victorian intelligence agencies and departments were small-scale, largely male endeavors staffed by soldiers and policemen, and they were maintained as peacetime departments with tiny budgets.[28]

In addition to Victorian intelligence changes, the British government set out to reform the Army and to fix the problems that had emerged during the conflicts of the 1850s. A multitude of committees and commissions studied the problems and made recommendations for change. Intelligence underwent scrutiny, as did military operations; the whole army's public image and recruitment began to be reformed. From a brutal band of men charged with enforcing domestic peace, the British army was transformed between the 1850s and 1860s into a respectable group necessary to Britain's security.

What led to this new articulation of the British soldier and his purpose? Most historians suggest that a combination of the increased ability of the police to handle civil disputes, the sympathetic press coverage of common soldiers serving in the Crimean War, and the sense of fear accompanying the Indian Mutiny of 1857 helped reform public sentiment.[29] Also important was the growth of "muscular Christianity," which rejected passive models of manliness and called for evangelical armies of God.[30] By the 1880s, imperial literature celebrated the exploits of hero- generals and common soldiers alike, and war assumed a distant and glamorous aspect for many men and women in Britain. As Edward M. Spiers notes in his excellent study of the late Victorian Army, "The army enjoyed unprecedented popular appeal and esteem during the last three decades of the nineteenth century."[31]

Accompanying the changes in regular army organization came an important shift in views of the role of civilians—both male and female—in military conflict. Volunteer forces were recruited after 1859 and many working-class and middle-class men joined these reserve forces over the next forty years.[32] In addition, the work of Florence Nightingale and her friend Jane Shaw Stewart helped create the first well-publicized, if not highly successful, female nursing service of the Victorian army in 1861.[33] The new Victorian army, its intelligence apparatus, and its developing professional nurses corps would all be tested as the nineteenth century came to a close with the Anglo-Boer War in South Africa.

WOMEN DISGUISING THEIR CLEVERNESS

Although Florence Nightingale's work is often celebrated as a revolutionary change in women's roles in war, this interpretation is misleading because women have never been absent from theatres of war. Women have wielded arms in battle, suffered the devastation of enemy invasion, and served armies in a variety of capacities. The women who have assisted armies, often labeled "camp followers," have been a particularly vital support group in times of war. Women not only performed service tasks as laundresses, cooks, and provisioners, but also provided emotional support for soldiers as their wives and prostitutes. For example, the British and German forces that came to North America to fight in the American Revolution brought thousands of women with them as auxiliaries. In May of 1777, there was one woman "camp follower" for every eight men in the British army in New York; by 1781, that number had risen to one woman for every four and one-half men.[34]

Women have also long been associated with information gathering and dissemination, whether through informal neighborhood networks of gossip or through the formal work of political espionage. Women have provided financial and political capital to various causes, often manipulating kinship networks to their advantage. Even a cursory look at aristocratic women's power brokerage in the medieval and Tudor/Stuart periods shows the ways in which women's behind-the-scenes efforts could prove useful to political and military leaders.

Evidence suggests that women performed supporting roles as informants, especially upper-class women who could easily and informally gather information in diplomatic and social gatherings. Women wielded considerable influence through familial and church patronage, and many used diplomatic gatherings as platforms for their own ambitions. Much of aristocratic intelligence gathering must be set in the context of a larger role of women in European state building.[35]

Non-aristocratic women could be drawn into roles as informers and couriers as well.[36] Women of modest means played a different kind of role in the intelligence drama of the early modern period. Through employment in offices and households as clerks, servants, governesses, or companions, women from a variety of backgrounds played a role in gathering political and military intelligence in European history. One such example is the French female agent employed as a cleaning woman in a German embassy in the 1890s; she found the initial note that began the infamous 1894 Alfred Dreyfus spy trial.[37] Some of these women took advantage of their invisibility to pass information, to participate in government plots, or to harbor fugitives. One woman, Jane Bradley, reported a plot against the government in 1679 while working as a barmaid at the Heaven Tavern in Westminster. For her role as informant, Bradley received a "gold coin" and permission to continue reporting suspicious activities. Less than a year later, Bradley uncovered another plot to discredit a nobleman, but found herself on trial as part of a larger conspiracy when she reported her findings. Eventually Bradley was acquitted.[38] Female agents like Bradley participated in small ways in the improvised network of espionage and intelligence of the seventeenth century, but their roles are not generally well documented.[39] The work of carrying information or gathering intelligence was dangerous and poorly paid, but especially during the English Civil War people worked as agents out of personal, family, or religious loyalty. As Alan Marshall has noted of the women employed as spies during this period:

> A number of women were also caught up in the wartime espionage trade and all too often took graver risks than the men by passing through enemy lines. They sometimes concealed information about their persons in the, possibly vain, hopes that the licentious soldiery would not molest them.[40]

If these women managed to escape molestation, they still had to worry about imprisonment as well as psychological and physical torture if caught by enemy forces. Marshall notes the case of one woman caught spying who lost several fingers to an interrogation that included torture with lit matches.[41]

The best-known example of a seventeenth-century woman spy was by no means the most successful of these early female agents. Hired by the British government, author and playwright Aphra Behn reported from Antwerp in the late 1660s. Under the code name "Astrea," Behn worked with male spies to gather information and send reports in cipher back to London in exchange for money.[42] Initially paid only £50 in

1666, Behn received written instructions to contact a freewheeling adventurer named William Scot in the United Provinces [Dutch]. In addition, her superiors asked Behn (with the assistance of Scot) to provide military and commercial information on the Dutch and to organize a group of informants and correspondents willing to report to the British government. Behn appears to have been rather ineffective in her activities, falling prey to Scot's manipulation and lapsing into serious debt. Apparently, Behn had to pawn jewelry in order to continue her mission and appealed to her superiors for another £100 for her living expenses.[43] Her real success came from her writing not from espionage.

Women could take on highly important roles in intelligence in times of war. Women's freedom from military conscription and their ability to move about in occupied territories made them ideal—but rare—agents. Women took on these roles in the domestic and foreign secret service networks developed during the revolutionary and Napoleonic periods. Women were particularly useful as international and domestic couriers—sometimes in disguise—because their intellectual abilities were often discounted by enemy forces. Female agents and couriers were drawn from a variety of national and class backgrounds, and their ages and marital status varied from young, unmarried women to middle- aged matrons to older widows.

One group of couriers operating in France and Britain included several women in notably important roles operated in France and Britain. Organized by Louis Bayard, a young Frenchman hired in 1795 by the British government, this network was one of the most successful of the revolutionary period. One important courier in Bayard's organization was Mme. Arabella Williams, a "courier of distinction" living in Paris and the widow of a British soldier. Known as *le petit matelot* [the little sailor], the nearly fifty-year-old Williams often successfully disguised herself as a cabin boy by donning sailor's clothing. She carried money and messages and hosted British visitors at her home near the Ministry of Foreign Affairs in Paris. As historian Elizabeth Sparrow notes, "Trusted implicitly by British ministers, she sometimes carried large sums of specie (money) besides dispatches, and was doing this at least from the summer of 1797, although no record has been found of a British government salary until July 1799."[44] Eventually, Williams's frequent trips to Britain with large sums of money brought her to the attention of French officials, and she was arrested in May 1801 leaving no further historical record.[45]

Married women also served as couriers, carrying money or messages from the British government to their husbands abroad. These women had good reason to travel without suspicion and could safely correspond with their spouses. Records also show that women ran safe houses, gathered information working as actresses or servants, and even served as *estafettes* (mounted couriers) in northern France. Louis Bayard's large organization also housed women who betrayed the British cause and became double agents, including his own lover, *La Sablonnière* (the sandy one).[46]

In the relative peace of the nineteenth century, intelligence networks shrank, leaving women less visible as agents and couriers during the Victorian period. Also, the male preserves of the newly created police and state intelligence organizations allowed little room for women. Women, however, did continue to play a role in the development and definition of espionage and information gathering. Females continued to bolster British efforts as informers in Ireland and the British colonies. This "human intelligence" was vital in understanding local sentiments, uncovering plots, and establishing a strong British presence in an area. Paying for the "prattling of old ladies," as C. A. Bayly termed this practice, often meant the difference between the successful control of an area or its rebellion. For small fees, female marriage brokers, midwives, prostitutes, and vendors all contributed information to colonial authorities.[47]

Women's travels were another way that women contributed to the fortunes of state intelligence organizations in Britain. Victorian lady travelers often gathered local information, sketched sites they had visited, mapped their journeys, and kept journals with snippets of local life. Women travelers, many of whom were accomplished linguists, scientists, or scholars, pushed for the recognition of their work through the multitude of societies that dealt with colonial issues. These societies were often consulted by a government intelligence establishment that lacked concrete information about some of the places that were part of the British Empire by the turn of the century. As advisors, lecturers, and experts, women scholar-travelers helped map and describe the British Empire in the late nineteenth century, although no women were formally hired as intelligence officers until the twentieth century.[48]

Gertrude Bell was the first woman employed by British Intelligence as a political officer. Born in 1868 the daughter of a leading industrialist, Bell began her work as an amateur "lady" traveler in the Middle

East. Although British law did not permit her to get a degree, Bell was awarded first-class honors in modern history at Lady Margaret Hall in Oxford in the 1880s. She began traveling with her aunt and uncle in the late nineteenth century before beginning her own journeys. An avid Alpine climber and Arabic scholar, Bell had both the physical stamina and the intelligence to succeed as a solitary traveler in the Middle East. Her first desert journey was in 1900, and she traveled back to the eastern Mediterranean frequently until her death at her Baghdad home in 1926.[49] Soon after her first visit to Petra, Palmyra, and Syria, Bell provided photographs, notes, and maps to the government's topographical and statistical division. Given the tensions surrounding the "Eastern Question" (the crumbling Ottoman Empire) in the period leading up to the First World War, Bell's intimate knowledge and analysis of the people and places she visited made her a valuable resource. Although she clearly provided information to intelligence officials and to learned societies in Britain, her role was not formalized until World War I when she was hired alongside David Hogarth and T. E. Lawrence in the fledgling Arab Bureau founded in 1916.[50] By the summer of 1916, Bell was an army political officer attached to the Indian Expeditionary Force. Recognizing the shift in her status, Bell wrote of her appointment, "I believe I am to have pay, but fortunately I need not wear uniform! I ought to have white tabs [sign of rank], for I am under the Political Department. It's rather comic isn't it."[51] Comic or not, Bell's appointment as a formal intelligence agent in 1916 merely made official the long- standing practice of using women to gain information about enemies and friends. As British intelligence came of age in World War I, circumstances forced British officials to recognize the usefulness of women and begin to employ them in larger numbers.

SNARING SPIES AND SUSPICIOUS SUBJECTS, 1899–1914

The stage was set for the expansion of the British intelligence establishment with the Anglo-Boer War from 1899 to 1902, which would be the late-Victorian army's longest, bloodiest, and most expensive war.[52] The War Office called on volunteers to serve in the war, eventually employing about 448,000 troops and over one thousand women nurses.[53] The war exposed inefficiencies and problems in the army organization, supply structure, and tactics. Fourteen thousand of the 22,000 British that died during the three-year conflict died from disease and complications resulting from the unsanitary conditions prevalent in the army encampments.[54] In addition to the logistical problems that became apparent, the prewar intelligence that had been gathered proved to be wholly inadequate in preparing the army to face the Boers. Although Director of Military Intelligence Sir John Ardagh's office had issued reports on a possible war in South Africa, the War Office largely ignored his warnings. Also, his underfunded office could not begin to compile the necessary statistical, technical, and topographical information that would have helped the British effort.[55]

When the war began, army leadership made do with the small cache of information from the prewar period. Then, in July 1899, the War Office dispatched a tiny force of ten men who had experience in scouting and field intelligence. With Boers using guerilla tactics and depending on their superior knowledge of terrain, information became a crucial element for the British army's success. By November 1899, several of the original ten male officers were unavailable, having been besieged in settlements such as Mafeking and Kimberley. The information they had gathered and communicated was often underutilized, and government officials in London thought the intelligence officers were exaggerating the size of the Boer forces. It was not until the arrival of Lord Roberts in South Africa as commander in late-1899 that the British government addressed intelligence in a more sustained manner. By the middle of the war, Britain had an organized Field Intelligence Department, which employed 132 officers and thousands of male and female civilians of both British and African descent. Additionally, the government instituted rudimentary signal and cable censorship, a pigeon post for carrying information, and press/postal censorship to control information dissemination.[56] The Anglo-Boer War confirmed that effective military intelligence clearly depended on the use of local informants and close governmental observation of the civilian population.

The Anglo-Boer War also demonstrated the devastating impact of civilian involvement in modern warfare. The civilian armies deployed in the war included Boer farmers, African farmers and laborers, Boer women, and British volunteer soldiers. Boer women and children were particularly active as nurses and in combat and intelligence, serving the Boer commando units in a variety of roles.[57] More than 116,000 civilians suffered through internment in concentration camps run by the British during the course of the war. The camps were poorly run and danger-ously unsanitary, leading to high casualty rates for the detainees.[58] In short, beyond their organizational experience, British military officials gained important insight from 1899 to 1902 into the success of civilian internment, press and postal censorship, and effective intelligence gath-ering and processing during wartime. All of these measures would be introduced within Britain itself during the First World War.

After the Anglo-Boer War ended, the War Office moved quickly to reorganize and revitalize the army. In 1902, Prime Minister Arthur Bal-four created the Committee of Imperial Defence to address concerns from the war as well as the issues of conflict preparedness.[59] Along with a major overhaul of military operations came new developments in in-telligence. By 1904, the newly created Directorate of Military Opera-tions had four sections: strategy, foreign intelligence, special duties, and topography. This organization would control intelligence gathering for the next five years until the creation of the modern Security Services.[60]

The Anglo-Boer War awoke Britons to the problems in army organ-ization and intelligence and reinforced notions of popular Victorian militarism. Anne Summers writes that the Boer War created the prospect of a nation "organized as a fighting unit."[61] Rather than demonstrating the dangers of a militarized society and the problems of imperial control, the war reiterated for many people the need for a na-tion of citizens, male and female, willing to serve their countries. The war also pointed to the necessity of males and females from all eco-nomic classes participating in the national and imperial project, setting the stage for the development of the modern intelligence apparatus.

As the War Office concentrated on reorganizing its resources and forces after 1902, officials and social reformers in Britain fretted about national security, preparedness, and racial health at home and across the British Empire. Domestic anxiety mirrored larger imperial and in-ternational changes, such as Britain's waning global power and Ger-many's developing industrial strength and its new navy.[62] In particular, concerns focused on improving Britain's military strength and control-ling foreign influences in the country. By 1910, the British government had embraced the militarization process, not only reorganizing the reg-ular army, but also developing programs for civilians. Combining social engineering, moral reform, imperialism, efficiency, and character train-ing, militarized civilian organizations were developed to assuage concerns about national degeneration and foreign invasion. Women trained as nurses in Voluntary Aid Detachments (1909), the First Aid Nursing Yeomanry (1907), and in the Girl Guides (1910), while men and boys joined the Territorial Force (1908), Officer Training Corps (1908), and Cadet Corps (1908) to learn soldiering.[63] At schools after 1908, schoolchildren celebrated Empire Day, and both girls and boys rushed to join the new Boy Scout organization when a celebrated Boer War hero and former spy, Robert Baden-Powell, launched it at an experimental camp in 1907.[64]

Baden-Powell and other reformers were concerned with reports that in the nineteenth century birthrates had dropped but infant mortality rates had remained high. Social investigators had recorded poverty and disease in cities, and the military failures and inefficiency of the Anglo-Boer War exposed what seemed to be physical and moral weaknesses in Britain. These concerns with the health and vitality of Britain coalesced in calls for a reassertion of the virility and power of the nation.[65] Society's ills were described in medical terms by a new generation of eugenicists, psychologists, and social scientists who theorized that Britain was a nation in decline. Clearly, these writers argued, the nation needed to regenerate and revitalize itself through sacrifice and eventually war, but it also had to root out "disease" in society. Increasingly, that meant attacking those who were "different." Legislation and popular opinion targeted those of foreign birth as well as male homosexuals, female "hysterics," and those with mental or physical disabilities. By 1914, war was seen as perhaps the final "cure" or "cleansing" for Britain's social ills and internal weakness.[66]

A common focus for these anxieties regarding the perceived degeneration of the nation was the fictional image of the spy. The sheer number of spy narratives that appeared in the decade before the outbreak of World War I pointed to a deep-seated suspicion in prewar Britain that evil lurked and needed to be ferreted out.[67] Coupling fears about German invasion with uncertainties about foreign immigrants (or aliens) at home, the media and popular authors created a Britain that was "invaded by an army of fictional spies."[68] Using the "spy panic" to spur people from apathy to alarm, prewar writers such as Joseph Conrad and William Le Queux published detailed tales of the machinations of German spies intent on undermining and invading Britain. In his study of spy fiction, Cecil Degrotte Eby counted the number of invasions of

Britain in books written between 1870 and 1914. Germany invaded Britain forty-one times, France invaded eighteen times, and even the United States invaded Britain in one book.[69]

One of the earliest spy stories was George Chesney's 1871 *Battle of Dorking*, but perhaps the most important book in launching the "spy craze" was Erskine Childers's *The Riddle of the Sands* (1903), which follows the adventures of two amateur English spies who uncover a German invasion plot. William Le Queux made his living detailing the possible invasions and plans of the Germans in works such as *The Invasion of 1910* (1906) and *Spies for the Kaiser* (1909). One historian claims that "[Le Queux's] aim was to kindle in his readers a conviction that German agents were hard at work everywhere, reconnoitering beaches and preparing acts of sabotage."[70] Alfred Harmsworth (Lord Northcliffe) also did much to fuel the craze in his newspapers such as the *Daily Mail*. The spy-catchers in popular fiction were often ordinary individuals who knew their duty to their country and who shared characteristics of bravery, intelligence, and patriotism.[71] Although enemy spies hailing from Britain itself were depicted in spy fiction, the greater threats were foreigners that had infiltrated British society and betrayed their adopted homeland.

While the stories of espionage were mostly fictional, they were told as sensational and "realistic" yarns in the great numbers of cheap newspapers and serial magazines available in the late-nineteenth and early-twentieth centuries. In reality, many of these writers' fictional claims influenced British officials in the formation of a formal secret service. The seriousness with which the government saw the threats points to spy fiction's importance in shaping prewar popular and national opinion. Historian Niall Ferguson has cataloged a number of senior British officials who appear to have accepted the premise of much of this spy literature. One such official used letters from readers to William Le Queux to bolster his theories about a massive German spy network.[72]

Panikos Panayi has persuasively argued that official acceptance of the spy panic echoed a clear and popular anti-alien mentality in British society. Panayi examines anti-German sentiment expressed in the literature, while Susanne Terwey looks at how Jews in Britain were targeted in espionage literature as a particularly virulent domestic enemy. Fears of foreigners accompanied restrictive legislation aimed at immigrants hoping to settle in Britain. Initially, the 1905 Aliens Act—the first major restriction of entry into Britain since the 1820s—severely limited immigration into the United Kingdom.[73] Then, when Britain declared war on Germany in 1914, the Aliens Restriction Act was passed, further restricting the rights of those of foreign birth, leading to mandatory registration for all aliens and the internment of some immigrants.[74]

In addition to legislation, British public and private officials responded to calls for national regeneration and change. The government created new institutions, including volunteer programs for improving the health and readiness of men of service-age and reducing infant mortality, nurse training for women, and the British Secret Service.

The Secret Service (later known as MI5 and MI6) was developed in August 1909, after a flurry of activity from individuals and subcommittees within the British Admiralty, War Office, and Scotland Yard. The new service was to stand apart from other government agencies despite having connections with the Home and Foreign Offices, the War Office, and the Admiralty. Director of Military Operations J. S. Ewart recommended in a 1908 memo the creation of the Secret Service because of the need to locate foreign agents, examine mail, and watch for enemy sabotage in case of war. If such an agency successfully tracked foreigners, Ewart reasoned, they could be seized on the outbreak of a war. He asked, in short, "How far can the civil departments of the state assist the Admiralty and War Office in tracing and ascertaining the residences and vocations of foreigners in the coast districts and vicinity of London?"[75]

Lieutenant Colonel James Edmonds, head of the small counterintelligence office before 1909, also argued for a secret office to combat the dangers of German espionage when he testified before a Committee of Imperial Defence intelligence subcommittee in 1909. Chaired by Secretary of State for War R. B. Haldane, the subcommittee was charged with considering Britain's competitiveness in counterespionage and foreign intelligence gathering. The subcommittee had representatives from all major government war and surveillance agencies including the Admiralty, Home Office, Post Office, Foreign Office, Military Operations, Naval Operations, Treasury, Foreign Office, and Metropolitan Police. After several meetings in the spring and summer of 1909, the subcommittee recommended the creation of an independent Secret Service, which would coordinate with all government departments and serve as a depository of intelligence information and as an intermediary between other departments.[76] Only a handful of people knew of its existence. Phillip Knightley notes the importance of the sub-committee's work in defining the shape and secrecy of British intelligence:

> Once the idea of protecting the government from the dirty business of spying by having a non-existent intelligence service had gained acceptance, the next step was almost automatic: the non-existent service and way in which it was created had to become a deep secret, otherwise the whole point was lost. So the secrecy that was to run like a *leitmotiv* through the history of British Intelligence began immediately.[77]

After much discussion and correspondence, five men met on August 26, 1909, at Scotland Yard to found the new Secret Service under the Directorate of Military Operations with assistance from Scotland Yard.[78] By early 1910, the fledgling organization had two sections in separate offices: a domestic counterintelligence office under the leadership of Captain Vernon G. W. Kell—an army linguist with experience in a variety of foreign countries and in criminal investigation—and a foreign intelligence branch led by Commander Mansfield G. Smith Cumming—a well-traveled naval officer.[79] Kell's office became MI5 (Military Intelligence, section 5) in 1916, while Cumming's branch was renamed MI1C (Military Intelligence, section 1C). These small offices were shoestring operations; Kell's office operated on less than £2000 in 1910.[80] Neither Kell's nor Cumming's organization was very large prior to 1914, but both were able to lay the groundwork for their wartime activities.

In particular, those supporting the Secret Service pushed hard for a revision of the 1889 Official Secrets Act that would allow Kell more latitude and power in arresting those accused of espionage or subversive activities.[81] The push for more governmental secrecy reflected larger changes throughout the western world. The meaning of espionage seemed to be in flux during this period as legislative codes regarding treason and espionage were revised in many nations. New codes dealing with espionage were enacted in France (1886), Italy (1890), Russia (1892–1893), Norway (1902), Japan (1907), and the United States (1911). In Britain, the Official Secrets Act of 1889 was the first visible sign of the shift in legal attitudes toward espionage, and although weaker than its twentieth century revision, the 1889 act represented a new era in intelligence work. Under the new laws, espionage was equated with high treason, and "a foreigner convicted of espionage [was] liable to the same penalties as a native-born subject."[82] The revised Official Secrets Act passed in 1911, gave Kell the power he sought to pursue spies, put the burden of proof of innocence on the suspect instead of the accuser, and eliminated the need for investigators to demonstrate proof of a suspect's treasonous intentions.[83]

The tougher Official Secrets Act and the new Secret Service Bureau did not end the debates about the danger of spies. In fact, Kell's office contributed to these concerns when it apprehended and tried a handful of spies in the two years before the war. Several Germans and one English naval officer were brought to court in highly sensational trials between 1912 and 1914.[84] These real-life spy dramas highlighted the imaginary stories of the adventures and treachery of spies published in the years before the war.

Humorists and cartoonists also entered into the debate over espionage in Britain, depicting spies in the most unlikely of places. Political cartoonists at *Punch* delighted in drawing absurd scenes of possible espionage, including villagers worried about a matron sketching pictures and Boy Scouts stalking imaginary spies intent on invading Britain. Perhaps the best parody of spy fiction came from a young P. G. Wodehouse, who in 1909 wrote *The Swoop! Or How Clarence Saved England, A Tale of the Great Invasion* as an answer to a play staged earlier that year about the invasion of England.[85] Clarence Chugwater, fourteen-year-old Boy Scout extraordinaire, leads his Scout troop to victory against nine invading enemies (all of which land simultaneously). Clever in its mockery of the spy genre, the book claims that Britain was so feeble in its military preparedness that only the Boy Scouts remained to defend it. Luckily, all of the other armies were also hapless and unprepared, including the German army that Clarence finally confronts, saying, "An hour ago your camp was silently surrounded by patrols of Boy Scouts, armed with catapults and hockey sticks. One rush and the battle was over. Your entire army, like yourself, are prisoners."[86]

Humor aside, when England declared war in August of 1914, spy paranoia soared with a rash of newspaper stories, books, and films. In the first few months of the war, cinema audiences were thrilled to see titles such as *The German Spy Peril* (1914), *Guarding Britain's Secrets* (1914), *The Kaiser's Spies* (1914) and *The Crimson Triangle* (1915). Like many prewar spy novels that featured evil yet pitiful German villains, these films often used "smart little Boy Scouts or even Girl Guides who were able to trick German spies of quite incredible stupidity."[87] Fueled by fictional stories, popular fears of a spy menace exploded when the threat of invasion and military espionage became real. Some Britons began looking for spies among their neighbors and turned violent against people of German ancestry.[88]

Spy panics in 1914 were not limited to Britain, with stories of spy mania emerging in most of the combatant countries. In Hamburg, Germany, a mob carrying sticks chased a foreign theatre troupe when the actors were rumored to be spies. English teenager Margaret Foote was holidaying in Germany when Britain declared war. She recorded in her diary how "spy-mad" Germans accused her and her friends of being Russian spies. Daisy Williams, temporarily stranded in Germany in August 1914, was arrested (although quickly released) on suspicion of being a Russian spy. Williams noted that even hanging a pair of gloves on the windowsill might lead neighbors to contact the police about possible signaling.[89] Englishwoman J. H. Gifford summed up the problem afflicting people in many of the combatant countries in her description of Belgium at the beginning of the war, "[They] became quite crazed on the subject and imagined a spy in every foreigner."[90]

Popular spy mania in Britain and other warring nations also infected major social and governmental institutions. For example, in September of 1914, Edinburgh University announced that it was firing all German-born members of its staff.[91] The British government passed laws that suggested paranoid fears of subversion, even going so far as to outlaw weather reports and chess-problem solutions in newspapers.[92] Newspapers themselves repeated rumors of spy activity, often running the stories under sensational headlines such as "The Spy Peril" and "Enemies in England." In an article praising the roundup of suspected spies and suspicious aliens, the *Times* noted that only "the cleverest and most dangerous" spies were left at large by September 1914.[93] Even Parliament held several discussions about the nature of the peril facing Britain from within, with the House of Lords debating the issue in November 1914 and again in June 1916.[94] The popular agitation caused by alleged spies created a sympathy for and fascination with government surveillance of the population.[95] As people reported the suspicious activities of their neighbors and politicians debated the spy peril, the Secret Service quietly rounded up the individuals on the list of foreign suspects it had been compiling since 1909, and Parliament passed its most extensive legislation curtailing citizens' rights since the Napoleonic wars.

CONCLUSION

The fortunes of the intelligence establishment in Britain up to the Anglo-Boer War were inextricably tied to internal and external conflict. In times of foreign war or civil disturbance, men and women of the nation declared their loyalties and participated in secret information gathering and dissemination, but usually only for the duration of the conflict. In peacetime, Britain's intelligence organizations were allowed to shrink and even stagnate. This precedent of "intelligence as needed" had been the model that the British government drew on until 1914, when war again loomed. This time, however, the length and scope of the First World War and subsequent twentieth-century militarization cemented the connection between militarism and intelligence, exposing the need for permanent security organizations and for women's formal labor in these establishments.

By 1914, all the elements were in place for the creation of a "watchdog" state with contingency plans coordinated for the various armed services, government offices, and industries, bound together in a publication called the "War Book," which had been compiled by a subcommittee of the Committee of Imperial Defence.[96] The Admiralty, the War Office, the Foreign Office, the Home Office, the Post Office, and the Government Press all prepared, at least on paper, for a continental war. What was not in place in 1914, however, was the trained labor for these endeavors. Britain had a small professional army, a motley group of territorial reserves, and tiny intelligence offices. Lack of funding and personnel for properly gathering information, and more importantly analyzing it, had plagued the nineteenth-century intelligence branches, so World War I leaders wanted to ensure the proper processing and dissemination of vital information. As the war dragged on, the labor resources for running a wartime state and a major modern war had to be redefined almost continually to account for men drafted into combat, and increasingly women became a viable and useful solution to intelligence staffing needs.

Women, who had been a small part of very small intelligence networks prior to the twentieth century now became a crucial yet invisible element in the creation of World War I spy organizations. There were many strong, educated women who were patriotic and willing to "do their bit" for a low salary, and it was these female workers on whom the British intelligence establishment precariously balanced. Abroad, women of divergent backgrounds were hired to run risks behind enemy lines to gather the vital technical and territorial information needed to fight the enemy. Even the modern image of the female spy that developed in popular media during and after the war reflected both the real participation and imagined roles of women as spies and intelligence workers. In the increasingly militarized world that followed the First World War, and especially after 1945, the gendered intelligence bureaucracy was a *fait accompli*.

2

DORA's Women and the Enemy within Britain

I have never been in such a situation as I have been today and I am nearly mad. I never thought my letter to my sister would be taken as a crime. . . .

—Martha Earle, May 14, 1918

IN SEPTEMBER 1918, Martha Earle was sentenced to one year in Holloway Prison under the Defence of the Realm Acts (DORA) for writing letters to her sister in Germany.[1] Her crimes, listed as twelve separate indictments, included providing information to the enemy and using a code in correspondence. Earle, a German by birth, married a British headmaster in 1908 and moved to England with one of her two grown daughters from a previous marriage. Due to her marriage, Earle automatically became a British citizen subject to the British monarch. The Naturalisation Act of 1870, revised as the British Nationality and Status of Aliens Act (BNSA) of 1914, stated that "the wife of a British subject shall be deemed to be a British subject and the wife of an alien shall be deemed to be an alien."[2] In short, wives took their husbands' nationality no matter what their loyalties; British women lost their citizenship if they married foreigners, and foreign women automatically became British citizens on marriage to a subject of the King of Great Britain.

The Earle espionage case and the issue of women's nationality raise important questions about the nature of women's relationships to their state and their husbands during World War I. If a woman could be transferred involuntarily from one country to another as if she were property, her loyalties were by definition uncertain and transitory. This chapter explores the tensions between state protection of women and its suspicion of them, paying particular attention to the focus on women spies as a particularly pervasive evil, despite the small number of arrests of women in Britain for espionage. With the perception of their shifting loyalties, women became targets of governmental regulation and control along with those of foreign birth. Anti-alien feeling, fear of the degeneration of the country, and spy paranoia all combined to create a gendered notion of both nationalism and subversion.

During World War I, espionage—in stark contrast to the newly emerging professional intelligence industry—was increasingly depicted as a perverse, morally corrupt, and effeminate activity. Newspapers identified the "enemy within" as those living in the "bosom of Britain" whose crimes against the state were described in sexual terms. Espionage was generally referred to as domestic, hidden, and sneaky—in other words, it was feminine. Intelligence, on the other hand, was professional, bureaucratic, and officially secret—or masculine in its endeavors. The gendered definition of espionage began with the prewar spy panics and solidified throughout the war period with strident anti-alien rhetoric, control of female sexuality, and one sensational libel trial.

DORA, ARA, AND OFFICIAL SECRECY

The First Defence of the Realm (DORA) legislation passed in August 1914 initially seemed to target only spies and traitors, but as the act was subsequently amended during the war, almost anyone caught speaking against the government or "causing alarm" could be arrested on suspicion. The counterespionage branch, MI5 (alone and in collaboration with other government branches and the police), was directly responsible for enforcing more than sixty of the DORA regulations. The Secret Service was given the power of search and seizure as well as the authority to clear areas of inhabitants, limit movement within and outside of Britain, and intern suspects and people of alien origin. Investigation depended on the careful tracking of suspicious activities and people, the availability of civilian informants and tips, and the restriction of citizens' privacy. Censorship commenced with the outbreak of war with suspicious mail being forwarded to a special office for investigation. In addition, MI5 could detain people who supplied intoxicants to His Majesty's Forces or who wore unauthorized medals or badges. Signaling and the use of fireworks were forbidden in certain areas, and all drill other than for official military exercises was halted.[3] Claire Culleton, in her study of working-class Britain during the war, lists some of the restrictions that DORA allowed:

> [DORA] suspended emigration; it regulated governmental control of the engineering industry, bridled workers' strikes, fixed crop prices, and issued to farmers compulsory tillage orders; it forbade the hiring of men between the ages of 18 and 60 in nonessential industries; it restricted processions and public protests; it monitored and censored the public press . . . it enjoined stringent curfews for single and for married women; it imposed limited hours of operation for pubs and other social establishments; it introduced the daylight savings order; it prohibited the chiming and striking of London's public clocks. . . .[4]

Under the umbrella of the DORA legislation, the list of controlled activities continued to expand throughout the war.

Women were particularly targeted by the DORA legislation as worries about venereal disease (VD) and prostitution mounted. The health of the nation's soldiers was a primary concern, but rather than police soldiers' sexuality, the state chose to regulate women's activity. Seen as carriers of disease, and in some cases, decadence, women's bodies were regulated for the protection of soldiers and the nation. Although crime rates plummeted during the war, prostitution arrests and VD infection rates appeared to rise, whether the changes were because of better policing or an actual rise in sexual activity is unclear.[5]

To the British government, regulation of national sexuality meant controlling women's activities through a series of legislative moves. Curfews were established for certain women, the age of sexual consent was raised from sixteen years old to eighteen years old, and police were given new rights to examine and detain women and girls. For example, DORA 35C and 40D established new versions of the nineteenth-century Contagious Diseases Acts, giving authorities the right to stop suspected women and administer gynecological examinations for venereal disease. "Loitering" girls were detained, advertisements for abortifacients became illegal, and pub hours were shortened.[6] By early 1918, it was a crime for a woman infected with VD to have sexual intercourse with a serviceman, even if he were her husband and even if he had given her the disease.[7]

These broad powers echoed some of the restrictive safety measures adopted during the Napoleonic wars, but the great level of intervention seen during World War I was truly unprecedented. DORA allowed the monitoring of all British citizens, but in combination with the revised Official Secrets Act passed before the war in 1911, intelligence and police "special" units had increased powers. The 1911 act made it easier to prosecute those accused of espionage by assuming a suspect was guilty unless proven innocent. This sweeping legislation, introduced deliberately on a Friday afternoon, passed quickly and with little Parliamentary discussion or consideration.[8] Despite supporting the Official Secrets Act, one intelligence official noted uncomfortably in his journal, "we talked of the new Official Secrets Act and the really scandalous way it was rushed through the House of Commons in one day despite a protest from 'Byles' that it upset Magna Charta . . . [which] is perfectly true!"[9] The act did change citizens' rights considerably. With its broader understanding of espionage crimes (including the crime of harboring a spy), police could enter individuals' homes, search them, seize materials, and arrest any person they believed suspicious, if necessary.[10] Counterespionage chief Vernon Kell gleefully noted in his report for 1911 and in the official wartime history of his counterespionage branch, Military Intelligence 5 (MI5) that the 1911 Official Secrets Act changed the whole nature of British counterespionage and preventive intelligence.[11]

Although British citizens were significantly affected by these changes, foreigners living in Britain during the war felt the biggest impact, especially with the addition of the 1914 Aliens Restriction Act. The legislative triumvirate of the 1911 Official Secrets Act, the 1914 Defence of the Realm Act, and the 1914 Aliens Restriction Act was especially injurious for non-British-born subjects, even those who were naturalized citizens. Foreignness was linked not only to treason, espionage, antigovernment activities, and subversion, but it also became a moral "disease" in British society that had to be cured, replicating the spy panics of the prewar period.[12]

The hostility toward foreigners partially legitimized in DORA became officially institutionalized with the Aliens Restriction Act (ARA). This act, like DORA, was broad ranging and difficult to enforce without major increases in personnel and financial resources. The ARA established rules for monitoring all alien activity in Britain, mandated their registration, required aliens to obtain permits for travel more than five miles from home, and designated areas prohibited to foreigners. Eventually, other legislation led to the establishment of a passport system within Britain and at all port controls. Many German language newspapers were shut down, and aliens were forbidden to own wireless or signaling equipment, cameras, and carrier pigeons. After October of 1914, the British government limited aliens' ability to change their names to more Anglicized alternatives[13] and by the end of the war even revoked the citizenship of some British-naturalized Germans and Austrians.[14]

Perhaps the most disturbing aspect of the British government's alien policy during the war was not requiring alien registration or increasing surveillance but the government's effort to remove aliens from designated areas and then from British society altogether. Beginning with the imprisonment of suspected spies, large numbers of German and other enemy alien men were held in internment camps for the duration of the war. Men of military age made up most of the nearly thirty thousand people interned. About twenty thousand of this group were repatriated during or after the war.[15] Alien internees, some of whom had sons serving in the British forces, lived in cramped quarters with poor diets and few privileges. As the war progressed, the quantity and quality of rations in the internment camps deteriorated until by early 1919, horsemeat was one of the main staples of internees' diets. Most of the interned men were held on the Isle of Man or on ships anchored off the coast of Britain in uncomfortable accommodations.[16]

The female threat to national security was more subtle—the government perceived that women were capable of infiltrating society and weakening it from within through marriage, childbearing, and sexuality. Officials particularly worried about foreign women transmitting syphilis or gonorrhea to British soldiers home on leave. To eliminate the female threat, the British government sought to deport female aliens. By January 1915, close to seven thousand women had been repatriated, and others—especially single women—faced pressure to ask for voluntary repatriation or risk deportation.[17] Women were not interned in large numbers, but women who were imprisoned often ended up serving for a short time in local lockups, women's prisons, or in Holloway Prison in London as they awaited deportation. The small group of women imprisoned on espionage charges and DORA violations were kept in a wing of the Aylesbury Inebriate Reformatory along with female convicts and two-dozen girls from a Borstal institution (a detention center for young adults).[18]

A good description of the internment experience for both men and women comes from the memoirs of socialist-anarchist and pacifist, Rudolf Rocker. Although of German birth, Rocker was imprisoned as much for his political leanings as for his nationality. This was apparent also in the arrest of his wife, Milly (an Ukrainian Jewish immigrant), and one of their sons. Rocker, arrested in December of 1914, describes the tedium and the sense of betrayal felt by many in the camps. He was held in a series of internment centers throughout Britain, including those at Olympia and Alexandra Palace as well as one of the "floating prisons" moored off the south coast. Despite his objections, Rocker was deported to Germany in 1918. Because he had left Germany before the war as a political undesirable, he was refused entry and spent the end of the war in the neutral Netherlands, returning to Germany only after the fall of the imperial government. Milly, arrested in 1916, was held without trial under DORA at Aylesbury. Their powerful friends in London, including editor of the *Daily Herald* George Lansbury and MP (Member of Parliament) Joseph King, lobbied without success on their behalf. In his memoirs, Rocker describes his and Milly's fury at their living conditions and their concern for their youngest son, an eight-year-old living parentless for much of the war with a succession of family friends. Rudolf said he found the internment camps demeaning and dehumanizing, and Milly addressed the advisory board considering her case in 1917:

> You have kept me in prison for fifteen months without trial. Why do you treat me differently from my [male] comrades Shapiro, Linder, and Lenoble? Why shouldn't we all be allowed to go to Russia? You know that I was arrested because of my political views. Yet I was put in prison with criminals, with prostitutes, with women suffering from disease, with whom I have to share toilet, bath, and crockery.[19]

She asked for deportation to the Soviet Union in 1917 but was refused because she wanted Rudolf to accompany her. It was not until after the war that she and their sons were allowed to rejoin Rudolf in Germany.[20]

Foreigners were targeted for imprisonment and removal even if they had cut all ties with their countries of birth and had embraced British citizenship. Wealth and position could sometimes buy leniency from the government, but not in every case. D. H. Lawrence and his

German wife Frieda were expelled from their house in Cornwall because of its proximity to Atlantic shipping lanes.[21] The German monks at Buckfast Abbey were put under unofficial house arrest for the duration of the war. To increase British nationalism, King George V held an official ceremony to declare himself the first in a new "English" line: the Windsors (which is still the Royal Family's official name).[22] In fact, people in positions of authority and public trust were often suspected of being the worst offenders, and letters to the editor, petitions, and media reports continued to call for the clean up of "highly-placed" traitors.[23] Often anonymous, these letters named prominent figures as traitors. One missive, sent to the Criminal Investigation Department (CID) in June of 1916, accused (among others) Margot Asquith (wife of the former Prime Minister) and eighty-year-old Mrs. Ashbee of Chelsea of espionage. The author went on to threaten violence, writing, "the PEOPLE have had enough." Although the CID officials noted the this letter seemed "the high tide of folly," they still thoroughly investigated its claims.[24]

Even highly-placed government employees often had difficulty helping foreign-born relatives and friends. James Headlam (Headlam-Morley from 1918 on) was a well-known historian working in the Propaganda Department and Political Intelligence at the Foreign Office during the war.[25] His foreign-born wife's rights were protected through her marriage to an Englishman, but he wrote a series of letters to ask for special treatment for his foreign-born servants and in-laws. In his letters to the British Home Office he repeatedly agreed to "take full personal responsibility for their inoffensive conduct and for their personal protection," while questioning the validity of the policy regarding aliens. Headlam tried to help one of his female employees, an Austrian, who was refused exemption from repatriation. He argued in his 1916 letter:

> On public ground there cannot possibly be the remotest cause for any suspicion that injury would arise from her being allowed to remain in this country. She is an extremely quiet, retiring person. . . . When she came to England she broke off all connections with her original home; she has a brother interned here and a neice [sic] married to an Englishman, and is most anxious to be allowed to remain.[26]

It is unknown whether Headlam's efforts brought success.

Ethel (in apprehensive whisper which easily reaches her German governess, to whom she is deeply attached). "MOTHER, SHALL WE HAVE TO KILL FRÄULEIN?"

This cartoon from *Punch* mocks the anti-German fears in England at the beginning of the war. [September 2, 1914.]

     Throughout the war, alien restriction, deportation, and internment policies were justified by the government as a "protection" both for aliens in Britain and for British citizens, yet the government did little to protect the women and children left destitute and subject to attack by the male internment policy. Although the Home Office had a Destitute Aliens Committee (in 1916 changed to Civilian Internment Camps Committee) to assist those in need, it was largely ineffective. Private aid schemes, especially a program devised by the Quakers, provided necessary assistance to those aliens left penniless and alone by the war.[27] The government's lack of an effective wartime alien aid policy seemed to mirror the popular anti-alien feelings in the general population. Public reaction to aliens varied from verbal insults to full-blown riots as Britons scrutinized their communities for "enemies."

     Some of this activity focused on worries about German spies in England. One London woman living in a household with eight other women recorded the hearsay about the spies nearby, writing on August 7, "Germans are being freely arrested as spies, many of them known to the police." By the next day, she was recording, "It appears there are a series of armed plots among Germans in London, but there is general confidence that the police have full knowledge and the situation well in hand."[28] Likewise, another woman recorded in her diary on 31 July 1914 that "a good many spies captured in the Island [of Wight]" and that there had been rumors that Germans had poisoned the water supply.[29] *Punch*, the British satirical magazine, parodied and fueled anti-German sentiment and spy paranoia in a series of cartoons throughout the war. Although downplaying the seriousness of the spy threat in humorous scenes, the magazine tacitly approved the practice of scrutinizing foreigners within Britain. One 1914 cartoon has children asking their mother if they will have to kill their German governess, while another scene a year later has an irate little girl holding beheaded dolls, which her brother has "killed" because they were made in Germany.[30]

Nurse. " GOODNESS ME! WHAT 'AVE YOU BEEN DOING TO YOUR DOLLS?"
Joan. "CHARLIE'S KILLED THEM! HE SAID THEY WERE MADE IN GERMANY, AND HOW WERE WE TO KNOW THEY WEREN'T SPIES?"

Punch represents the anti-German riots and spy paranoia that shook London in October 1914. *Punch* Library, London; October 21, 1914.

Home Office records documented both complaints about attacks on German residents (especially women and children) and official apathy to such behavior, while letters poured into newspapers asking for enemy spies to be rooted out.[31] By September 1914, almost nine thousand complaints had been lodged with the London police against Germans.[32] In order to demonstrate the cross-class extent of the spy menace, the London *Times* noted that those already arrested in August 1914, included:

> Hairdressers, German naval pensioner, bookkeeper, music-hall artist, German Consul, engineer, waiter, pastor of German seamen's mission, subaltern, student, cook, mariner, cabinet-maker, photographer, director of margarine works, director of oil company, professor of languages, and ship's chandler.[33]

Such reports were aided by "leaked" information about thousands of suspected spies at large in the country. Although all foreigners were suspect, enemy aliens and especially Germans bore the brunt of the violence.[34] Britons now saw themselves not so much in opposition to the French (as in the eighteenth and nineteenth centuries), but as foes of Germany, the new enemy to be watched.[35] Germans within Britain faced discrimination and attack as fears over the war and the power of the German nation rose.

This anti-German sentiment ran high throughout the war, fueled by newly formed organizations such as the Anti-German Union (later the British Empire Union) in 1915. These types of organizations held meetings to pressure Parliament to intern or deport aliens and sponsored publicity campaigns that exposed German sympathizers. For example, a 1917 petition from the British Empire Union (Oxford Branch) to J. A. Marriott, MP, asked for "internment without delay of all enemy aliens," excepting only Englishwomen married to Germans. Another anonymous leaflet received in the Home Office in January 1917 suggested that the British "Coddled the Huns" and demanded that the "Hidden Hand" and "gigantic spy system" be unmasked.[36] A variety of demonstrations were held during the war to try to influence governmental policy. One such meeting in Trafalgar Square in July 1918 called for the "immediate internment of all aliens of enemy blood, whether naturalized or unnaturalized" and featured signs that proclaimed "A clean sweep!" and "Intern them all!" At this same demonstration, letters of support were read aloud and published in the newspapers from such diverse personalities as Rudyard Kipling, the Bishop of Birmingham, and the Prime Minister of New Zealand.[37]

Periodic outbreaks of anti-alien rioting occurred during the war in a variety of areas around the country. The first riots in August 1914 featured isolated attacks on German residents and businesses with one larger riot in Keighley, Yorkshire at the end of the month. More serious were the October 1914 riots that devastated parts of South London, and that began in Deptford. Rudolf Rocker described these riots in his memoirs:

> In October mobs collected in the streets, in the Old Kent Road, in Deptford, Brixton, Poplar, and smashed and looted shops which they thought were occupied by Germans. There were real pogroms. . . . The police were helpless. The troops had to be brought in before the outbreaks were put down."[38]

Although the October riots created havoc in the communities affected, the most serious and widespread rioting did not take place until May 1915, after the announcement of the sinking of the *Lusitania* by a German submarine. In that month, riots with widespread damage broke out in Lancashire, the Midlands, Yorkshire, Derbyshire, South Wales, and London.[39] Police could not contain the violence, so the Cabinet announced measures to intern all enemy alien males on May 13, 1915.[40] In addition to these community riots, individual attacks were common both via print and in person. Alien shopkeepers and service workers were shunned and British employers sacked German and Austrian employees. The *London Gazette* even published a list of names of those who had anglicized their German names.[41]

Anti-foreign sentiment, fear of decadence, and suspicion of women combined in 1918 for one of the most notorious trials of the decade. Perhaps the best (if most extreme) example of the fears engendered during the war, the trial pitted Noel Pemberton Billing versus Maud Allan in a libel case during the summer of 1918. Billing, a Member of Parliament for East Hertfordshire and publisher of the right-wing newspapers the *Imperialist* and the *Vigilante*, claimed in print that there was a "Black List" of 47,000 traitors and spies in high positions in Britain. The article, which ran in the *Imperialist*, stated that the German leadership used this list of known traitors and degenerates to recruit highly-placed spies among the British citizenry. Billing tied foreignness to sexual deviance, playing on public fears of disorder and sexual promiscuity. In the "black book of sin" that the newspaper claimed to have discovered, the article exclaimed, "In Lesbian ecstasy the most sacred secrets of State were betrayed. The sexual peculiarities of members of the peerage were used as a leverage to open fruitful fields for espionage." Billing and his colleagues published these sensational and extraordinary claims hoping to draw a libel suit and the publicity that would follow.[42]

Because the original article did not provoke a libel suit, in February the *Vigilante* followed the *Imperialist's* earlier claims with a now-infamous news article entitled "The Cult of the Clitoris." This follow-up article implied that many of the suspects on Billing's "Black List" could be found attending "private" performances of Oscar Wilde's play *Salome*, starring dancer Maud Allan. The author claimed these men and women were morally degraded, perverted, and dangerous to the state.[43] The choice of *Salome* was deliberate, tying the allegations to an earlier libel suit Oscar Wilde brought against the Marquess of Queensberry and the gross indecency trial that followed. Wilde, as the author of *Salome* and as a convicted "sodomite," triggered public memory and media attention to these new claims. Banned in England during Wilde's lifetime, *Salome* was being staged anew in a limited run in London. The play retold the biblical story of Salome (who persuaded Herod to give her John the Baptist's head on a platter) as a tale of sexual power and perversion. Maud Allan, a well-known Canadian exotic dancer who had performed throughout Europe and the producer of *Salome*, J. T. Grein, brought libel proceedings against Billing in 1918, which gave him the national platform that he had hoped to gain.[44] Although the prosecutor attempted to show that the play's themes—passion and revenge—were universal, Billing kept diverting the court's discussion with innuendo and accusations that had little to do with the libel in question. Maud Allan, accused of immorality and lesbian proclivities, became a central figure in this national spectacle as an outsider (Canadian), an exotic dancer (she was compared to Mata Hari, who had been executed less than a year before in Paris), and the lead actress in a play whose central themes were symbolic castration and sexual perversion.

The trial opened in May of 1918 and attracted national and international media coverage, airing Britain's anxieties over decadence and espionage—vices that were firmly linked in the case. As the London *Times* noted in a post-trial editorial on June 5, 1918,

It is safe to say that no lawsuit of modern times has attracted such universal and painful interest as the deplorable libel action which terminated yesterday at the Central Criminal Court. Not only in London, but even more in the provincial towns and countryside, the daily reports have been read and discussed with almost as deep anxiety as the news of the war itself. . . . But the case very soon developed, as it was intended to develop, into a whole series of promiscuous innuendoes, in which pro-Germanism was united with every sort of unnatural vice, against many thousands of English men and women, some few of whom were actually named in Court.[45]

As the *Times* noted, the case linked foreign birth and sympathy with homosexuality, promiscuity, and immorality. This connection echoed the prewar and wartime spy fiction that historian Nicholas Hiley describes as pornographic in its storylines, imagery, and situations. Both Edwardian pornography and spy fiction, he argues, functioned in hidden worlds and operated as wish-fulfillment for readers, especially middle-class adult and adolescent males.[46]

The titillating content of the Billing libel case was never in question. Witnesses in the trial ranged from Lord Alfred Douglas who adamantly denounced the play and the lover (Wilde) he had formerly praised, to Billing's own lover, Mrs. Eileen Villiers-Stuart, who named prominent Liberal politicians to be among the 47,000 degenerates and traitors. When Villiers-Stuart took the stand, Billings, who was representing himself, asked his lover to confirm names in the book. She positively confirmed Mr. and Mrs. Asquith, Mr. Haldane, and Mr. Justice Darling (the presiding judge in the case) as Billing called out each name.[47]

At the end of the weeklong trial, the jury found Billing not guilty of libel, vindicating his accusations and shocking those who had been attacked such as Maud Allan and Margot Asquith.[48] Espionage was branded as a decadent trade peopled with the immoral and abnormal. As scholar Jodie Medd astutely notes, "With 'loved ones' at the front engaged in a war that defied representation, those at home witnessed a sexualized scene of strife upon which they could displace anxiety and emotion."[49] Beyond being a diversion for fears of losing the war, the trial also served as a reminder that Britain's internal enemies and dissidents were being watched. Although many media accounts deplored the sordid spectacle of the case, few questioned the connection between aliens, sexual perversion, and espionage, and even fewer called for a halt to such allegations. The London *Times* emphasized the "positive" side of the case, saying if "public men and women" are reminded "that countless eyes are watching their doings and their associates," then the trial and scandal were worthwhile.[50] Four years after DORA and seven years after the Official Secrets Act, such surveillance seemed necessary to the maintenance of the nation's morality and security. More important, however, the case seemed to support the notion that there were clear links between espionage and sexuality, especially women's passions.[51]

A "RULING PASSION": WOMEN SPIES IN ENGLAND

When war was declared on Germany in August of 1914, Kell's counterespionage branch was ready with a special war list of suspected spies who were immediately put under surveillance or detained by police or both. On the list were a few women, only two of whom were immediately arrested on August 5. Both had been implicated in spy cases prior to the war, and they joined a handful of women already in prison for prewar espionage activities.[52] Despite only 243 women being detained, watched, or prohibited from military zones as possible spies by the end of 1916 compared to the more than one thousand men on the same list, there continued to be worries about the particular dangers of female spies, and especially alien spies.[53] Intelligence officials viewed female espionage as domestic and occurring in private spaces. Therefore, in some ways, it was seen as more dangerous than male espionage because it was hidden. The women who were imprisoned for espionage were usually caught through domestic arrangements—through private letters tagged by censors or through tips from concerned acquaintances or family members. Those most closely scrutinized by MI5 were "pro-German" women and "women intimate with [British] soldiers or officers."[54] Given the current state of war, the latter category encompassed most of the female population of Britain!

Media images of women emphasized their "naturalness" as spies because of their shifting loyalties, seductive powers, and access to intimate spaces. Yet women who spied were also depicted as unnatural creatures who had betrayed their own natures. These competing images created a strange tension and ambivalence in the definition of female spies. Causing even more confusion, most of the women tried in

Britain for espionage were not native born, which made their activities neither unnatural to their natures nor natural to their shifting loyalties.

Intelligence officials often portrayed female spies as ruled by their passions and incapable of clear thinking and moral decision making. The few cases of women arrested as spies that do exist are well documented and demonstrate how female aliens were a source of considerable anxiety. The focus on single, foreign women as an evil influence reflects British concerns with race, sexuality, and national safety, and the fear of Britain's future resting only on the honor and service of its native-born women. As Margaret Darrow notes, women were seen in only one of two roles: either domestic, serving mothers or nurses, or public women inappropriately embracing the war as spies, traitors, and prostitutes.[55]

Although women in espionage were considered to have an advantage over men because of their seduction skills, they were also depicted as overly emotional and prone to romantic entanglements. Underlying these stereotypes was a fear of female sexual betrayal with the possible serious consequence of the instability of the nation. In other words, women were alternately soft, pliable nurturers and hard, intractable, vixens, reflecting confusion about women's true calling in a militarized wartime state.[56] In fiction and sensational "histories" of espionage during the war and interwar periods, women spies were depicted as people on the margins of society: foreign governesses, actresses or dancers, prostitutes or drug addicts.

The curiously named author E.7 repeated in his 1939 book *Women Spies I Have Known* all the clichés about both the calculation and the weakness of women spies. In his description of Lu-Lu the Dancer (Louise Herbaut), E.7 claimed, "she was up to all the tricks of the Boulevards an expert in the gentle art of painless extraction—whether she was drawing money, diamond rings or just the price of a good dinner out of some fascinated client. . . ." Yet, the seduction specialist Herbaut had to be "initiated" by E.7 and his partner so that she would know how to extract information. All of E.7's work came to naught, however, when, "Louise, who we imagined had a little lump of rubber in the place where her heart should have been, fell in love with the man she was employed to vamp."[57] In a similar vein, Ferdinand Tuohy published articles in a variety of newspapers in the 1920s denouncing the effectiveness of female spies. Tuohy claimed that women spies were "*voyantes*" who "are apt to fall in love all over the place, being of an adventurous bent, when only instructed to have 'affairs' with certain individuals hand-picked for them. . . ."[58] Popular opinion held that women spies were out for money, power, or position unless they were working for Britain, in which case their motives were either patriotism (as with Nurse Edith Cavell) or revenge (usually for a beloved's death). Archetypal female spies arose in media reports, popular histories, film, and fiction before, during, and especially after the war: the calculating "Fraulein Doktor," the martyred saint, and the *femme fatale* (see chapters 5 and 6).[59]

In the majority of cases, the reality of women spies captured in Britain did not mirror their fictional representations. Most interned women were foreigners who were imprisoned under DORA and never publicly tried or charged, making it difficult for historians to analyze their cases. The handful of women who were tried officially for espionage before and during the war provide more detailed information on how female spies were perceived in Britain. Women spies were considered clever and tricky, yet also weak and inept, and intelligence reports depict them as both hard-hearted and romantically susceptible. In fact, the female spies seemed a difficult puzzle, a paradox for many of the writers who recorded their cases.

British intelligence officers suspected the Germans of using females as spies, but they differed in their assessment of the extent to which women were employed. Some former agents thought spycatchers should be suspicious of foreign governesses and women who toured the country in motorcars, noting that those were favorite recruits of the Germans.[60] In a lecture on intelligence methods Lt. Col. James Edmonds noted that, "The use of women in procuring intelligence for Germany is very considerable, and extends from ladies . . . down to the professional '*horizontales*,'" while Constance Kell, wife of the MI5 chief, claimed that "women were occasionally used by the Germans as agents if they were possessed of a ready wit . . . but their usefulness was somewhat limited."[61] Hamil Grant, whose 1915 history of espionage was quite influential among wartime intelligence officials, claimed that, "woman as a rule fails as a secret service agent" because she acts only for reasons of love or revenge and is virtually incapable of experiencing the "platonic" patriotism that drives men.[62]

In reality, the women imprisoned for espionage offenses shared one trait. Most of those convicted and detained on espionage charges were born outside of Britain in enemy or neutral countries, such as

Switzerland, Germany, or Austria-Hungary. Some of these women were interned without trial based on prewar associations with spies or suspected espionage activity, while others were caught and tried at the Central Criminal Court during the war. Many were eventually deported in 1918 or after the war. Included among the list of undesirables were Martha Earle (who appeared at the beginning of this chapter), her daughter Eleanor Polkinghorne, Louise "Lizzie" Wertheim, Louise von Zastrow Smith, Lina Heine, Heddy Glauer and Marie Kronauer—all of whom were German-born women. Also arrested for espionage were French-born Albertine Stanaway and a Dane (naturalized as a Swede) named Eva de Bournonville. British women suspected of espionage activities were often put under surveillance, reported to family members, or in one case, sent to a convent for the duration of the war. Aliens were more susceptible to official internment on suspicion alone.

What characteristics drew the interned spies together? Most were caught through their correspondence, either by vigilant censorship employees or by anonymous tips from relatives or neighbors. Heddy Glauer, implicated in the spy case of her lover who was imprisoned in 1912, corresponded with police before being turned in by her landlady for traveling more than five miles from home without a permit in 1915. Later, her former lover denounced her, claiming she was a forger.[63] Several of the women were arrested after censorship employees found an unusual code in each of their letters to relatives and friends abroad. Additional circumstances also directed suspicion toward them, with Earle's estranged son-in-law sending letters to the press about his "hostile German" relatives, for instance. Smith sent pro-German newspapers to relatives through the South African mail, ignoring the fact that this practice was illegal.[64]

Secret ink was also a downfall of some women spies. Authorities worked hard to detect secret inks, find substances that would make invisible writing visible, and develop their own secret inks that could not be detected. Almost all inks had easy reagents, although at one point in the war the British Secret Service thought that semen might prove to be perfect as a secret ink because it did not react to any of the normal chemicals.[65] One can only imagine how officials thought women spies might obtain such ink! Spies such as Lizzie Wertheim and Eva de Bournonville were caught because of their use of common secret inks such as lemon juice. Officials searched Wertheim's room and discovered perfume and talcum powder raising the supposition that she was using these fixatives with secret lemon juice ink. De Bournonville's secret ink correspondence was detected by censors and led to her capture. When she was arrested in late 1915 she had cakes of soap with potassium ferrocyanide (for secret writing) in her possession.[66]

British officials had trouble classifying the women spies, alternating between condemnations of their passionate or cunning natures and pity for their romantic or familial attachments and obligations. Glauer, for instance, was described as an "excitable woman, entirely without principle, governed by her passions" in one part of an official report and as motivated by "love, revenge, fear, self-interest and love of her child" later in the same document.[67] In his history of the Secret Service, former intelligence official George Aston describes Eva de Bournonville in similar terms. He claims to have included her in the book "principally to show the strength of the 'ruling passion' of her kind. She wrote a letter to ask if she might have in prison her manicure set and part of her large wardrobe, adding rather pathetically: 'Please kindly hang up my evening dresses. . . .'"[68] In discussing the same case, Scotland Yard's Basil Thomson described de Bournonville as "the most incompetent woman spy ever recruited by the Germans" but added that German treachery had made her "imperil her life for £30 a month."[69] MI5 official historians accused entertainer Pauline Slager of "beguil[ing] the police with worthless information" while her mother, Catherine, was caught forwarding information to Germany that Pauline and her other daughter Eleanore had collected.[70] In all these descriptions, male intelligence officers vacillated between pity for these women as victims and fury over their treachery and betrayal.

Other female spies were classified as dupes for their male companions, pointing the way to a useful strategy for women to avoid more serious punishment. Maud Gould, who was arrested while carrying military information, was released when she claimed not to know what she was carrying for her husband, despite the fact that she had also been caught disposing of scraps of paper after her arrest. Officials suspected that she was at least "a willing decoy" given her "brazen" behavior, but they allowed her to claim ignorance of her husband's activities.[71] Lizzie Wertheim was sentenced to penal servitude after her male accomplice (who was executed for his role) confessed after the verdict that "I took a very great advantage towards her. We became friendly; in fact in a few days it turned into a love affair."[72] Albertine Stanaway was interned but never formally tried because of lack of evidence when she was caught sending materials for her lover who was imprisoned in France. As the official report records, "Regarding Stanaway there is no certainty except that she seems to have really loved Rothendt and risked much for him."[73]

Male police and intelligence officials treated all women spies with a mix of suspicion and condescension. Although angry when they perceived women to be lying, the officials seemed more inclined to give them the benefit of the doubt. Their dismissal of the abilities of female spies often allowed the women to manipulate trials and sentencing to their advantage. In a strange twist on the Glauer story, one of the female official historians for MI5 noted that male officials were a bit naive. She added an editorial note to her history of the case, writing,

> Regarding the case of Heddy Glauer it seems strange it was not investigated more thoroughly in the beginning. . . . Another observation that forces itself upon the recorder is that in the case of a highly strung, excitable woman, the help of one of her own sex in appraising the case might be of value. She gave infinite trouble by petitions and actions which would have been more easily interpreted by a woman.[74]

Not only does the author suggest that female officials would have seen through the devices and stratagems of women spies, but she also mentions another characteristic that the women spies often had in common: boldness. Officials overwhelmingly depicted them as unnaturally bold, especially in their demands for treatment after arrest and in their petitions for release. Milly Rocker, who had petitioned for release or deportation to the USSR, is an example of one woman who tried to use the media to publicize her plight. She repeatedly called on friends in the Labour movement, such as politician George Lansbury, to help with her requests.[75] Another American woman caught carrying messages for the Germans, Gertrude Evelin, "wrote many hysterical letters while in prison, the general trend of which was: 'I am going to commit suicide if you detain me any longer.'" She was not released and repatriated until April 1919.[76]

According to official reports, the women interned at Aylesbury Prison (the main prison for female DORA or ARA violators and accused spies) did not seem to be aware of the seriousness of their crimes, often asking for better diets, improved clothing, more exercise, and access to other prisoners. In seeking better conditions for themselves they experienced small triumphs. One victory for the prisoners was an increase in the number of letters they were allowed to receive per week. At first they could have only two a week, but after repeated complaints the number was raised first to three letters a week and then more following further petitions.[77] Individual female prisoners, even those convicted of espionage by juries, were allowed some privileges. Evidently, de Bournonville and Wertheim were given the privilege of talking occasionally after "an application was made on [de Bournonville's] behalf."[78] The women's demands for better treatment led to a loosening of restrictions until the Aylesbury Prison governor complained that the internees were troublesome and hard to control. In a June 1917 plea for help, governor S. F. Fox wrote to the prison commission, "Ever since the Aliens have been interned here the condition of affairs has been unsatisfactory and is now so bad that supervision has been reduced to almost a farce. The grounds of this place are now at the complete disposal of the Interned women from 6:30 A.M.–9:15 P.M." More disturbing, Fox continued, were the "notes . . . found under cabbage leaves, and signs, and dumb language [is used] which [is] not understood by the Officers. . . ."[79] The women had found a way of fighting the confines of their imprisonment, and they capitalized on whatever leverage they could gain.

Lina Heine was one such troublesome internee accused of espionage in August 1914. She confessed guilt after being interned, claiming that her imprisoned husband was innocent and should be released. He was not released, but instead died in prison on December 1, 1914. After his death and her transfer to Aylesbury, she started a campaign of "endless petitions" to the government for release or repatriation or both. Heine also appeared to enlist the help of a male alien (Austrian), who, on his repatriation, published an article about British prison cruelty in the death of her husband. The Foreign Office had to answer to an American ambassador who investigated the claims on humanitarian grounds at the request of Austria-Hungary.[80]

Despite official complaints, many of the women denied being bold or opportunistic, sometimes pleading not guilty and claiming not to have understood that what they did was illegal. Whether the women really did not consider their crimes serious or whether it was a strategy to gain sympathy from British officials is unclear. At her trial, de Bournonville testified, "I did not think that I did do any harm to anybody with that [information]."[81] In a similar vein, Earle told Scotland

Yard, "I have done nothing to do this country any harm." Both women stated repeatedly that the information that they communicated was of little value. Earle, who was sixty-four years old at her trial and whom MI5 officials described as "something of an invalid," admitted to sending letters with code words to her sister in Germany, but claimed it was an old family code and that she was just reporting on life in London.[82] Earle, convicted of espionage and sentenced to prison, sent no information of military value, was never paid, and was never proved to be supplying secrets to anyone except her sister.[83]

In all the cases of women arrested in Britain, however, the most damning statement that could be made was that a woman was pro-German or anti-British. When Louise Herbert, a fifty-five-year-old curate's wife from Darlington, appealed her conviction for breaching DORA, she was denied appeal as a "person of German sympathies." She admitted that if she had had the means she might have passed information to the Germans, but claimed not to have done so. In court, a police superintendent noted that in addition to her obvious German sympathy, "he had never seen in the appellant's house photographs of Lord Roberts, Admiral Jellicoe, or Sir John French, or pictures of the 'Invasion of England,' or the 'Charge by the Argyll and Sutherland Highlanders.'"[84] The superintendent implied that Herbert was dangerously unpatriotic. Herbert was imprisoned for being pro-German and for not actively supporting the war despite having had little opportunity to pass on important information to anyone of authority in Germany. Espionage, treason, and sedition in World War I were crimes of intent, and as one scholar notes, "The rhetoric of war demanded that all women visibly demonstrate their national loyalty."[85]

The case files mention over and over again that petitions for release were being denied because the women in question were too pro-German. The denials reflected a genuine fear of subversion in a tense wartime state but also demonstrated a deep anti-alien feeling, especially because many of the British-born women accused of espionage were left free from internment. For example, Patricia Riley Hentschel, the British-born wife of a German citizen, was tracked for possible espionage activities from 1909 through the end of the war but was never interned. Hentschel was arrested and released before the war and in the trial of an accomplice even admitted to a role as a "beguiler," telling officials that, "She herself acknowledged this part: she was to find out, she said, those officers and non-commissioned officers who were in need of money and open to bribery." Hentschel was allowed to relocate to Wey-bridge, change her name, and live her life (under surveillance) outside the walls of Aylesbury Prison.[86] Officials deemed one British young woman to be "foolish," and her actions were reported to her mother. May Higgs, another British subject, sent a letter to her mother in Holland in July 1915, which was intercepted by the postal censors. In it, she offered her services to the Germans. Although she was briefly interned in 1916, "eventually she was sent to a convent for the duration of the war."[87]

Those responsible for tracking suspicious activity in Britain—MI5, police, port officials—wavered in their opinions of women's abilities as spies. Official condescension toward the weak and ineffective female spy alternated with fear of women's sexual wiles and ruthless ambitions. Former intelligence officer during the war Ferdinand Tuohy wrote a newspaper account of women spies and their work in 1926. His assessment encapsulates the arguments about women spying both for and against Britain in the war:

> In effect, women spies fail both in the head and in the heart, and also in character composition for the business on hand. Women are fundamentally inaccurate. They experience a constant "urge" to be working in the limelight, jibbing at the patient compilation of dull details which forms the basic job in spying. They talk—that is, are inherently untrustworthy—vanity usually being the propelling motive. . . . The root difference is, one supposes, that a woman, to be a spy, must be an adventuress by nature; whereas a man agent can just be any unit, stepping from a train at Victoria Station each morning around 9 A.M.[88]

Tuohy's assumptions reflect the larger cultural understanding of women's role in intelligence work and in wartime. Women were considered fatally flawed, either through their romantic natures or their vanity. Just as their national loyalty supposedly changed with the nationality of their husbands, their personal integrity and their very natures were unstable and suspect. Either women were inept but respectable, or they were dangerous and effective sexual adventuresses. In either case, officials claimed women's inherent weaknesses made them a bad bet for intelligence work.

In the gendered language of twentieth-century espionage, female espionage was inextricably tied to sexuality, and these women remained dangerous precisely because they made men vulnerable. Sexy prostitute-spies could bring men to their knees and make them willing to betray their countries, while the naive romantic woman spy made men vulnerable because they inspired pity. As A. A. Hoehling notes in the introduction to his sensational study, *Women Who Spied*, "There will be female spies as long as men remain vulnerable to the wiles of attractive, willful women. . . ."[89] Ironically, the same officials who voiced concerns about women's suitability for espionage hired females in large numbers for wartime intelligence work both at home and in enemy territory. While condemning enemy female spies captured in England as "unnatural" women, British male intelligence officials praised the work of their fine female agents working in France and Belgium.

CONCLUSION

Britain's concern with monitoring and controlling foreigners made it extremely difficult for enemies to establish any successful espionage networks in the British Isles during the war. However, the vigilance of the police and counterespionage offices, combined with censorship, DORA, ARA and other legislation, created a precedent for intense government secrecy, the invasion of citizens' privacy, and unconstitutional infringements on personal rights such as trial by jury. Intolerance of foreigners was institutionalized during the war, leading to a series of racist and prejudiced laws in the interwar period allowing the government to continue a wartime policy of registering and defining foreigners.[90]

Women were a particular problem for the British government in its attempt to define "true" citizens. As people without permanent nationality, their citizenship depended not on whether they were born British, but whether their husbands were British. One scholar calls women of the period "place-holders for men," capable of reproducing male citizens but not of entirely fulfilling that role themselves.[91] This ambivalent relationship between the state and its female citizens was exacerbated during the war by "sexual anger" directed toward women occupying new roles in society and the workplace.[92] Vague fears of degeneration, a hidden spy menace, and an "enemy within" found a convenient scapegoat in the imagined female spy, a sexualized and predatory woman. These images had incredible staying power in the public consciousness despite the few real women spies captured or charged.

Altogether, the British only formally charged about thirty spies during the war but compiled a much larger series of lists used to identify espionage activity. By the end of the war they had a massive registry of all the aliens in Britain—a "Defence Black List" with over thirteen thousand names, more than twenty- seven thousand files, and 250,000 individual cards in the MI5 registry.[93] These lists, files, and cards included personal information, identifying characteristics, suspected illegal activities, and sometimes photographs or other supporting material. The government's plans to track all traitorous, subversive, or unusual activity in Britain required large numbers of clerical workers.

While efforts between 1909 and 1914 had yielded a small list of suspects who were arrested immediately on the declaration of war, larger tasks faced the British government after the outbreak. The government had to control ports and communications, manage and track foreigners (both enemy aliens and neutrals), suppress dissent and domestic subversion, investigate DORA violations, and proactively gather intelligence at home and abroad. Military men not eligible for active service were obvious choices for this work, but the intelligence departments soon had to turn to untrained older male scholars, boys too young to enlist, and finally, educated women. By 1918, the Directorate of Military Intelligence and the Postal Censorship Branch were staffed with thousands of young women, many of whom were as knowledgeable in foreign languages and history as their male superiors.

3

Women behind the Scenes

Let us now praise women clerks,/Clerks of little showing,
For their work continueth,/And their work continueth,
Broad and deep continueth/Greater than their knowing . . .
And we all praise famous men/Ancients of the office
For they taught Intelligence/Tried to teach Intelligence,
Taught us all Intelligence,/Which is more than knowledge.

—S. Callow (1920)

IN HER "Song of the Women Clerks (with apologies to R. Kipling)" in
the first issue of *The Nameless Magazine* privately published in March
1920, Miss S. Callow tried to capture the novel experience of women
working in the spy-catching bureau of the British War Office. MI5 was
the organization primarily responsible for counterespionage in Britain,
and its job was to track and investigate suspicious activities in Britain
while coordinating intelligence information and reports from a variety
of sources. MI5 employees were expected to keep their work and its location secret, especially because the branch housed a massive card registry of known and suspected espionage activity in Britain and abroad.
At MI5, more than six hundred educated women were entrusted with
government secrets between 1915 and 1919. These women (and teenage
girls) worked alongside male civil servants, military personnel, and
special secret service officers at the London MI5 headquarters in Waterloo House, No. 16 Charles Street, Haymarket.[1] As clerks, supervisors,
report writers, translators, printers, searchers, messengers, and historians, women made it possible for a tiny spy-tracking office created in
1909 to become a massive information clearinghouse by the end of the
war. As Callow's song points out, women clerks worked long hours in
the service of the state in the war years performing the detailed work of

maintaining and updating intelligence records for their use by British and Allied military and civilian authorities.

MI5 was only one of a score of secret offices that employed women for sensitive intelligence work during the First World War. This chapter examines how women's temporary labor, which was both cheap and efficient, made it possible for British military intelligence to grow into a complex bureaucracy by the end of 1916. The women of the secrets sections, despite their youth (most were under thirty) and inexperience (some had no previous clerical skills), became the heart of an intelligence establishment, employed in virtually every aspect of information- gathering work. But while these women were entering intelligence across the country and across Europe, they were in a paradoxical position. Despite being recruited to handle state secrets and national security issues they remained ineligible to vote or hold political office. The realities of wartime conscription, the demands of modern bureaucracy, and the technological changes in communication and information processing had forced the state to turn to well-educated but disenfranchised women, albeit those of a superior class, for labor in its secrets industry.

Prior to the outbreak of World War I in August 1914, the few women working in the War Office were limited to working as typists. Subordinate to male clerks and without hope of promotion, female typists were marginal to the functioning of the Secret Service and other intelligence sections.[2] In general, intelligence offices were small organizations with few permanent staff members. In fact, the entire Directorate of Military Operations (that included intelligence) employed just over one hundred people in 1914. The war brought major expansions in both operations and intelligence, leading to the creation of a separate Directorate of Military Intelligence (DMI) in January of 1916 that had a staff of more than six thousand by 1918.[3] With the mobilization of men for the armed forces and male conscription after January 1916, opportunities opened up for women who were soon employed in every part of the DMI as well as in intelligence sections of the Foreign Office, Admiralty, and Army headquarters.[4] These legions of young women worked in a variety of capacities during the war, some temporarily replacing men and others working in newly created jobs.

The convergence of the growth of the modern secret state and the expansion in educational opportunities for women meant that females played an important role in shaping the twentieth-century professional bureaucratic intelligence industry. Women designed and ran the spy-tracking paperwork networks, staffed and shaped postal censorship, and played a role in developing state propaganda and cryptography. The intelligence community, popularly understood as a male preserve, rested on the backs of female laborers. Although women entered many wartime occupations such as policing, munitions, and transport, their work in intelligence helped create and structure this emerging industry.

Despite the fact that women were valuable assets to the state as necessary workers in an information-based bureaucracy, their labor was undervalued both during the war and after it. In all sections of the civil service, women entered paid government positions during the war and opened the doors for future women to engage in such work; however, the wartime female workers also created a precedent for gender discrimination in hiring, employment practices, and compensation that was hard to erase. No departments demonstrate this temporary feminization of work and exploitation of young female labor better than the secret service sections under the auspices of the War Office and the British Admiralty.

RECRUITING THE "NAMELESS CLUB"

A dramatic example of the relatively rapid expansion of jobs for women is MI9, or the Postal Censorship Branch, which began using women in September 1914. This important security work was increasingly entrusted to women, with MI9 employing more than thirty-five hundred women on its payroll in November 1918, compared to only thirteen hundred men.[5] Women were employed as examiners, clerks, translators, chemical testers (for invisible inks), and censors, and some even held supervisory roles. MI9 handled an incredible amount of correspondence including all non-military incoming, outgoing, and transit mail (correspondence passing through Britain on its way to other countries).

The Post Office was one of the few civil service branches that had employed women in a variety of occupations before the war. Women had held positions in the Post Office since 1870 when it inherited a group of women employees from the private telegraph companies it absorbed. A report on female employment in 1871 made it clear that women workers were successful in these positions because they were willing to work for low wages in clerical jobs, were often better educated than their male counterparts, and were drawn from "a superior class." The report also noted that women were less troublesome, less inclined to strike, and less likely to remain in their jobs long enough to draw a pension. Finally, the report concluded that "aggregate pay to the females will always be less than the aggregate pay to the males . . . [but] the work will be better done by the females [because of their class]."[6] On the eve of war in 1914, the Post Office had apparently accepted the report's conclusions because it employed approximately fifty-eight thousand women.[7]

Despite the Post Office's history of employing women, civil mail censorship itself was subsumed under the authority of the War Office, so it was not entirely clear what the place of women would be in this new work.[8] Bowing perhaps to the inevitable need for workers, the War Office, "which had previously employed women to a limited extent, now recruited them in large numbers on a temporary basis, and other [civil service] departments followed suit."[9] In censorship, particularly, women were needed almost immediately in September 1914, to deal with the volume of mail piling up for examination. As the chief censor noted in his report on wartime censorship,

> From an early date in the war none but men over military age or found unfit medically were employed, except in a few exceptional cases, in the censorship. In order to save man power and to utilize their special abilities women were employed in the censorship from very early days.[10]

Women were also employed in Room 40, Old Admiralty Building, which served as the ears of the Navy. Room 40 (later known officially as I. D. 25) was responsible for decoding enemy messages and ciphers for Naval Intelligence. Directed by William Reginald "Blinker" Hall after October 1914, Room 40 was an odd office that ran three watches for a twenty-four hour schedule. The cryptographers were a motley crew of language instructors, university dons, scientists, and barristers, many from wealthy backgrounds. In addition to the men hired to decode enemy messages, women were hired in 1917 to perform secretarial tasks, unload message tubes, and help with decoding. The staff, fondly dubbed by some as "Blinker's Beauty Chorus," only employed women with naval connections or personal recommendations.[11] As one male cryptographer noted in his memoirs, "the typists were ladies passed under the microscope of every kind of social and political scrutiny . . ."[12] Some of the women were university graduates, several were daughters of admirals or other naval officers, and most were relatively young, single women with significant foreign language skills. Of the women hired, a few remained with the office in the interwar period, and several returned to work in cryptography during World War II.[13] Other intelligence branches that employed women included overseas passport control offices and the British Mission in Paris, the Propaganda section, the Translation Bureau, Military Press Control (press, photography, and cinematography censorship), and MI1B (which deciphered enemy wireless messages).

MI5 may be the most surprising employer of large numbers of women. When Britain declared war on Germany in August 1914, Kell's spy-tracking office was composed only of about two dozen office employees (four were female), but it quickly expanded and reorganized to deal with its multitude of wartime duties.[14] The office was put under the direct control of the War Office and named MO5g (which it would be called until 1916 when it was renamed MI5), and new officers and clerks were added to the staff. The office continued to expand and evolve until by the time of the armistice, MI5 had more than eight hundred employees and eight branches, each with a variety of subsections.[15] Women worked in all the branches of the London office, overseas, and in domestic ports, but they were most visible in the "H" Branch, records administration. MI5's Registry—a huge card file of suspects and information—was staffed entirely by women after November 1914. In his memoirs, Compton Mackenzie describes his visit to the MI5 registry in London during a trip home from his intelligence duties in Athens:

> I asked for the dossier of some rascal. . . . One rosy- cheeked young woman hurried to the boxes of the card-index, and returned presently to equip another rosy-cheeked young woman with the necessary clue to send her scurrying across to an enormous chest of drawers whence with another clue she in turn hurried over to a third rosy-cheeked young woman, who with the final clue to the whereabouts of the required dossier opened a filing-cabinet to bring the culprit's misdeeds to light. . . . "I'm so sorry, Major X——," said the rosy-cheeked young woman in charge of the sanctum sanctorum of filing-cabinets, "but I don't seem able to find the man you want."[16]

The Electric Bells having broke, the G.G.'s (*not* Grenadier Guards) sit outside Maj. D.'s door in case he wants them.

The Nameless Magazine, published by former women employees of MI5 (Counterespionage), parodies their teenage Girl Guide messengers in this 1919 cartoon. Imperial War Museum Department of Documents.

This humorous story of official overkill and bureaucracy demonstrates the eager bustle of the young women employed in the Registry. Despite its failure to produce Mackenzie's suspect from its files, the Registry functioned more or less smoothly as a repository of information on activities tracked by MI5 during the war.

In addition to women clerks and secretaries, teenage girls were also employed by intelligence to run messages between offices in the building. Early in the war, Boy Scouts had filled these positions in many sections, but at MI5 they were "found to be very troublesome. The considerable periods of inactivity which fell to their share usually resulted in their getting into mischief." So, the office replaced the Boy Scouts with Girl Guides on September 4, 1915, and the girls "proved more amenable and their methods of getting into mischief were on the whole less distressing to those who had to deal with them than were those of the boys."[17] Girl Guides also replaced the Boy Scouts as messengers in the censorship offices.[18]

The Guides of MI5 worked daily from 9 A.M. to 7 P.M. with little time off, they pledged "on their honour not to read the papers they carried," and signed a contract with the permission of their parents and Girl Guide captains. The Girl Guides were paid ten shillings per week plus dinner, and most were fourteen to sixteen years old. Organized into a company with their own captain by January of 1917, each Guide patrol within the company was assigned to a floor. Their duties included carrying messages and filling inkpots, and they were expected to parade every Monday afternoon on the roof of Waterloo House.[19] Some older Guides were given additional duties, but in general the girls waited for messages, sometimes too eagerly if staff publications are to be believed. The Girl Guides show up in many privately printed works and are often parodied for their intensity regarding their duties in the offices, as shown in this MI5 cartoon. Miss M. S. Aslin summed up the experience of working with teen girls for nine hours every day:

> She speeds from floor to floor, bearing messages of good will, and no obstacle is too great for her to fall over in her devotion to this happy task. Released for the moment, she retires to her attractive little sitting-room, where she reads and writes or converses quietly(?) on high topics with her friends.[20]

In short, the Girl Guides were soon familiar figures in the War Office secrets industry, and their work continued through the peace process with a contingent serving in Paris with the British delegation.

A small number of women were employed by the intelligence directorate to perform non-clerical jobs, manual tasks, and skilled or semi-skilled work. Women cleaned most of the intelligence offices, although many of the rooms at Room 40 were notoriously off-limits to cleaning for much of its existence. Canteens were staffed and supervised by women, as was the tea club at Room 40 run by Joan Harvey, a "lady secretary."[21] At MI5, women were hired temporarily as searchers to frisk female passengers at the ports before this duty was assumed by a contingent of female auxiliaries from the Women's Army Auxiliary Corps (WAACs) in 1919.[22] From January 1917 until the end of the war, a woman managed the photographic section of "H" Branch, and Kell's female secretary assumed responsibility for managing the office's finances in April 1916. Women staffed the switchboard, ran the lifts, charred and cooked, and served as chauffeuses for MI5's three motorcars. By the end of the war, a "lady doctor" was even engaged to attend to the needs of the staff. Some of the Girl Guides were also trained to clean and repair typewriters in the office.

Perhaps one of the most important and taxing jobs in the office also fell to women late in 1916. The Misses Ewen, two sisters who were members of the Women's Printers' Association, took control of the printing section, doing what they could with an antiquated hand press and few supplies. As the official historian of MI5 "H" Branch notes in her report on the printing section, "It is probable that here this much derided faculty of women for using substitutes for recognized tools stood them in good stead, male printers would possibly not have been bothered with such makeshifts. . . ." Happily, the printers got a new machine and a staff of fourteen women and two men to oversee it before the war's end.[23]

Several women were given positions of real authority in the offices. University-trained women wrote précis of sensitive materials, compiled reports, translated information from abroad, and served as official historians. In fact, five women wrote most of the historical report on MI5's service during the First World War.[24] Other valuable women with significant responsibilities were the officers' secretaries, many of whom were promoted to the rank of officer near the end of the war. Although they were well educated and competent, these women had to struggle to be recognized as colleagues rather than drudges. As MI5's historical report records, "It has been remarked by a secretary that in the early days of MI5 some of the officers were inclined to look on their secretaries as mere shorthand-typists, and that some even were prejudiced against women workers. . . ."[25]

The two highest-ranking women in MI5 were Controller of the Women's Staff, Edith A. Lomax and her assistant Elsie L. Harrison who together oversaw a massive organization of documents and people during their several years in the office. At the height of the war the two women handled all personnel matters for the hundreds of women and girls at MI5 while overseeing the processing, classification, and retrieval of more than ten thousand documents per month. For almost two years the women's staff was divided into three shifts in order to staff the office almost twenty-four hours a day, making Lomax and Harrison's management and coordination of employees even more difficult.[26] The night shift (10:00 P.M. to 7:00 A.M.) was abandoned in August of 1916 because of its excessive cost and frequent work stoppages from air raid warnings.[27]

Women had important supervisory roles in branches outside MI5 as well. In Room 40, Lady Sybil Hambro, the wife of an important businessman, was a cigar smoking, "formidable head of the secretarial section."[28] At MI9, a female supervised all the women working as examiners or in higher-ranking positions. Women with special skills in languages or science were also hired as technical experts and translators, while some rose to positions of authority as deputy and assistant censors.[29] Charlotte Bosworth reported after the war that she obtained her job as a deputy assistant censor because of her excellent skills in German and French, but it was her knowledge of German script that got her transferred to Paris for "special" work.[30]

In smaller offices in neutral and allied countries abroad, women were often essential to the running of the offices. Eileen McNeill (later honored as a Member of the British Empire (MBE) for her war service) was sent to Holland to type espionage reports coming in from secret service agents working for the British General Headquarters (GHQ) behind enemy lines.[31] Lady Claire Milne, awarded the British Empire Medal (BEM), performed similar duties in the London office of the GHQ secret services.[32] Likewise, the British Mission in Paris—the official liaison to other Allied services—was staffed largely by women in both the trade and espionage sections and supervised by thirty-year-old Miss Mary Harris.[33] Viscount Mersey, appointed in May of 1916 to lead the British Mission in Paris, made special mention of his dedicated female staff, saying they were "young women from all ranks of society" who worked hard "from morning to night and hardly ever made a mistake." He also singled out Harris for her ability to know "something, at any rate, about every one of the twenty thousand dossiers which we eventually possessed. . . ."[34]

Despite their important and responsible work during the war, women were almost invariably compensated at much lower rates than their male colleagues. The male breadwinner ideal—which assumed that only men supported their families—was firmly in place and was exacerbated by the higher economic status of many of the women, which caused many officials to treat them as "patriotic" workers not needing a living wage. It was assumed that women worked in clerical occupations only for patriotic reasons, amusement, or pin money.[35] This attitude gave rise to wage discrepancies that cut across the intelligence industry and that were unapologetically explained in official histories, memoirs, and reports.

For example, the women employed in naval cryptography in Room 40 were paid much lower wages than their male colleagues. In a 1919 salary listing, male officers earned between £350 and £500 per year, while the highest paid university-educated women in the office received only £200 per year. Typists, tubists (who retrieved coded messages from tubes), and secretaries received even less.[36] Despite their poor wages, one of the chiefs of Room 40 mentioned female typists' indispensability to the office in his memoirs, recording, "expert typists were admitted when the need for their help was almost too apparent. It should be noted . . . that the last should have been the first or at any rate let it be said that every expert cryptographer must possess at least one typist skilled in sorting filing and analyzing."[37] As this official noted, clerical availability and accuracy made intelligence dissemination possible; without this key function, vital information could sit endlessly in a basket waiting for analysis.

As in the Admiralty's cryptography sections, women in other offices were hired almost exclusively as temporary workers, leaving them without job security and with lower wages than their male colleagues. One stark example of the unequal treatment of female employees was the war bonus award system of 1915, in which cost-of-living bonuses were awarded to civil servants doing war work. Women war workers insisted that it cost the same for men and women to live in wartime London, but men were still awarded a higher bonus.[38] Censorship employees were granted compensation bonuses for "special usefulness" but these bonuses also reflected gender inequity. In March 1916, male examiners received £1 extra per week, while female examiners performing the same duties received only a 10 shilling bonus. This disparity is especially striking because female examiners more often read in foreign languages and, in the words of Chief Censor A. S. L. Farquharson, were "more meticulous and probably more conscientious."[39] Women did get lower wages, but it should be noted that male employees worked one half-hour longer each day because of labor agreements, and on average they examined a greater bulk of mail than women did. Farquharson attributed men's greater productivity to their longer hours and the simpler nature of the mail they examined (often in English or in the specialized technical fields in which they were trained).[40]

Wages in the censorship division (MI9) also generally reflected gender inequalities despite the fact that women made up more than 75 percent of the total workforce. Men in MI9 were paid per annum, while women in most positions were paid weekly. Even the four most senior women only received £5 per week as assistant censors, their fifty-six male counterparts receiving between £400 and £500 per annum. Graham Mark notes, "This indicates that the lady staff, even at their top level were employed on a weekly basis, whilst the men had greater job security and nearly double the salary."[41] For ordinary examiners, men received £4.4s maximum average pay per week, while women got only £2.17s.[42] It is not surprising that the wage discrepancies were also reflected in other wartime occupations. For instance, male munitions workers' wages averaged double the wages of women in the industry by April 1918.[43]

Work in government intelligence also meant hours of detailed and monotonous work with few holidays. In MI9 women officially worked from 9:30 A.M. to 5:00 P.M., with an hour for lunch and a twenty-minute tea break, but in practice, overtime hours could increase the workday. Each woman could look forward to one and a half days off per week, if the schedule was operating properly. Freya Stark described her work in MI9 in a series of letters to her mother in January of 1917, noting less generous hours and less holiday time than the official report records: "I can only write Sundays, as I really do feel very tired all the week, and usually sit and look at the fire in my spare time." Stark noted in a February letter,

> I have just had two days' holiday (they give one weekend every six weeks) and I am so annoyed because I had to spend most of it in bed, stifling a cold. The W.O. [War Office] insists on all windows being open, and as there has been fog, snow, and all sorts of weather lately, it wasn't at all pleasant . . . it is very strenuous. . . .[44]

The censorship offices were cold because of official attempts to limit illness from infectious disease. Housed in a poorly ventilated building, the windows were kept open all year. Conditions were often cramped because of constant expansions of staff in the offices. Many of the women had to sit elbow to elbow and vied for space at the long eleven-by-four-foot tables. Stark noted in her diary that luckily only one of the seven other women at her table was "insufferable," but that there were about 300 other examiners in her room. She continued, "I feel a kind of suffocation and long for a breath of solitude and a clear skyline and the coolness of wind that has come from spaces without a human voice."[45] An anonymous censorship worker recorded that she truly earned her £3 per week by learning "how to sit next to someone I cordially detested without slapping her; and, what was perhaps more important, how to sit next to someone I liked extremely, and carry on an animated conversation with her, without being detected."[46]

At MI5 (counterintelligence), women were scheduled for eight or nine-hour days, but they often worked seven days a week and overtime was common. Most got a day off every other Sunday and one half-day free each week. In a 1920 report, the new women's controller Hilda Cribb noted that the strain of work was alleviated in several ways beginning in the spring of 1915. The women's staff was allowed to have one week off after three months of work (three weeks vacation per year), and women were encouraged to learn typing or shorthand so they could vary their duties in the office. The Registry work of filing was especially tedious, and Cribb recorded that, "The work of looking-up was so fatiguing that no one was able to keep at it for too long at a stretch. . . ."[47]

For their hours of work, the women of MI5 were paid less than their male counterparts from the beginning. In October 1915, most of the female clerical staff received between £7 and £10 per month, with a few women earning slightly above or below that range. The superintendent (later the controller of woman's staff) Edith Lomax was paid £20 per month in October 1916 and only just over £29 per month by February 1919. Throughout the war Lomax received less money than male officers with comparable duties in the office, most of whom were paid about £33 per month.[48]

In order to pursue their war work at MI5, women staff members often took lodgings near the office in local hostels or boardinghouses.[49] Late in the war women also took advantage of low-cost meals offered by MI5's canteen late in the war and by the "K" Club, a members-only restaurant down the street from Waterloo House that served government workers cheap food.[50] Women of MI5 improved their lot slightly in the latter years of the war by arguing successfully for higher wages based on a merit system of pay, but interestingly enough, they had to enlist the services of their male branch officers to point out "the right of a Government woman clerk to a living wage."[51]

II. AS SEEN BY THE FEMALE STAFF.

A militant MI5 file clerk chases an elusive spy file from the hundreds of thousands of personal dossiers that the Registry clerks maintained. Interestingly enough, the file is also female. *The Hush-Hush Revue.*

Wage issues and the hours of wartime clerical work aside, women continued to enter temporary civil service jobs for a variety of reasons. Some wanted to perform service work during wartime, some wanted the excitement of paid employment, and others needed something to help pass their time. Their reasons were fueled by calls to patriotism. For example, postal examiner Florence Rees and her coworkers were instructed that their objective was to protect the men risking their lives "from betrayal by enemies in our midst," which was probably a powerful motivating force.[52] By January of 1918, approximately 144,600, mostly middle- and upper-class women were employed in civil service positions, and by November that number had risen to 235,000, or 56 percent of the total staff.[53] These women, especially those in intelligence, were privileged in many ways; their sex allowed them exemption from the draft and their class backgrounds opened doors for them in the secrets community.

GENDERING AND CLASSING INTELLIGENCE WORK

Who were the women that chose to work in the intelligence offices? For the most part, only "girls from 'good families'" were hired for the sensitive work of spy tracking.[54] Women from the ranks of the elite and upper-middle-classes were recruited from the women's colleges at Oxford and Cambridge, elite schools such as Cheltenham Ladies College, and well-known high schools. Women who had private tutelage or foreign educations were also sought if they had good references. Some women employed in the intelligence offices were hired based on specific skills (such as language, typing, or both), but those qualities were sometimes less important than good character references. Poet May Wedderburn Cannan had considerable clerical and writing experience from working with sensitive materials in the editorial offices of Oxford University Press when she applied to work for the British Mission in Paris, but she still had to provide references testifying to her character. She used a well-known professor, Arthur Quiller-Couch, a woman involved in the Red Cross, Lucie Raleigh, and A. S. L. Farquharson, head of the War Office's Postal Censorship Branch, to vouch for her.[55]

Women applying for work in the censorship branch were also carefully screened for language skills and for more intangible qualities. Freya Stark described the process in a series of letters to her mother. She set up an appointment for a language interview and was tested on November 1, 1916, stating that she knew French and Italian well. The examiner told her that they really wanted people with German language skills and gave her "an unintelligible bit of manuscript to read." Stark noted that the standards must have been lax because she passed. Once the language exams were completed, "a terrible looking document arrived from the War Office . . . asking [her references] to guarantee me in all sorts of virtues: and to say that I am temperate, honest, and capable of keeping secrets of a 'highly confidential nature.'" Two weeks later she was offered the position.[56]

According to MI5 historical reports, qualified applicants for the office had to possess sterling character references. They were expected to possess honor, intelligence, diligence, tact, good schooling, and reticence. Most of those hired were single women between the ages of twenty and thirty, although married and older women were employed if they had special qualifications or particularly strong connections.[57] Women workers at MI5 were chosen at first through recommendations from schools such as Cheltenham Ladies' College and Somerville College, Oxford, but it was often difficult to attract university women to such poorly paid positions. Most of the women eventually hired were public school or college women, some referred by institutions and others recommended by women in the office or by other government departments. As former Registry worker Mrs. D. B. G. Line remembered, "Candidates for these posts were selected by private recommendation and there was never any advertisement." She had gotten her job when her aunt had recommended her to a friend who happened to work at MI5.[58] Those nominated for positions had to be interviewed by the lady controller to insure that they were trustworthy, discreet, and suitable for such work.

Although some positions required office skills such as typing or shorthand, no previous clerical experience was required for many of the jobs at MI5. The ability to hold one's tongue seemed to be the paramount qualification, and the women of MI5 had to be prepared to prevaricate when asked about their work or its location. Mrs. Line recalled telling people she worked "where Nelson looks like Mephistopheles," because that was the view of Nelson's column in Trafalgar Square from the roof of the MI5 building in Haymarket. From that angle, the statue of Lord Nelson appeared to have horns.[59] Male officials worried most about this aspect of the work, often fretting that women would brag of their jobs or chatter to friends about state secrets. Yet as Hilda Martindale notes in her study of women in the civil service, "It was realized, to the surprise of some of their men colleagues, that women could keep a secret and did not divulge confidential information."[60] Women, in fact, received praise from many male bosses after the war for their hard work, precision, and reticence.

For clerical and supervisory work, male officials turned to upper-class women who were considered more trustworthy and reticent, assuming their backgrounds assured their patriotism and devotion to honor. Females who had been exposed to "old school" ties, values, and nationalism presumably knew the importance of keeping secrets for the common good. More important, however, women of the upper classes could be depended on to go quietly when the time came, back to their families, to positions in women's education, or to future husbands.

The roster of women who worked for the intelligence agencies during the First World War was an impressive one. Writers and poets such as Marjory Hollings, May Wedderburn Cannan, and Elinor Jenkins joined the intelligence service, as did the daughters of university dons, admirals, and merchants. The women employed at I. D. 25 alone included the headmistress of Christ's Hospital for girls, wives of doctors and businessmen, university graduates, daughters of well-known magnates in banking and industry, and daughters of the landowning gentry. In many cases, the women outranked the men in wealth, education, and birth. Many former debutantes got a very different education during the war than what their families had planned for them, especially because they were joined by men drawn from a range of class and occupational backgrounds, including everyone from artists and authors to aristocrats.[61] Consider the situation of Olive Roddam, the daughter of a wealthy Northumberland landowner whose family found her an intelligence position to help her forget the death of her fiancé in 1914. She was hired at I. D. 25 to serve as secretary to cryptographer A. D. (Dilly) Knox. A brilliant recruit from Cambridge, Knox was known for the eccentric habit of breaking codes while sitting in a bathtub installed in the tiny room he used as an office. Perhaps unsurprisingly, given the nature and hours of such work, Roddam and Knox married in July of 1920.[62]

Of those who were not already affianced or married before the war, many left their work to marry. In fact, so many of the women became housewives that the editor of the "old girls" magazine for MI5 workers felt it necessary to add an encouraging note for the spytrackers-turned-housewives in 1921:

> If there was one vocation which, as wider vistas opened before the eyes of the twentieth-century woman, a natural reaction tended to belittle it was the world-old calling of the housewife. The war (one of its few merits) has changed all that. The woman of today realizes that the care of the home needs as much skill and training, and is as honorable as any other profession, and that cooking can be a fine art and "house work" an opportunity for intelligence and initiative.[63]

However, a number of women also found joy in paid work and looked for ways to continue meaningful employment after the war in the civil service or other industries. Some used education as a postwar destination: L. Gracey and J. Constant went from the MI5 Registry to Oxford University to study physics and English respectively. Carrie Morrison hoped to become one of the first woman solicitors, and Gladys Hill studied her way toward becoming a surgeon. Those with the family wealth to support it or with husbands in diplomatic posts traveled to destinations such as France, Kenya, Italy, India, and Egypt.[64]

A few women made national names for themselves in their postwar work. Hilda Matheson worked in intelligence from 1916 to 1919 for MI5 in London and Rome and later went on to work as the political secretary to Lady Nancy Astor (the first woman to sit in Parliament), as a British Broadcasting Company (BBC) presenter from 1926 to 1931, and as a secretary for the massive Oxford African Survey project—all before returning to intelligence work during the Second World War.[65] May Jenkin, a university graduate hired at I. D. 25, also joined the BBC after the war.[66] Freya Stark, who worked for a short time in the censorship division, became a well-known traveler and writer in Syria and Iraq, following in the footsteps of Gertrude Bell, who also did intelligence work during World War I.[67]

Some of the female workforce would have been content to continue their jobs in intelligence. Despite their lower wages and difficult working conditions, many women enjoyed their work and hoped to remain working after the war's end. Cribb described the hopeful feeling among the staff before the end of the war and their disillusionment after the war:

> The conditions of work had always been made as easy as possible under the circumstances, and the consideration the women's staff in particular received, not only with regard to hours of work and sick leave, but also with regard to pay—which was at a higher rate than most government offices—made them feel that the Authorities took a real interest in their workers. . . . But, alas! This was a vain hope for a bomb was soon dropped upon us in August [1919] when the Authorities had instructions to cut down considerably by 30th September, and great was the sorrow on August 27th when a third or more of the staff received a note that their last hour had come.[68]

As with MI5, MI9 also had to clear out its examiners and censors by the summer of 1919. Although supervisory officials tried to help the censorship employees find work, few women and virtually no men were given permanent clerical work with the Post Office. Other women followed some of the "higher censorship officials" to clerical positions at the Ministry of Pensions, which faced the massive job of sorting paperwork. During the demobilization period, male censorship employees tried to protest their imminent unemployment and slowed their work in the office to a crawl. In an interesting maneuver, the supervisors of the censorship office replaced the men with women "who were drawn from a higher class and were more loyal than the men" and so "got over the difficulty." The fact that women were more acquiescent and less likely to feel entitled to combine in unions or to agitate for better treatment contributed to the sense that females were "suitable" for temporary war work.[69]

Some women in the censorship branch ruefully noted the disappearance of their jobs in the 1919 memorial book published for employees. In a poem called "Ten Little Censorettes," the author describes the slowly dwindling staff, "One little Censorette found her work was done. She got demobilized and then there were None." Another wrote a fake classified advertisement touting her skills to prospective employers:

> Young lady, refined, excellent conversationalist, accomplished tea maker, nearly three years' war work, Government office. Fair knowledge of the rudiments of card indexing, desires a like position.
> —Mabel, c/o Chells, Brixton.[70]

As with most other temporary women's work during World War I, most intelligence positions were eliminated with the national demobilization of 1919 to 1920. Most women foresaw losing their work, and some went straight into married life and unpaid domestic labor in the home. Even the Ministry of Reconstruction's Women's Employment Committee of 1919, created to find opportunities for women's employment, agreed that women were needed to rebuild Britain's homes. The committee, while recognizing that "women's employment in clerical work [was] revolutionized by the war," and women would most likely do much of this sort of work in the postwar world, was explicit in its condemnation of married women working outside the home. Composed of both men and women, the committee recommended equal pay for equal work but said that "every inducement, direct and indirect, will be given to keep mothers at home."[71] Single women were also shunned at the end of the war as brazen, "with 3 inches of powder on their faces," and selfish not to give up their pin money to make room for ex-servicemen.[72]

By the end of 1918, as many as 750,000 women had been laid off with only a rail pass and two weeks pay for their efforts. As historian Gerard De Groot notes, "Women workers had become pariahs. They were simultaneously criticized for accepting unemployment benefit rather than taking up work and for refusing to give up jobs rightfully belonging to men."[73]

Even women who hoped to remain in their wartime positions or to find similar work found the postwar civil service a grim place to be. In her study of interwar civil service opportunities for women, Meta Zimmeck found fundamental inequalities in recruitment, grading, advancement, compensation, and pension arrangements. Women were excluded unfairly from administrative posts, downgraded from wartime positions, and paid, classified, and promoted on a separate scale from men. Structural inequality in the civil service and in the larger employment pool meant that female employees were younger, paid less, and had better educations than their middle-aged, better-paid, male colleagues with substandard skills and education. As a result of discriminatory policies and low pay, no regular pay increases, and poor opportunities, the number of women in the civil service plummeted in the interwar period in intelligence and all other government branches. The total female staff in both permanent and temporary positions in the civil service hovered around 25 percent of total staff from the early 1920s to the outbreak of World War II. It was not until after World War II that women flooded into clerical work, but even then they were still often denied administrative posts and promotions.[74]

The women of the secret services offices who did manage to find work went to various postwar positions knowing their work had been useful in the war, yet mindful of their status as "women" workers in intelligence. A good example of the gendered division in the office staff was the creation of postwar clubs for MI5 workers. Kell and his male colleagues formed the I.P. (Intelligent People) Club in 1919, but "no ladies present" was the rule; only past and present male members of the staff were invited to attend.[75] In retaliation, the female staff created its own organization, noting ruefully that they should have named themselves the Ladies' I.P. (or LIP). However, they called their organization the Nameless Club, a play on both their "secrets" work and their status, with "many members having already been put away [demobilized] and the fate of the rest hanging in the balance."[76]

Despite the rush to demobilize women, in private communications the War Office recognized the benefits of keeping a trained staff of women on hand in case of future conflicts. During the demobilization period officials considered a plan for paying retaining fees to members of the clerical staff so they would agree to be immediately available if necessary. Additional consideration was given to a plan in which graduates of elite girls' schools would register as a "reserve class of the

Special Intelligence Service" with a retaining fee.[77] Although neither plan was adopted, officials realized their dependence on women's labor and that "the clerical staff in the Special Intelligence Service in many cases do work of equal importance to that of junior officers and must be selected with as much care. . . ."[78]

CONCLUSION

World War I made it clear that modern spy networks and intelligence agencies should be based on the surveillance of a nation's population and the principle that intelligence agencies rely on information gathering and processing. Surveillance information is not useful however, unless the results can be organized, analyzed, and disseminated to the appropriate civil and military authorities. In wartime Britain the rudiments of a modern counterintelligence system emerged at MI5 but did so only with the cooperation and effectiveness of the women working for the agency. As MI5 chief Vernon Kell wrote in a letter to the "Lady Controller," the success of counterintelligence operations depended on the labor of both men and women in the agency and the department "*increased* its value by employing a staff of women."[79] Countless obscure and "nameless" women did their part to keep Britain safe by accepting the mundane work of listening to, sifting, recording, and maintaining mounds of detailed personal information in an age of carbon copies and file cards.

The British government recognized the work of this "nameless" group of women by conferring honors on some of the MI5 female workforce and clerks from overseas offices. Edith Lomax, the MI5 controller, was named first a Member and then an Officer of the British Empire for her services to the War Office, while her assistant Elsie Harrison received the honor of MBE. Fifteen other women who had worked for most of the war at MI5 received distinction when they were mentioned in the *London Gazette* for their war work.[80] Most of the women, however, received no recognition, and their contributions to the intelligence gathering of World War I remained hidden in the classified documents of the British government until being opened in 1998.

Women's wartime employment helped create and solidify a gendered hierarchy within the British civil service. By using carefully controlled policies of the dilution of the labor force, the government employed women without affording them the benefits of seniority, pension, and equity.[81] By effectively declaring the women "temporary" and hiring them outside of the established civil service system, the government set a precedent for employing women as a "special" group. From the end of the war until 1946 a marriage bar was in place, requiring women to resign from civil service posts on marriage.[82] This policy virtually ensured the continuation of wartime employment practices that offered young, unmarried women entry-level positions and paid them lower wages than those given to male employees of similar rank. Until 1935, women in the British civil service were excluded from equal pension arrangements and received only a marriage "gratuity" as a sort of dowry if they left to marry after serving at least six years.[83]

In short, female office workers shaped the future of intelligence operations, but they also participated in the long- term structuring of women's civil service work in Britain and helped to create a gender-segregated wage and benefit system that lasted beyond the next world war. Although many historical studies define women as marginal to the "real" business of espionage and intelligence gathering, women's services were crucial to the development of twentieth-century British government secrecy, and their labor enabled intelligence to grow into the modern organizations and structures we see today.

4

Soldiers without Uniforms

> Soldiers without uniforms, we have not known the intoxication of combat where we advanced elbow to elbow to the seductive clarion call, nor the nights of battle triumphant. But we have known violent struggle . . . we have seen the voids created in our ranks, the fear of arrest, tracked by the German police, we have wandered in our cities. . . .
> —Jeanne Delwaide, Agent 20 of *La Dame Blanche*

UNLIKE THEIR BRITISH COUNTERPARTS who tracked spies from the safety of an office buildings, women in occupied territories labored as soldiers in the field for the British intelligence establishment. As Jeanne Delwaide described it, spying for the British in wartime was heroic, terrifying, and fulfilling all at once.[1] Women agents were hired for the dangerous tasks of gleaning information from the Germans occupying their nations, coding and transporting that information, and organizing sophisticated spying networks under the eyes of their enemy. Employed by British, French, and Belgian intelligence offices, thousands of women participated in large and small ways gathering information and resisting the German occupation of Belgium, Luxembourg, and northern France. Women often provided an important component to intelligence and escape networks because their movements aroused fewer suspicions than the activities of men.[2] This chapter addresses women's espionage behind enemy lines largely through the examination of one of the many intelligence services run by Allied governments in occupied Belgium.

Each expeditionary force and various branches of the military and civilian offices of governments had their own intelligence services at the fronts. The British ran three discrete organizations: two Army General Headquarters (GHQ) branches, one at Folkestone run by Maj. Cecil

Cameron and one in London organized by Maj. Ernest Wallinger; and one War Office branch in Holland led by Capt. Richard Bolton Tinsley. None of these branches cooperated well with the others and their hostility endangered the work of the agents in these services.[3]

La Dame Blanche was one of these services, funded and managed by the British War Office through representatives in Holland and staffed by more than one thousand Belgian and French civilians.[4] Named after a legendary female specter that was supposed to herald the destruction of the Hohenzollern dynasty, *La Dame Blanche* (The White Lady) organization sought also to destroy the German Hohenzollern Empire but through hard intelligence work rather than ghostly intervention.[5] *La Dame Blanche* was an intricate network of information gathering that was focused in east and south Belgium as well as in the occupied north of France and was staffed by men and women patriots.

Founded by three men in Liège, Belgium in 1916, the network tried to find a government sponsor among a dizzying array of national intelligence organizations operating out of neutral Belgium, northern France, and Holland. When *La Dame Blanche* leaders went looking for a sponsor they ran into bitter competition among British intelligence groups and additional rivalry in "parallel systems controlled by . . . French and Belgian Allies."[6] After first approaching the French, Belgian, and British Army intelligence services, *La Dame Blanche* chose to attach itself to the British War Office (Tinsley service) in 1917, partly because the War Office had money to pay its agents.[7] Their British contact and chief of operations was a South African man, Capt. Henry Landau, who had joined the War Office intelligence staff in 1916.[8] After obtaining a formal affiliation with the British, *La Dame Blanche* recruited couriers, territorial observers, trainwatchers, and other personnel to aid the Allied war effort with much-needed information on German morale, troop movements, and technology. Regardless of age, social class, or sex, Belgians could enroll as soldiers by taking an oath of loyalty and thus actively participate in resisting German occupation. Providing enlistees with soldier status was a crucial recruiting tool because it helped legitimize covert intelligence work and promised recognition for its members after the war. For men, this was particularly important because of the societal expectation that they serve their countries in a military capacity if possible. For women, *La Dame Blanche* permitted its female recruits to function in so-called masculine roles, such as spy, courier, and saboteur. Women civilians in occupied zones had to deal with dual fears of rape and accusations of intimacies with the enemy,[9] and the active resistance of *La Dame Blanche* gave them a way to end their powerlessness and to protect themselves against rumors of collaboration.

The gendered army of intelligence workers created in the service was unprecedented in British history. These workers—a military force of foreign soldiers—included minors, old-age pensioners, and even nuns. Yet the composition of the service was no accident—the leaders of *La Dame Blanche* recognized that their occupation by Germany had made all Belgians participants in the war. Rather than being excluded or consigned to secondary functions, women were employed at all levels of the organization. *La Dame Blanche*'s three male leaders, fearing capture, deportation, or both, wanted a service that could run entirely on womanpower if necessary. The leaders developed a shadow executive body comprised entirely of women who had the skills and knowledge to assume control of the service should they need to. This "feminine reserve" functioned in leadership roles throughout the organization but was also designed to take over if the men were arrested.[10] Although women were also subject to arrest, the chances of the older women being deported as forced labor seemed slim.

LA DAME BLANCHE AND BELGIAN RESISTANCE

When scholars of the First World War discuss Belgium, they usually refer to the early months of 1914 when German armies came crashing through the country en route to Paris. Called "poor little Belgium" or "brave Belgium," the nation is depicted as a victim of Teutonic aggression and European power politics.[11] German atrocities against civilians, deportation and forced labor of Belgian civilians, streams of refugees, and the trench-filled landscape near Ypres are familiar descriptions of Belgium's situation during the war.[12] Less familiar is the active role that many Belgians played in resisting German occupation and aiding the Allied armies. In fact, when Belgian resistance is mentioned it usually refers to the heroes and heroines of the Second World War, not the First, despite the significant clandestine networks that developed during World War I.[13] Between 1914 and 1918, Belgians resisted occupation and gathered information for Allied armies in a variety of ways, yet little of this activity has been studied or analyzed in major histories of the war.

Why has Belgian civilian activity during this period been so invisible? The "poor little Belgium" depicted in war propaganda as a woman raped by invading armies played such a powerful role in the narrative of World War I that the notion of an active Belgian resistance movement challenges the vision of Belgium's victimhood. Describing rapes and mutilations of women and children in lurid detail, news accounts and political cartoons portrayed Belgium as a woman violated. Historians John Horne and Alan Kramer note that both the British *Punch* and the French *L'Illustration* published drawings of "a brutal German soldier, presiding over the burning ruins of a Belgian village and astride the corpses of those most symbolic victims, a woman and a child."[14] The occupation of Belgium became the symbolic penetration of its body politic, now gendered female in war depictions, making the nation a pitied victim of German aggression. This vision of the Belgian war experience left little room for stories of civilian heroism after the fortresses at Liège and Dinant had succumbed to German forces.

This conflict in narrative may account for why few scholars have used the rich archives of the Patriotic Services of World War I stored at the Archives Générale de Royaume (AGR) in Brussels.[15] What those hundreds of boxes of material demonstrate, however, is that thousands of Belgian men and women, from different social classes and of different ages risked their lives to defy the German army by gathering intelligence, carrying messages, smuggling Allied soldiers to safety, disseminating pro-Allied propaganda, and refusing complicity. These activities, which went virtually unrewarded and unrecognized by the postwar Belgian government, need to be studied in order to explore the ways that Belgian resisters and intelligence agents influenced the course of the war and set a precedent for later collaboration between resistance networks and foreign governments in World War II.

La Dame Blanche (LDB) demonstrates only one part of the wartime activities of Belgians but is nonetheless a fascinating case study for historians of the Great War. Not only do a wealth of records document its members' backgrounds, war service, and motives, but both men and women were formally militarized. Before allying themselves with the British War Office, *La Dame Blanche*'s executive council insisted on formal militarization for *all* members of the network. In other words, the agents of *La Dame Blanche* wanted to be recognized not as "vulgar spies" but as soldiers in the *Corps d'Observation Anglais au Front de l'Ouest* (English Observation Corps of the Western Front) who took an oath and registered for service. In fact, the directors of the network forbade members from using the terms "espionage" or "spy." Instead, *La Dame Blanche* personnel used the label "agent" or "soldier" when referring to themselves in their roles as military intelligence gatherers.[16] The agents' concern that they might be mistaken for spies motivated by greed rather than soldiers with patriotic intentions was echoed in British official correspondence. As Major Wallinger (GHQ Intelligence) noted in a memo, "In view of the popular conception and misuse of the word 'spy,' I am sure it is not generally recognized that the persons in [an] invaded country who have in the past, and who are at present giving us information concerning the Germans are amongst the finest type of patriots."[17] To help reinforce the respectable service credentials of these anonymous fighters, the British government formally recognized and reimbursed *La Dame Blanche* after the war as an auxiliary army to the Expeditionary Force. LDB soldiers submitted claims for expenses, hardships, prison time, and wages, which were settled in a lump sum by the postwar intelligence staff. In addition, the whole network received British War Medals and Order of the British Empire decorations.[18]

When *La Dame Blanche* leaders demanded militarization from the British government in 1917, what they wanted was to be an auxiliary branch of the army, complete with ranks, battalions, discipline, and enlistment. The government, following past practice in wartime, had created an Intelligence Corps to accompany the British Expeditionary Force (BEF) in 1914, but the Intelligence Corps was composed of regular army personnel, not foreign nationals.[19] Despite getting a lukewarm reception from the British, *La Dame Blanche* did organize itself along military lines into three battalions, eight companies, and a number of platoons and squadrons, basing most of its divisions on geographical location. In addition to the larger military structure of battalions, each town with a rail line was given a number. Those numbered locations formed the basis of platoons. For example, Battalion III centered in Brussels (#100) had four companies organized by location. Figure 4.1 shows a map of the extent of *La Dame Blanche*'s mastery of train lines by late 1918. The enlistees who pledged the LDB oath of service were also organized by ranks received from their leaders—corporal, lieutenant, soldier, etc.—but the British authorities during and after the war refused to accept this ranking system. Although British intelligence officials eventually recognized the militarization of the corps, they refused to recognize LDB's ranking hierarchy, perhaps because in many cases women outranked and supervised men. As with the development of the network itself, the ranking system was based on service to *La Dame Blanche* alone, not on age, sex, or social status. To examine the structure of the service more closely and look at the demographics of the organization, I will focus on one specific battalion of *La Dame Blanche*.

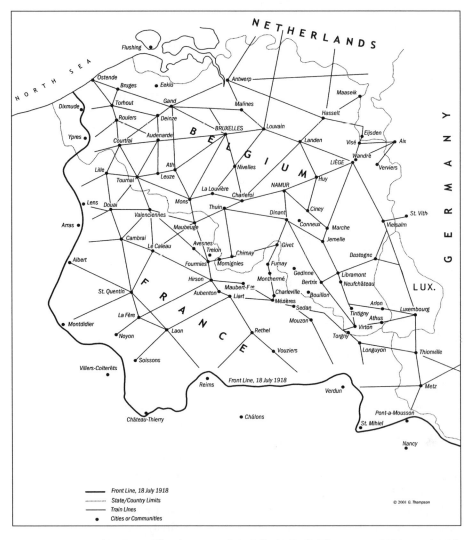

Extent of *La Dame Blanche* network in July 1918. G. Thompson, 2001, used with permission.

Battalion III was the smallest of the three battalions, with about 190 documented agents and auxiliary civilians in its official records, but the battalion was important because of its surveillance of several important rail lines linking Brussels, Malines, Mons, and Charleroi. The battalion was headed by a single woman in her forties, Laure Tandel, who along with her sister and *La Dame Blanche* assistant Louise, ran a school in Brussels. Laure Tandel had a reputation for defying the German authorities early in the war, and, in 1916 she spent a year in the German prison of Siegburg for her work on the radical underground postal network *Le Mot du Soldat* before she took over the command of Battalion III. The *Le Mot du Soldat* was begun by two Jesuit priests and provided a link between Belgian soldiers at the front and their families in the occupied zone.[20]

In addition to the Tandel sisters who commanded the battalion, women held many of the major executive positions in the service. Of the members of Battalion III, fifty-nine were women—about one third of the 190 total.[21] Thus, Battalion III serves as a useful microcosm of the larger organization because in *La Dame Blanche* as a whole, women also made up around 30 percent of the total.[22] Women in both Battalion III and the larger network were the main couriers who transmitted reports between agents and cities. More than a dozen women in Battalion III undertook the dangerous work of maintaining a regular correspondence between battalion headquarters in Brussels and *La Dame Blanche* commanders in Liège.

Specific information about the composition of *La Dame Blanche* can be drawn from service records that document the age, occupation, location, and war service of all its members. In a survey of the ages of agents (see figure 4.2), it is striking that such a broad range of people became involved; in Battalion III alone, the agents ranged from sixteen to eighty-one years old. Most members of Battalion III seem to have been between the ages of twenty and forty-two, although there were also a considerable number of men and women in their forties and fifties. The average age of agents in this battalion ranged from thirty-seven to thirty-nine years old. For men, these numbers may simply reflect the nature of fighting war—men in the twenty-eight to thirty age range were mobilized under universal male conscription in 1914, but older and younger men were trapped in occupied Belgium and unable to leave to join regiments in France.

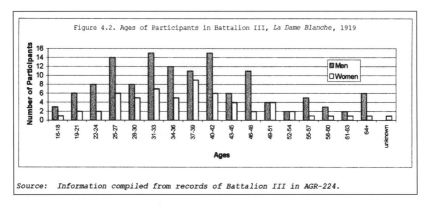

Figure 4.2. Ages of Participants in Battalion III, *La Dame Blanche*, 1919

Source: Information compiled from records of Battalion III in AGR-224.

La Dame Blanche's membership was drawn from a variety of age groups, including children and the elderly. This chart shows only one section of the organization. Tammy Proctor.

For women, service in *La Dame Blanche* depended on factors besides age. The network's service records included the marital status and maiden names of women participants, providing an interesting snapshot of the women drawn to this intelligence unit and its networks. Of the women in Battalion III, more than 60 percent were unmarried and 7 percent were widowed (the remaining being married). These statistics combined with age figures suggest that independent, older women were more likely than younger women to work as formal soldiers in Battalion III's corps.

The diverse occupational backgrounds of *La Dame Blanche* are also apparent in the service records. For example, near Liège there was a group composed almost entirely of aristocrats, while in Battalion III's 7th Company positioned near Ghent, most members were male engineers or civil servants. Nuns were employed in the larger service, especially as prison visitors and informants. In Chimay, nuns passed information they gleaned from conversations with wounded German soldiers in their convent, which had been turned into a hospital by the Germans.[23] High officials were sometimes recruited as well, such as Alexandre Neujean, the chief of police in Liège, and Juliette Delrualle, the daughter of the Belgian Director of St. Leonard's prison.[24]

As an example of the many occupations of the soldiers of *La Dame Blanche*, see the breakdown for the 190 members of Battalion III in Figure 4.3. The twelve male railway employees were invaluable to the service because of their access to the national rail network that the Germans used to move troops and supplies. Workers in skilled trades and manual laborers, engineers, and educators were all involved in this particular branch of *La Dame Blanche*. The majority of women reported themselves as "without profession," leaving them time to work in some of the labor-intensive jobs in *La Dame Blanche*, such as trainwatching and traveling with reports. The clustering of members around certain occupations can be attributed partly to members recruiting trustworthy friends or acquaintances to the network.

What do all these statistics say about the makeup of *La Dame Blanche*'s Third Battalion? First, the majority of women in the battalion were unemployed or employed in education, sales, or domestic work. The battalion leaders themselves were educators, which may account for the large number of recruits from that sector of society. The majority of men were drawn from trade, manufacturing, transport, and utilities industries, with a significant number of skilled craftsmen, engineers, and civil service officials. Some occupations were directly related to cer-

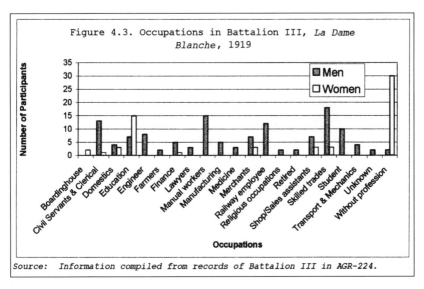

Figure 4.3. Occupations in Battalion III, *La Dame Blanche*, 1919

Source: Information compiled from records of Battalion III in AGR-224.

Most women in *La Dame Blanche*'s Battalion III were either without profession or were involved in education, while the men that volunteered came from a wide spectrum of occupations. Tammy Proctor.

tain kinds of espionage activity; railway employees, for example, were asked to report on troop movements by train, and landladies were often asked to feed and clothe fugitives. Almost all of the men and some of the women who joined *La Dame Blanche* were employed, so intelligence work was completed in addition to their other responsibilities. When financial hardship or the work demanded it, members were paid by the battalion commanders using funds smuggled into Belgium from Captain Landau's headquarters in Holland.[25] Battalion III reflected the same variety of "respectable" occupations, ages, and social standing seen across *La Dame Blanche* network.

FAMILIES OF PATRIOTS

The reasons that members gave for becoming part of a British intelligence network were as diverse as their occupations, ages, and backgrounds. Some members were involved from the beginning of the war in anti-German resistance, either through feeding, hiding, and smuggling Allied soldiers out of Belgium, or through publication and dissemination of illegal propaganda, such as foreign newspapers or underground papers, such as *La Libre Belgique*. For many men and women, working for British intelligence was just another way of helping Belgium rid itself of the German occupying army and ending the war. A subset of young men joined *La Dame Blanche* because it was extremely difficult for men of military age to leave the country to join the Belgian Army, especially after the Belgian frontiers were closed with barbed wire and high-voltage fencing in 1916. Some of the youngest males in the network joined because they were too young to become regular army soldiers even if they had managed to find their way to Holland.

Despite the diversity of their motivations, one of the most common reasons that men and women joined *La Dame Blanche* was for the sake of familial or personal ties. A defining feature of *La Dame Blanche* was its prevalence of familial and kin connections, which cemented loyalties and provided convenient recruiting pools for new members.[26] The need to fight in the war either to forget the pain of a loved one's death or to avenge that death motivated some members to risk their lives in joining the network. Others wanted to protect themselves and their families.

One family of five women joined Battalion III to act as couriers, transcribers, and letterboxes (receiving and passing on messages).

Anna Kesseler, a widow in her mid-fifties, lost her only son in battle near Anvers in 1914, which spurred her and her four daughters to help British intelligence. As Battalion Commander Laure Tandel noted in her postwar report, Kesseler was "a patriotic and courageous mother who had already lost her only son," but who "did not hesitate to authorize her four daughters to take an active part in the *La Dame Blanche* service. . . ."[27] All five women worked for the service, and two of the daughters, Germaine and Maria, served as regular couriers between Brussels and Liège and ran the battalion's secretariat in Brussels. Because of their positions as important links in the network, they were assigned ranks of sergeant (Germaine) and corporal (Maria) despite being only twenty-three and twenty-one years old, respectively.[28] The Kesselers were not unique in *La Dame Blanche*, as a family that worked together throughout the network.

Family connections were an important part of *La Dame Blanche* and other intelligence groups; many members of a formation were often related through blood or marriage. This was especially true of agents working the railway observation posts—the rail lines needing twenty-four-hour surveillance. Often it was easiest for a family or a couple working in shifts to maintain the twenty-four-hour schedule from a residence situated near the lines. The Latouche family—father (a former railway employee), mother, and two daughters age thirteen and fourteen—maintained a crucial post in Fourmies that overlooked the rail line from Aulnoye-Hirson from September 1917 to the end of the war.[29] The two daughters watched during the day, while their parents took the night shift. All intelligence agents feared a police search, so the Latouche family devised an innovative way of keeping track of the soldiers and equipment they observed. They recorded troop information in the form of foodstuffs, listing troop movement and equipment on pieces of paper similar to grocery lists. On the scraps of paper German soldiers were recorded as beans, horses were chicory, numbers of cannons became coffee beans, and so on. Completed lists were stashed in the hollow handle of a broom.[30] Landau notes, "A remarkable feature not only of the Hirson Platoon, but of the whole 'White Lady' organization was family cooperation. Husband, wife, children, even the dog (watching at the door), and often the furniture (a hiding place for compromising documents), each played a part."[31]

Another family, the Arnolds, worked an observation post in Gouvy from July 1917 to November 1918. Paid ten to fifteen francs per day by

British Intelligence, the Arnolds—father, mother, son, and daughter—kept up a shift of watches on the rail line, noting troops and equipment as it passed. The parents took turns watching, and once a week the father carried the information to a letterbox. Gerardine, the thirteen-year-old daughter of the house, explained her role in her postwar report:

> When friends or strangers were at the house and my parents were hindered from fulfilling their mission, my brother [aged fifteen] and I replaced them. At other times, one could not determine exactly that which was on the railcars or the kind of troops, then we would play on the bridge or along the tracks and we would come report what we had seen.[32]

In another case, Julie and Adolphe Barnich, a brother and sister from Luxembourg, rented a room with two small windows above a café next to the train line in Capellen. For four months, from November 1917 to February 1918, the two worked twelve-hour shifts with Adolphe carrying messages by foot to a weekly rendezvous. Twenty-two-year-old Julie described this dismal life in a postwar report:

> There is nothing more horrible than long winter nights in a room without light in forced idleness . . . fighting drowsiness and fearing to fail in one's duty. The next day taking up again the same life, with nothing, not relaxation nor distraction to come break the somber monotony of this existence. . . .[33]

Julie had to give up this dreary life when Adolphe fell ill and died of a bronchial infection in the spring of 1918.

Such family and individual trainwatching posts made up the backbone of the information networks of La Dame Blanche and other Allied services, making possible much of the larger work of intelligence gathering. Although useful logistically to organize trainwatching posts around families, the nature of these units made the work particularly dangerous because all the members of a family could face arrest, imprisonment, or death. Perhaps families risked disaster because of the comfort they received from working alongside loved ones. Parents could keep an eye on children. Also, patriotism was a powerful motivating force, and La Dame Blanche agents often wanted to prove their patriotism to relatives and friends. Most likely, however, family and close personal friends were the most trustworthy people to enlist as helpers in a secret life.

Beyond trainwatching, families also cooperated in running letter-boxes (drop-off points for information), safe houses for traveling agents, or courier networks. For example, the unmarried Weimerskirch sisters ran a bookstore in Liége that functioned as a letterbox for *La Dame Blanche* and as a liaison for an information service inside St. Leonard's Prison. This bookstore remained one of the most reliable links in the service, functioning without detection until the end of the war.[34] In another Liége safe house, tragedy struck a family when two young brothers—Louis and Antony Collard—were captured, imprisoned, and executed for having intelligence reports in their possession.[35] Their father and two of their sisters were also involved in intelligence activities, and one of the daughters enrolled in *La Dame Blanche* after her brothers' imprisonment. Sadly, she died soon after the war from an illness contracted after she was imprisoned. All five members of the family spent some time behind bars for their activities, and three died for their intelligence work.[36]

One of the most unusual formations in *La Dame Blanche* featured several closely-connected aristocratic families. Platoon 49 was conceived as one of three special overlapping groups that provided connections between battalions and areas not well integrated into the service; it was centered around the château de Conneux, near Leignon. The de Radiguès family at Conneux become involved almost immediately in the war effort in 1914 with four sons managing to join the army at the front. The remaining family members did their part in the war by caring for wounded French soldiers and helping them escape to Holland. This escape service, known as the Service de Monge, relied on a series of aristocratic homes and abbeys used as safe houses for soldiers brought by guides to the Belgian-Dutch frontier. The service was organized and led by the Vicomtesse Gabrielle de Monge and functioned from November 1914 to April 1916 before dissolving in a series of arrests, imprisonments, and executions. De Monge herself was sentenced to three years of hard labor for her role as a guide, but not before she and another guide had conducted nearly four hundred soldiers to the border.[37]

By the time Platoon 49 was formed in 1918 with many of the old de Monge network, the only family members at Conneux not imprisoned or not at the front were Thérèse de Radiguès and her three daughters,

Belgian Vicomtesse Gabrielle de Monge de Franeau, born in 1883, ran a successful organization for passing information and people out of occupied Belgium and into the neutral Netherlands from 1914 to 1916. She was arrested and condemned to three years of hard labor in a German prison in 1916. The remains of her network regrouped and became a section of *La Dame Blanche* in 1918. The Imperial War Museum Department of Documents.

Marguerite (age twenty-six), Marie-Antoinette (age twenty) and Agnès (age fifteen).[38] Led by Thérèse de Radiguès, Platoon 49 gathered and ferried information between locations in eastern Belgium and also sent individuals into new areas to organize additional trainwatching posts. Two young comtesses, Françoise and Anne de Villermont (age twenty-two and twenty-four respectively), were charged with setting up a post at Givet, while Marie-Antoinette de Radiguès and Baroness Clémie de l'Epine (age twenty-five) traveled on foot sixty miles round-trip through occupied territory to establish a new unit at Charleville. The platoon leader, Thérèse de Radiguès noted that the platoon's total contribution to the work of *La Dame Blanche* was small, but that it was still important to the functioning of the service in Liège and around the Belgian-French border in the east. This platoon illustrates the range of backgrounds involved in intelligence, from tavern owners, railway engineers, and teachers in Brussels to elite families around Leignon who all described themselves as "without profession."

Exploiting and capitalizing on family ties were easy and safe ways to develop intelligence networks, especially because informal flows of information already moved through these kin webs. Enlisting families, although sometimes dangerous, also ensured an extra measure of loyalty and perseverance. Parents protected children, siblings shielded each other, and longtime family friends could be depended on in emergencies. The use of families to gather intelligence by *La Dame Blanche* drew on these relationships and made the service more secure.

MILITARIZING CIVILIANS

Beyond the familial webs that helped forge relationships in *La Dame Blanche* was the most powerful motivating force for members: militarization. In order to become a formal soldier of the service, men and women took oaths of loyalty, either as soldiers (for the majority) or as attached civilians. The oath was a simple one:

> I declare and enlist in the capacity of soldier in the Allied military observation service until the end of the war. I swear before God
> to respect this engagement,
> to accomplish conscientiously the offices entrusted to me,
> to comply with the instructions given to me by the representatives of the Direction,
> not to reveal to anyone (without formal authorization) anything concerning the organization of the service, even if this stance should entail for me or mine the penalty of death
> not to take part in any other activity or role that might expose me to prosecution by the occupying authority.[39]

The oath was a point of pride for the men and women who took it, and it lent credence to their patriotic service, reassuring those who still saw intelligence work as less than honorable. Although *La Dame Blanche* emphasized honor and egalitarian principles, the oath suggested the hierarchy of military service. Once sworn, the oath bound members to their pledge and promised serious consequences for those who violated it.

The oath also gave structure and purpose to the organization and insured that members would give up other resistance work such as employment by competing intelligence organizations, circulation of propaganda, and operation of escape networks. By controlling members' outside activities, *La Dame Blanche* tightened security and ensured that members arrested for other illegal activity would not be able to give evidence on LDB service.

Members, although not uniformed for obvious reasons, were encouraged to carry themselves as soldiers and to act appropriately. In addition to the oath they took, members were formally registered, given small lead identity badges with the seal of the Corps, and assigned false names for their work.[40] For example, one of the network chiefs Walthère Dewé was known as van den Bosch, Gauthier, and Muraille to agents, which helped maintain security if anyone was arrested.[41] The directors distributed copies of rules, including general operating procedures and instructions on what to do if arrested or interrogated to new *La Dame Blanche* soldiers. Finally, members were given important information on German uniforms, weapons, and regiments, plus a code list for encrypting the information they gathered.[42]

Militarization was a key part of the success of *La Dame Blanche* because it helped enforce loyalty and threatened a postwar court marshal for any who betrayed the organization. Military status also reassured those who enlisted that their work would be officially recognized. Gendered analysis of the organization and reports suggests that for men especially, soldier status gave them the hope of legitimacy after the war, or as one member put it, "We are to be . . . soldiers like the 'others.'" Being part of the fraternity of combatants, not a civilian "shirker," was crucial to men's identity as citizens and patriots.[43] Herman Chauvin, one of the network chiefs, noted the importance of militarization in helping recruit new members. He wrote after the war,

> Receiving the oath of a soldier was for the newly enlisted certain proof
> of the usefulness of the work that we were demanding; it represented,
> for after the war, the recognition of services rendered, official protec-
> tion in case of accident, the prospect of being acknowledged as broth-
> ers in arms by the valiant soldiers at the front. . . .[44]

Militarization was crucial precisely because it conferred legitimacy on the organization. *La Dame Blanche* agents saw themselves not as spies or resisters, but as soldiers in service to the cause, risking their lives just as those on the front lines did. Although the men and women of *La Dame Blanche* were officially non-combatants, they were still soldiers who had remade their homes and businesses into battle zones. After the war, the network chiefs of *La Dame Blanche* were "flooded with demands" from agents asking for proof that they had been formally enlisted in the observation corps.[45]

This postwar process was complicated, however, by the presence of large numbers of women in the service. Although militarization had seemed to bring legitimacy, the British government balked at militarizing the women in *La Dame Blanche* when the necessity of spying ended in 1919. Although it had recently created the Women's Auxiliary Army Corps (WAAC), the British government in London did not favor granting women soldier status in Belgium, despite the promises made by intelligence officers such as Landau, who had operated in Holland. Only vigorous lobbying by several British intelligence officers and the repeated requests of *La Dame Blanche* chiefs led to the eventual official acceptance of militarization for the women of the service.

To bring about the acceptance of the militarization of women, the chiefs had threatened not to accept their own militarization if the women, who had served under the assumption that they were soldiers, were not recognized as such. In a contentious letter to London written in February of 1919, Landau pleaded the case for the women agents, saying that they "ran exactly the same risks as the men." He also suggested that militarization was really important to the women, "having so had the military spirit drilled into them, that they are much keener on it. . . ."[46] Likewise, in his report on the role of women in his company, Commandant Leopold Blanjean wrote that when it came to a sense of duty and moral force, women were more likely to accept the challenge of joining the service and were therefore deserving of military status. He claimed that when he recruited members, men hesitated, but women did not. In fact, he found that in decision making, "the man is nothing, the woman is all," suggesting that women often determined whether a couple or a whole family would join the cause.[47]

Where enlistment offered men a sense of legitimacy in their own eyes, it offered many women the excitement of active service in roles generally filled by men. *La Dame Blanche* was a chance to join men on an equal footing in wartime service. Irene Bastin, later Soeur Thérese de l'Enfant Jesus, and her friend Marie-Thérese Collard were enlisted in May of 1918, only seventeen and eighteen years old respectively. Irene described her feelings as she took the military oath:

> We had the honor of becoming soldiers ... [but] Marie-Thérese dared not believe in this good fortune. That night she could not sleep, and she said to me many times: "At last that which I have so desired is realized, I am going to work for our nation and as a soldier."[48]

Thérèse de Radiguès, leader of Platoon 49 and the mother of several of its female members, describes her sense of purpose and engagement in the corps. Her reminiscences reinforce the notion that the perilous endeavors they engaged in energized many of the women: "The feeling of danger hanging over our heads night and day did not dishearten us, far from it, it seemed that the greater the danger became the more enchanting was our work."[49] The notion that war was an exciting and liberating experience for many women is not a new concept. Feminist scholars have demonstrated that women felt an intoxicating excitement in the sense of purpose and usefulness the war provided for them.[50] The First World War created a brief interlude of increased freedom for some European women before the realities of the postwar world led to a backlash of anger and resentment against women, especially those who had replaced men in jobs.[51]

Women in *La Dame Blanche* felt a sense of mission and intoxicating liberation, and they tested their mettle before firing squads and behind prison bars. Prison became both a political act of defiance against the German occupying force and an act of solidarity with other women soldiers—a statement of female power in the face of adversity. Gabrielle Petit, a Belgian working for British intelligence, famously captured the act of national and female defiance at her execution for espionage, when she said, "I will show them that a Belgian woman knows how to die."[52]

This sentiment is echoed in postwar accounts of the audacity and courage of women agents who were captured, many of whom were imprisoned in Belgian jails or in the German prison at Siegburg, near Köln. A few were executed, but women were more likely to receive sentences of hard labor rather than execution for espionage and treason. It is difficult to estimate the number of women imprisoned for intelligence work during the war, but at least three hundred female political prisoners moved through Siegburg Prison alone in the last years of the war.

Siegburg was a combined men's and women's prison near a number of munitions factories on the outskirts of Köln, Germany in the heart the Rhineland industrial zone. As the war progressed, the prison often experienced Allied air raids, almost daily from May 1918 on.[53] Designed to hold three hundred women, the first political prisoners cohabited with the female criminals already housed at Siegburg, but as the number of political prisoners rose, the criminals were moved out.

Wealth and social position were not sufficient for commuting sentences, although some prisoners received concessions such as a single cell or the freedom of wearing non-prison garb. The women held in Siegburg, however, were from remarkably diverse backgrounds and represented the range of people drawn to intelligence work. As prisoner Louise Thuliez wrote of Siegburg,

> All classes of society were represented in the prison, from the humble working-woman to the aristocrat, from the peasant who had never before left her native village to the city lady accustomed to a life of luxury and ease. There were even some nuns. . . . The prisoners came from all parts of occupied France and Belgium. Sometimes there were whole families in prison. Madame Ramet, a Belgian, whose son had been shot, was there with her two daughters, Mme. Denoel with four. . . . Our common misery created bonds of affection that survived the war. . . .[54]

The women confined at Siegburg for their political activities (running escape networks or working in intelligence) used their common bonds to stay alive, maintain morale, and continue their work of resisting the Germans. A souvenir found from Siegburg describes some women who spent Easter 1917 encouraging hope and writing a "fantasy menu" of delicacies that they would enjoy after their release.[55] Four women at Siegburg escaped while on a work party outside the prison walls and later sent a gleeful and insouciant postcard to the director of the prison.[56] Some women sentenced to hard labor refused to make shell fuses for munitions to be used against Allied armies. The ringleaders of the boycott, Marguerite Blankaert and Louise de Bettignies, were put in solitary confinement, but the strike held. Women with political or social connections wrote letters to high officials, and soon other work was found for the prisoners.[57]

The prisoners lived and worked in difficult conditions, which strengthened their sense of persecution and their determination to "soldier on." Their daily rations were 175 grams of black bread and a serving of what they called "insect soup" or "mouse soup." In the spring of 1917, the prisoners (officially declared "prisoners of war" by the Allies) began receiving a military biscuit ration.[58] Medical aid was rudimentary, so any women who gave birth often did so locked in her cell with no assistance. At nine months of age, the infants were sent to wet nurses in the town, and the prisoner only got to visit their babies once a month.[59] When typhoid broke out in the prison late in the war the women banded together to nurse the ill and agitate for better food and conditions. Because the German prison authorities feared contagion the female prisoners laid out their dead, carried coffins, and staffed the infirmaries during the epidemic.[60] These experiences hardened their resolve and reinforced their sense of serving as soldiers and prisoners of war.

Jeanne Delwaide, also a prisoner at Siegburg, was arrested in 1917. Delwaide was a important catch for German authorities; she had been involved in a multitude of resistance activities early in the war and was among the first twenty agents recruited by *La Dame Blanche*. Had the authorities persuaded her to speak she could have put LDB in grave danger because she knew the true identities of the three chiefs of the service. One of the chiefs, Walthère Dewé, sent a coded message to her in prison through a chaplain warning her to remain silent. He wrote, "Remember you are a soldier. Remember your oath. Deny everything." Delwaide admitted to German authorities that she helped Allied soldiers escape, but she denied all knowledge of espionage during almost seven months of detention and interrogation before her trial. As Henri Bernard notes in his biography of Dewé, "Jeanne held [the chiefs'] lives in her hands and never spoke."[61]

Like Delwaide, other women took risks to keep their military oaths. When Jeanne Goeseels was arrested with four *La Dame Blanche* agents and several intelligence reports were found in her house she tried to claim ignorance of the agents' activities. She succeeded in saving herself and two of the men from execution. Goeseels, a pious and respectable middle-aged matron, told police that one of the men was her lover and his companion was a traveling friend. She claimed that none of them knew anything about the two other "lodgers" and the reports they had in their possession. Under repeated interrogation and verbal abuse, Goeseels remained silent.[62] Her willingness to accept the scorn of her interrogators and her bravery in rallying her companions by reminding them of their *La Dame Blanche* oaths made her a celebrated heroine in the organization after the war.[63]

Stories of the hardships the women endured, their bravery, and their silence helped solidify the image of the female soldier in the intelligence service.

With models like Eglantine Lefebvre, a courier for *La Dame Blanche* who delivered reports until the day she collapsed and died from a serious illness,[64] female agents in the service sought to serve their nation and demonstrate that their patriotism was as strong as that of men. In some ways, the women seemed to go beyond the call of duty, perhaps feeling the need continually to prove their readiness for the work of a resistance soldier and intelligence agent. Undoubtedly, their military oaths and the thought of a postwar court martial helped steel their resolve, but women had clearly shown their suitability for intelligence work by maintaining silence in prison and honoring their pledges. Women saw their war service and their reaction to adversity and imprisonment only as reinforcements of their case for militarization and as legitimizing their postwar demands for military decoration. As Jeanne Delwaide said in her public acceptance of a British Empire medal after the war, "We have done our duty—as good British soldiers—and we have done it with joy, with no other hope but the assurance that our modest services would not be unnecessary to the great common cause. And today you come to tell us . . . our patient labor was not in vain. . . ."[65]

CONCLUSION

Although it is hard to gauge the network's overall effectiveness, British officials attested that *La Dame Blanche* had been a success during the war, particularly in providing information on the 1918 German offensive. One British officer went so far as to claim that the service had gathered up to 75 percent of the intelligence that Britain received from German occupied territory in the latter part of the war.[66] Altogether, more than six thousand agents are documented as having served British intelligence during the war but many more went unrecorded.

In terms of recognition, one of the officers in charge of liquidating the postwar organizations claimed that more than three thousand British War medals for military service were awarded along with £50,000 to settle postwar claims for prison pay, expense reimbursement, and family hardship. *La Dame Blanche* itself had more than one thousand documented and official members. These agents were awarded Order of the British Empire decorations (many of them in the military division) in formal investiture services at Brussels, Ghent, Lille, and Liège, and *La Dame Blanche* was listed as a "Volunteer service attached to the British Army in France (COA [Corps d'Observation Anglais])" in official honors publications in Britain. Each agent presented a special postwar commission with credentials and claims for money and signed a "declaration of satisfaction" after being paid. These declarations were binding, and agents who later tried to claim additional funds were turned away.[67]

In a larger sense, wartime intelligence networks such as *La Dame Blanche* helped define the twentieth-century development of the concepts of espionage, resistance, clandestine activities, and military intelligence. In fact, because of its success *La Dame Blanche* was resurrected in the Second World War as the British *Clarence* network of resistance and intelligence gathering, and many of the network's former agents joined the fray again.

World War I had set the standard for militarizing civilians in enemy territory and in using female intelligence agents, so the same reaction to Nazi occupation in the 1940s was natural. The challenges of organizing civilian networks behind enemy lines during World War I arose again in the Second World War in finding men and women willing to staff the networks and legitimizing their espionage activities. As in World War I, the networks had special significance for women because they allowed females access to active patriotic service in occupied territory and belied misconceptions about women's unreliability and weakness. As Henry Landau argued after the war, "allied women spies were just as brave and efficient as the men."[68]

If wartime intelligence networks were so successful, why have the experiences of men and women intelligence agents, resisters, and political prisoners disappeared so thoroughly from our vision of the Great War? Scores of ordinary folk opened their homes and risked their lives to assist Allied soldiers and governments, yet their experiences largely have been forgotten by scholars. The memorials to these patriots exist

The memorial to *La Dame Blanche* and its leader,
Walthère Déwe, sits hidden on a hillside in
Liège, one of the forgotten monuments to Belgian's World War I resistance to German occupation. *Photograph by Todd Shirley.*

in cities and towns across Belgium, but local residents often have no
conception why these men and women are memorialized. The records
of *La Dame Blanche* suggest that a closer examination of the gendered experiences of civilians living in occupied territory during the Great War
might help explain why, as Margaret Darrow queries, if World War II
made heroes and heroines out of those in occupied territory, World
War I did not.[69]

One reason the women of *La Dame Blanche* went mostly unrecognized and were largely forgotten is that in occupied territories such as Belgium the line between combatant and civilian was blurred, and the experience of occupation undermined expectations about women's role in warfare. The nature of the terms "home front," "nation," and "soldier" fluctuated in the First World War. As several historians note, the neat division between home and battlefront is a convenient device for authors and historians but does not precisely capture the experience of the war.[70] The women of *La Dame Blanche* had no concept of a home front because their own homes became fronts when their nations were occupied. The civilians who lived with the enemy sought to find meaningful ways to fight their occupiers and to aid their nation's soldiers even as it seemed that their nation had disappeared.

The soldiers of *La Dame Blanche* do not appear in the official histories of the war or in military overviews of the conflict even though these men and women risked their lives and considered themselves combat soldiers. The cultural debates over who fought and how during the First World War were especially pitched in the newly-liberated Belgium of the early 1920s. For the women of *La Dame Blanche* especially, soldiering for Britain in the Allied cause, while it did not bring them the recognition at home that they sought, did give them impeccable credentials after the war and a profound sense of accomplishment.

The LDB soldiers without uniforms did not become heroines in the historical record, and were soon replaced in even the most popular writings about the war by sensationalized images of a different kind of female soldier. Historian Joanna Bourke argues that, "female soldiers threatened to devalue the sacrifice made by their male counterparts" and the fear arose that women would kill men's warrior ethic.[71] Bourke's argument is persuasive given that most lasting images of women intelligence workers are either as spy-seductresses or victims and martyrs.

5

Spies Who Knew How to Die

And I will show them that a Belgian woman knows how to die.
　　　—inscription on the Gabrielle Petit monument in Brussels

OF THE WOMEN who risked their lives to gather intelligence on their enemies, hundreds were arrested or detained for questioning, but only a few paid with their lives. These few, however, were the subject of countless books, news articles, monuments, and films after the war, and if any of the names of espionage heroines from the war are remembered, it is this small number of martyrs. As with Gabrielle Petit who was remembered for her brave words as she was led to her execution, these female spy-martyrs and resisters are depicted as brave defenders of their nations who never compromised their countries under the pressure of their impending deaths. The stories that remain of these "modern Joan of Arcs" weave narratives of mental strength, protection of co-conspirators, and defiant attitudes toward their executioners.

This chapter examines several prominent female intelligence agents, their deaths, and their memorializations to illuminate the ways that women's service to the state was represented in contemporary accounts and in postwar commemoration.

Just as soldiers engaged in dangerous work, women used their feminine invisibility to their advantage but also masculinized themselves by taking on the "male" work of gathering information in war zones. British officials praised their daring and inventiveness while the women were alive, but these agents became victims of foreign aggression in the official discourse after their capture and execution. Death refeminized them. Innocence, patriotism, and brave stoicism became hallmarks in postwar tales about these women, violated by the bullets that pierced their chests as other innocents had been violated by invading

German armies. Belgian, French, British, and American accounts all speak of the atrocities of German officials against "innocent" women in occupied territory, often ignoring the women's culpability and guilt in the crimes of which they were accused during the war. Descriptions of spy-martyrs usually emphasized the moral character, generosity, patriotism, and naive spirit of the women who died for their nations. Why are these women celebrated more than the female agents who survived the war without detection or capture? The key to their success is their deaths; they are women who died in a war fought to protect them. In the ideas of the time, if soldiers fought to protect their nations and if women reproduced and nurtured those nations, was it not an atrocity to execute these good women? The execution of women during World War I provided governments with ample propaganda in the battle for morale at home.

The British, in particular, manipulated the image of female spy-martyrs for propaganda purposes, using their deaths at the hands of the enemy to claim a moral high ground. Although the British widely used female spies and sent them into danger in the occupied territories, they did not execute enemy women spies caught on British soil. By constructing an image of the executed female spy as an innocent martyr sacrificed to German aggression, allied propagandists reinterpreted the roles of female secret service agents, making them heroic victims rather than gallant soldiers.

"BLACK WAR'S WHITE ANGEL"

Perhaps best known and most often commemorated of all the women spy-martyrs of the Great War is Edith Cavell, a nurse who was not even technically a spy. She did not gather intelligence for the British or serve as a courier or letterbox, rather, she participated in the operation of an escape network for Allied soldiers trapped in occupied Belgium. Despite the fact that her war work was mostly humanitarian aid—hiding and smuggling refugees—Cavell is one of the best-known women of the war and is often described as a spy. After her death in 1915, her case was debated internationally as Allied governments fueled the discussion with propaganda about her death.

Cavell's background and personality did not lend themselves well to romantic description in the media. Raised in an ordinary middle-class family, Cavell grew up in a small village near Norwich, Great Britain. Well-educated and trained for nursing, she spent her prewar life as a governess, nurse, and nursing instructor. In 1907, she was asked to run a newly instituted nurses' training school in Brussels. The school prospered under her tutelage, and reports from the period note her iron control, strict rules, and efficient administration of the institution. When war was declared, Cavell, forty-eight years old and well-established in Brussels, remained at the school to care for the sick and wounded and to teach new nurses.[1] Perhaps her story would have remained unknown had she continued with her hospital and training work, but her activities changed in November of 1914 when she agreed to hide two English soldiers who were separated from their units in battle.

From that first experience until February of 1915, Cavell continued to harbor groups of refugees as they came to her and helped them obtain new identities and couriers to help them escape German-occupied Belgium. Her work expanded in late February when her hospital joined a larger escape network based in northern France near Lille and southern Belgium near Mons. Along with more than three dozen compatriots, Cavell operated a successful escape service from her Brussels nurses' training school to the neutral Netherlands. The network depended on "guides" who moved the men from place to place, several safe houses including two chateaux on the Franco-Belgian border, and "chemists" who produced forged identity papers. Cavell's school was the heart of the network: it lodged and hid refugees and became the pick-up and drop-off points for the guides. The network included a variety of people, but several of the most active volunteers were well-born women. Cavell was joined by Belgian aristocrat Princess Marie de Croÿ, Frenchwomen Louise Thuliez (a schoolteacher), and Comtesse Jeanne de Belleville. De Croÿ and her brother, Reginald, harbored soldiers in their chateau and helped forge new papers for them, while de Belleville served a similar function at her home in Montigny-sur-Roc. Thuliez guided the soldiers from their hideouts to other couriers or to Cavell in Brussels, while Cavell hid and nursed the soldiers in Brussels and helped to arrange their escapes. Two other important members of the group were Philippe Baucq, an architect who helped plot escape routes and organize guides, and Hermann Capiau, an engineer who guided many of the soldiers to Cavell in Brussels.[2]

Suspicious about all the movement in and out of the school, the German authorities conducted a thorough search of the premises on

June 14, 1915, but found nothing incriminating. The authorities also had additional information on Baucq, who was distributing the illegal paper, *La Libre Belgique*. On July 31, Thuliez and Baucq were caught at Baucq's Brussels home with thousands of copies of *La Libre Belgique* and incriminating evidence of their resistance activities. They were immediately arrested.[3] Over the next few months, thirty-five members of the network were arrested and imprisoned at St. Gilles Prison in a suburb of Brussels. Cavell was arrested on August 5, 1915, questioned, and placed in St. Gilles. Although the exact number of soldiers who benefited from the Cavell network is unknown, most historians agree that at least two hundred were saved during the organization's short history.[4]

Cavell confessed almost immediately that she had helped hide and transport soldiers, signing three separate depositions in her first two weeks in prison. She and the other thirty-five prisoners were tried between October 7 and 11 in Brussels. Of the prisoners, thirteen were women and most were Belgian. At the trial's conclusion, twenty-six members of the group were found guilty of varying degrees of treason and five of these were condemned to death, including Cavell, Baucq, Belleville, Thuliez, and Louis Severin, a chemist. Baucq and Cavell were executed early on the morning of October 12, but the other three had their sentences commuted after successful interventions on their behalf.[5]

The Germans immediately sought to use Cavell's case as a cautionary tale for those living in occupied territory. Through proclamations and posters, occupying authorities publicized the execution in order to discourage resistance activities and secret service work. J. H. Gifford, an Englishwoman running a convalescent home in conjunction with Cavell's institution, recorded in her scrapbook diary German attempts to dissuade resistance. After Cavell's execution, Gifford wrote about the warnings the Germans posted around the area that said, "Whoever knowingly aids in any manner *whatsoever*, an enemy of Germany in concealing his presence whether by giving him lodging, by clothing him, or by giving him food is liable to the same punishment—*Death*— or penal servitude."[6] These posters, dated October 12, 1915, stated that the "Governor-General of Brussels brings these facts to the knowledge of the Public that they may serve as a warning," and were signed by General Von Bissing, the governor-general himself.[7]

The Germans may have thought that Cavell's death would provide a good warning for others behind enemy lines, but the international

This postcard is an example of the sensational propaganda distributed by Allied nations that made Edith Cavell a martyr. The text on the back (not shown) reminds audiences that Cavell was "cowardly murdered by a German officer," twisting the truth of her death by firing squad and making her a passive victim of German aggression.

public outcry that followed the news of her execution soon convinced them of their error. Edith Cavell's death set off a firestorm of protest from both Allied and neutral nations and sparked a wave of propaganda. Cavell became a sensation overnight as the embodiment of the innocent woman wronged. In scores of news accounts her death was examined and mythologized. One New Zealand paper reported that Cavell's death had created "a thrill of horror and righteous hate throughout the World."[8] The *New York Times* gave the Cavell execution front-page headlines on October 16, 1915, running daily updates for the next two weeks and publishing a multi-page special feature with photographs on October 31. Part of the media frenzy was triggered by British statements—which later turned out to be misleading—that the Germans had knowingly misinformed Brand Whitlock, the American Minister in Brussels, who had asked to be kept apprised of the proceedings of the case. Whitlock later issued a statement claiming his words and actions had been misrepresented, but the damage was already done.[9] London's newspapers were practically unanimous in their expressions of horror and grief. Calling Cavell's death "one of the most appalling wickednesses yet perpetrated in this war," and a "foul and damnable infamy," the British media called for vengeance and for Germany to be treated as a "pariah" among nations.[10]

In addition to major news coverage around the world, Cavell's image was widely used in propaganda posters, postcards, and recruitment efforts, especially in the British Empire and France. Memorial services and concerts were held in France and Britain, and a market for Cavell souvenirs emerged.[11] Cavell's biographer noted that regular army and territorial enlistments in Britain rose substantially in late October and November of 1915, theorizing that the exaggerated stories regarding Cavell's death played a major role in army growth.[12] Newspapers reported a rash of enlistments in the British army, especially after King George issued a statement that claimed that "[r]ecruiting sergeants are unanimous in saying that Miss Cavell's heroic end has made an irresistible appeal to those men who needed some strong emotional stimulus before taking up arms. . . ."[13] The timing of Cavell's death was fortuitous for a government seeking to boost its numbers of enlisted men. In fact, in January 1916, only a couple months after Cavell's death, the British began conscripting soldiers.

The British government also tried to use Cavell's execution to highlight their own policy of sparing accused women spies from death sentences, and London papers reported the comparatively light treatment of a German-born woman in England. Only a week after Cavell's death, Louise Herbert was sentenced in British courts to a six-month prison sentence after admitting that she tried to spy for Germany.[14] German officials fought charges of their inhumane treatment of Cavell, issuing statements to the foreign press about the fairness of the proceedings and the dangers of knowingly violating rules in a war zone. Germans also accused Britain of hypocrisy, noting that the British had been guilty of far worse treatment of women in the concentration camps of the Anglo-Boer War. In letters to media and to local authorities in occupied zones, German officials raised the cases of several women executed by the French and Belgians in 1914 and 1915, noting that no one had censured them for executing women accused of espionage.[15] In the war of words, Germany used all the ammunition it had to refute the claims that Cavell's execution was an atrocity. The German case is outlined in an English translation of a German newspaper account:

> The execution of Miss Cavell . . . was made the occasion of a prolonged and bitter newspaper attack upon Germany. . . . But the story, to which such melodramatic details as weeping soldiers, brutal officers and final death by pistol shot were added, served its temporary purpose in diverting attention from the British blunders in the Balkans and at the same time in stimulating enlistments in Kitchener's armies. . . . Solemn horror was expressed that in the twentieth century a court martial should condemn a woman for a military crime and that that death sentence should be executed. The hypocrisy of this last is patent. Has not England for months imprisoned and starved women who merely sought the franchise?[16]

By noting Britain's treatment of female suffragettes prior to World War I, German apologists bolstered their case that they treated women and men equally in cases of espionage and treason. Despite such tactics, Germany pardoned some women in the months that followed Cavell's death so as not to cause additional backlash from the international community.

Why was Cavell's such a powerful story for the propagandists to use? One explanation may be that Cavell provided an individual focus for the stories of German atrocities in Belgium; her story encapsulated the experiences of others living under German control.[17] Another reason for her popularity may have been her status as a nurse, which made her execution seem all the more terrible. As a "healer" and an "angel of mercy," she seemed an unlikely candidate for a spy, who in popular minds was associated with vulgarity, immorality, and greed.[18]

Perhaps the most persuasive case for the Cavell myth's longevity is the nature of the story itself—told in 1915 when the war's length and brutality were only beginning to penetrate the consciousness of both national leaders and the public alike. Portrayed by propagandists as a victim murdered by the Germans, Cavell fit one of the images of womanhood that war fostered: the unprotected female, innocent and violated. Using images of endangered women in fiction and in news accounts to rally the British populace around causes and to inspire patriotism had a long tradition. During the Indian Mutiny-Rebellion of 1857, news reports lingered on tales of women's martyrdom, justifying "male retaliation" and "enabling British vengeance to appear all the more virile."[19] As Cannon Schmitt noted in his study of Gothic fiction, "women are always also figures whose victimization calls forth Englishness from (implicitly male) spectators."[20] In short, depicting women as helpless victims reinforced the nation's call to men to protect women from foreign aggression.

Robert Underwood Johnson's poem, published in the *New York Times* in weeks following Cavell's death, captures the victim myth that she embodied:

> *Room mid the martyrs for a deathless name!*
> *Till yesterday, in her how few could know*
> *Black War's white angel, succoring friend and foe—*
> *Whose pure heart harbored neither hate nor blame*
> *When Need or Pity made its sovereign claim.*
> *Today she is the world's!*[21]

In the weeks after her death, Cavell was transformed from an active resister to a passive pawn, providing a powerful story for women in wartime and a motivating force to men.[22] Perhaps for this reason that Cavell is often shown in posters kneeling, praying, or collapsed on the ground as supplicant and victim.

Key to her image was her purity (as an unmarried woman) and paradoxically, her maternal instincts (as a nurse). She was often depicted as a much younger woman, giving power to the image of her as violated innocent. She could be anyone's daughter, sister, or mother. As Florence Nightingale had told her readers in the 1860s, "every woman is a nurse," bolstering the notion that nursing was a natural occupation for women,[23] and during World War I, nursing was widely perceived as "feminine, maternal devotion." Cavell's death was useful propaganda for the British because it echoed popular images of Florence Nightingale. In effect, British propandists argued that the Germans had killed both a mother of the nation and an unsullied virgin; they had murdered the "lady with the lamp."[24] Edith Cavell was in many ways the perfect victim.[25]

MARTYRED HEROINES

Like Edith Cavell, several other executed women became symbols in the propaganda campaigns of the war. Age and nationality varied, but most of these women shared one characteristic: they were unmarried, standing alone, and unprotected in reality and in legend. Their unmarried status left these women open to two descriptions in the propaganda wars: either they were pure victims or unpure adventuresses. Women in the second category—represented most notably by Mata Hari—are examined in chapter 6. Those who were celebrated in postwar ceremonies and statues were the former—the unsullied patriotic "girls" of the secret service, cruelly executed by the enemy. Most of these heroines were guilty of the crimes for which the Germans had executed them. The Germans were well within their rights under international law to execute these women after their trials for espionage, sabotage, and treason, yet, like Cavell, most of them became icons of the female victim of war. Beyond vague protestations of their heroism, the real celebration was of their torture and deaths, not their heroism and ingenuity.

The women who generated the most horror and outrage were *fusillées*, executed by firing squad for their crimes. Although the manner of their deaths inspired a certain horrified fascination and a cult of commemoration after the war,[26] young women who faced this fate were particularly noted in public discourse. Often depicted in lurid or romanticized terms, their stories of execution always included rumors that could be oft-repeated. With Cavell, multiple stories circulated: that she had fainted when being led to the post; that an officer shot her with a pistol in the head; that one soldier in the firing squad was executed for refusing to fire on her. All the tales made sure to note the little Union Jack she wore over her breast as she was led to die.[27] In addition to detailed stories of their last hours and executions, the women's supposed last words were often recorded, sometimes even on their gravestones or monuments. Cavell's monument is inscribed with her now famous words, "Patriotism is not enough. I must have no hatred or bitterness for anyone." Lastly, the *fusillées'* stories always included a reminder that these were heroic women but they also possessed the feminine qualities of frailty, nurturance, virtue. Described as merciful angels and pure maidens, the executed women embodied femininity in the commemoration of their deaths. Numerous postcards of Cavell show a womanly woman quaking before a German soldier.

The Edith Cavell memorial just north of Trafalgar Square in London. The stark white figure of
Cavell emphasizes her innocence, while the
plinth behind her is inscribed with her patriotism and humanity. *Photograph by Tammy Proctor.*

These characteristic stories of the *fusillées'* last moments appear
with regularity in postwar accounts of their deaths. An examination of
a few of these women's stories helps illuminate the way their executions created a script for female participation in war as spy-martyrs. As
martyrs to the Allied cause, these women spies and resisters came to
represent the failed conquests of Germany. With unbent wills, the
women had suffered humiliation and violation at the hands of the
enemy, but they reasserted their feminine virtue in postwar accounts.

These women became a useful counterpoint to the enemy within expressed in the alternative account of female spies—unpure and treacherous women. These kinds of women might be undermining the nation with their treachery and perversion, but heroines like Edith Cavell knew how to die like true women and true patriots.

Who were these dead women patriots sacrificed to the Allied cause? Many of them lived in German-occupied zones and were drawn into British Secret Service work by familial obligation, patriotic fervor, or a desire for revenge against their enemy. While several of these mar-

Edith Cavell's Norwich memorial echoes her place in British history as a recruiting tool for soldiers. The soldier pays homage to her memory on the field of honor with gun in hand.
Photograph by Nancy Arden McHugh.

tyrs faced death by firing squads, one of the most famous died from an illness contracted in a German prison. Of this list of honored dead, two—Louise de Bettignies and Gabrielle Petit—became household names immediately after the war, and many others were celebrated in local areas.

Spy-martyrs appeared in various guises throughout occupied territory after the war, and their actions are commemorated in monuments set in town squares and cathedral courtyards throughout Belgium and northern France. Both men and women are memorialized—but women are often depicted in the statuary as grieving widows and mothers, civic symbols such as Marianne or Liberty, or angels hovering over soldiers or graves. The figure and memory of Joan of Arc was also used in these memorials of female spy-martyrs.[28] But all of the women, though martyrs and symbols during and after the war, are virtually unknown today. The monuments to their deeds still stand, but most people do not know the stories of the women memorialized in street signs and statues.

Most of the females executed by the Germans for espionage or treasonous activities during the war were ordinary women drawn into the war by their circumstances. Instead of granting unconditional commendation to these heroic women, postwar writers emphasized their status as women, thus playing down their strength and courage. Antoine Redier, makes it clear that although women spies' actions were admirable, there was something shameful for men about women showing such presence of mind and heroic fortitude:

> These numberless girls who, on a small scale, did the same work as Edith Cavell, sometimes saw terrified expressions on men's faces. [The women] who spent nights on the roads conducting numbers of men of military age and of every tongue—French, English, Flemish—towards the northeast—these women, though heroines of the war, were frail creatures enough, and had the intuitive yearning of their sex for protection in danger. It is humiliating to think that when danger did arise it was generally the women's presence of mind and resource that saved the situation.[29]

Men's failure to assume the role of protector had left women to defend themselves. This circumstance caused feelings of inadequacy in many men—a possible explanation of the ambivalent attitude with which women's espionage activities were greeted.

Thousands of women resisted German occupation on a daily basis, from refusing their services to communicating secret information to Allied armies. Hundreds of women spent time in local jails, lock hospitals (for venereal disease) or German prisons during the war. While many women were punished for their actions, only some of the women committing the more serious crimes were executed for their actions. Acting as a courier or a *passeur* (a frontier courier who passed over the border into neutral territory) was one job that could lead to execution because of its highly treasonous nature. Courier duties were widely assigned to women agents because they could often find excuses to move about freely, such as selling produce, attending at births, and visiting family. Young girls seemed to have been particularly valued as couriers because they were often overlooked or dismissed as harmless.

Leonie Rameloo and Emilie Schattemann were Flemish teenagers from peasant families who were living on the Belgian-Dutch border when the war came in 1914. Their small village, Bouchaute, was in the northwest, only a short walk from the frontier between occupied Belgium and neutral Holland during the war. At first, the border was guarded by patrols of soldiers and searchlights, but beginning in 1915, barbed wire and electric fences were installed. The intelligence services in occupied territory could function only if they had a means of getting information gathered in Belgium and northern France to their agents in the Netherlands. The spies needed what British Secretary of Foreign Affairs Sir Edward Grey called a "keyhole into Germany."[30]

To facilitate the transfer of information, a series of passages were arranged across the Belgian-Dutch frontier. All of the Allied intelligence services had offices in the Netherlands where the information could be processed and where informants could be instructed and paid. Although the passages became places where refugees and information could get through to neutral ground they were dangerous and unstable. The 200-volt fences claimed "some 3000 victims," not including those executed for attempting to get through the fences.[31] Many *passeurs* donned rubber suits and gloves to pass under the electric wires or used frame devices to create a safe hole through the wires, and others used bribes (usually money or drugs) or deception to get sentries to let them pass.[32]

Rameloo and Schattemann helped pass people and information through to Holland. Prior to the erection of electric fences, the two women led spy couriers and refugees across the frontier and performed courier duties between Bouchaute and Ghent. When the frontier passages became more difficult to cross, the two women and their male companion, Isidore van Vlaanderen, continued to pass information by throwing messages over the border where they were retrieved by agents in Holland. Their activities were discovered in 1917, and the trio was arrested and tried by the Germans. All three were shot in September of 1917 in Ghent; Rameloo and Schattemann were only twenty-one and twenty-two years old respectively, at the time of their execution.[33] These women were celebrated in postwar accounts of female resistance, and their names are inscribed on a memorial in their home town of Bouchaute today.

The deaths of Rameloo and Schattemann were surprising given their ages and the fact that other female couriers captured by the Germans were only sentenced to life imprisonment. The apparent randomness of death sentences for women contributed to the feeling that executing women for espionage was morally wrong. In the case of Edith Cavell, she and her associate Baucq were executed, while those such as Louise Thuliez—some of the people most responsible for the network's success and most enmeshed in actual espionage—were given clemency. Perhaps Rameloo and Schattemann were executed because of the success of their activities, because authorities wanted to send a message to border communities, or maybe because their status as poor peasants meant they had no powerful people who would intercede on their behalf. Whatever the reason, their honorable status as martyrs—two innocent girls killed for their patriotism and goodheartedness—was secure in the postwar climate of retribution.

Elise Grandprez, a woman living in the French-speaking Ardennes area of eastern Belgium, was another such local martyr of the war. Grandprez was an unmarried woman in her forties who lived at home with her mother in the town of Stavelot. Grandprez, along with two brothers (Constant and François), a sister (Marie), and some neighbors, became involved in resistance and espionage activities. The family first helped soldiers hidden in the Ardennes, but later they became major suppliers of information on German troops, engaged in train and territorial observation, ran a letterbox, and served as couriers. The front for their activities was Constant Grandprez's work as a tanner, which he continued while working for British intelligence. His work allowed him to travel freely between towns in the area, giving him access to more information. Elise's jobs in the family espionage organization were varied: she served as a supervisor, trainwatcher, and courier, but her real contribution was as collator and transcriber of information. She, and to some extent her sister Marie, transcribed reports in invisible ink onto ordinary objects such as packing paper, box covers, and book pages. The reports were then carried to the chief of the intelligence service in Liège.[34]

The Grandprez network remained successful until March of 1916 when their Liège contact Dieudonné Lambrecht was caught by the Germans and shot. Almost a year later in January of 1917, the Grandprezs—Elise, Constant, Marie, and François—along with their accomplices the Gregoires (a married couple), were imprisoned on charges of espionage. Elise and Constant Grandprez and Andre Gregoire were condemned to death, and held in the fortress of the Chartreuse in Liège, where they were executed by firing squad in the summer of 1917 while the others received various prison terms.

In newspaper reports of the deaths, headlines often emphasized Elise's death over those of her brother and Andre Gregoire, echoing reports from 1915 about the execution of Edith Cavell, which virtually ignored Philippe Baucq's death. The *New York Times*'s headline simply read "Shoot Woman As a Spy" while the London *Times* noted, "Belgian Woman Shot As a Spy." Both articles described the victims in the same way, placing the woman at center stage—"Mlle. Grandprez and her brother"—in their description of the events.[35] Although Constant Grandprez was in some ways the ringleader of the organization and although he and Gregoire had also been executed beside Elise, the media seized on the German execution of a woman.

The story of their deaths, published in Belgium after the war, emphasized Elise's moral strength in a time of fear. While her brother and Gregoire sat in their cells and contemplated their fates, Elise was busy. Each day when a nun would visit, Elise would ask for a hair ribbon—a black ribbon one day, a red the next, a yellow the following day. When the time came for their executions, so the story goes, Elise produced from the neckline of her dress three small Belgian flags that she had made from the ribbons while sitting in her cell. She pressed a flag on each of her colleagues and counseled them to "have courage" and "go forward." When her brother asked her to slow her pace so he could keep up with her walk to the firing range, she complied. As befitted a spy-martyr, Grandprez was patriotic and strong to the end, mothering the unfortunate men and providing moral guidance. Her biographer's

The monument for Elise Grandprez and her companions in Stavelot, Belgium depicts a young girl tending a grave not a heroic spy or soldier. The memorial, like many others in Belgium, stresses Belgium's victimization during the war, not its resistance to occupation. *Photograph by Tammy Proctor.*

description of Elise Grandprez's last moment keeps with her role of the spy-martyr; she "raised her hand toward the sky and cried: 'Courage! Vive la Belgique!'" After the war, the bodies of the Grandprezs and that of Gregoire were exhumed from their graves at the Chartreuse and moved to Stavelot. A monument sculpted by Maxime Real del Sarte was erected in their memory.[36] The monument depicts a young woman tending a soldier's grave, nurturing and caring for it as was a woman's duty, providing moral strength after the war as Elise Grandprez had done in her last hours.

MODERN JOANS OF ARC

In addition to stories of local female bravery and the Edith Cavell story, the First World War also produced "national heroines" from the ranks of British intelligence agents. The two most successful and celebrated of these agents were undoubtedly Louise de Bettignies and Gabrielle Petit. One Belgian official noted in 1919, "France has Joan of Arc. Belgium has Gabrielle Petit," while another author described Louise de Bettignies as the "Joan of Arc of the North."[37] British intelligence officer Walter Kirke noted in his diary that de Bettignies was known as a "regular modern Joan of Arc."[38] The comparison of female spies to Joan of Arc is interesting given her role as a spiritual figure similar to Therese de Lisieux and the Virgin Mary for soldiers and civilians in World War I. Joan of Arc as an image of a female warrior and victim was also canonized just after the war.[39] Like Joan of Arc, Petit and de Bettignies were women of heroism and vision who were tortured and killed for their audacity. Also like Joan, they shed their feminine frailty and assumed the more subversive, androgynous role of soldier. Joan of Arc stood as a figure of spiritual vision and strength but also as a dangerous gender-bending woman, and certainly her legacy was a mixed one.

These two "Joans" were of radically different backgrounds, personalities, and fates, but both encapsulated the myth of the female spy-martyr that the postwar world craved. Both were known for their ingenuity, courage, and defiance of German authorities, both suffered imprisonment and betrayal, and both died as patriots working for the British intelligence service. Their biographers hastened to note they were virtuous and pious women, but their deaths legitimized their activities in a way that would not have been possible had they lived.

Gabrielle Petit was born in Tournai, Belgium, in 1893 to a middle-class family, but she lost her mother at a young age and was sent to an orphanage, where she was abandoned. While still in her teens she moved to Brussels and worked as a governess and shop assistant and boarded with families. When the war began, Petit was engaged to a soldier who was wounded at Liège in 1914. Her first dangerous assignment was helping him cross into the Netherlands to rejoin his regiment. During that trip she gained information, which she then communicated to British Intelligence. Impressed by her efficacy and accuracy, intelligence officials offered to hire her to gather and carry information. Beginning in the summer of 1915, she worked with the British Secret Service around Tournai and Maubeuge, moving around in disguise under a variety of false identities. Her job included observing local areas, recording information on troop movements, and obtaining technical information. According to British intelligence Petit was a successful agent until her arrest in February of 1916.[40] Imprisoned at St. Gilles Prison, Petit was tried in March and executed by a firing squad on April 1, 1916, at the age of twenty-three.[41]

Often describing her as a soldier, her biographer noted her strengths: "This young girl was a soldier, an unassuming soldier, but a tenacious soldier with an iron will, always ready to submit to torture for the honor of the flag."[42] Like the strength of Joan of Arc, Petit's assets were represented not so much by her courage, efficiency, and success as an agent, but by her willingness to suffer and die for her country. This vision of her was strengthened by her final words, recounted in news accounts and written on her Brussels monument. Defying the authorities, Petit reportedly told them that they would see how a Belgian woman could die and refused to be blindfolded, shouting, "Vive la Belgique! Viva le . . ." as she was shot.[43] Her monument reflects this defiance, depicting an unbowed young woman, chin high in a "bold stance."[44] A tribute to all Belgian women in the war, the memorial stands as powerful symbol of the Belgian nation itself, uncringing and defiant after the torture and humiliation of occupation by the enemy.

Like Belgium's Gabrielle Petit, France's Louise de Bettignies also stands as a national heroine. Considerably older than Petit, de Bettignies was born in 1880 in St. Amand, France, the seventh child of a well-off manufacturing family from Lille who had fallen on hard times. Raised as a devout Catholic, de Bettignies worked as a governess and considered joining a Carmellite order prior to the war.[45] She spoke

Gabrielle Petit was twenty-three years old when
she was shot by the Germans for espionage. She
became a Belgian national heroine after her
1916 execution.

French, German, Italian, and English, and had been educated at Girton
College in Oxford, England. Before the war she worked in Italy and
Poland as a governess, and she had even declined an offer to teach heir
to Austro-Hungarian throne Archduke Franz Ferdinand's children. She
led an active life and was often described as fit and lively, as well as in-
dependent-minded and intelligent.[46]

De Bettignies was approached early in the war by both French and
British intelligence but chose to work for the British because of the
promise of a salary. Assuming the false name of Alice Dubois, de Bettignies spent time in Boulogne and Flushing being trained in codes,
inks, military information, and other important tools of the trade. Her
closest accomplice was a young woman from Roubaix named Leonie
Vanhoutte, known by the alias Charlotte. De Bettignies's service for
the British began formally in February of 1915 and continued until her

The stance of the Gabrielle Petit memorial in Brussels emphasizes Petit's youth, defiance, and patriotic martyrdom. As a memorial to Belgium's women, it is inscribed with her famous words, "and I will show them that a Belgian woman knows how to die." *Photograph by Tammy Proctor.*

arrest and the break up of her network in October of 1915. Her British superiors had only praise for her work, calling her a "really high-class agent" and noting just before her arrest that her work was splendid. One intelligence memo sought to describe her contribution: "I cannot speak too highly of the bravery, devotion, and patriotism of this young lady. Her service[s] to the British Intelligence . . . were simply invaluable."[47]

The network she ran was truly diverse and effective, covering the area around Lille and passing information about military emplacements, troop movement, and airfields. De Bettignies ran many personal risks, traveling to Britain fifteen to twenty times and into other high-risk zones, but she also supervised the work of a range of people from young girls to elderly men and women. In the months that she worked for British intelligence, de Bettignies showed audacity, courage, ingenuity, and intelligence; in short, she was a true soldier without uniform in the occupied zones. Her information was efficiently gathered, clearly transcribed, and effectively communicated to her superiors. Her postwar biographers, however, tend to focus not on her soldierly qualities or intelligence but on her purity, patriotism, and femininity. One author emphasized her essential femininity early and often in his account of her work: "Louise was the most womanly woman one could imagine. . . . There was nothing of the amazon about her." He continued by noting that de Bettignies and her female compatriots were virtuous: "Coquettes they may have been but prostitutes never . . . [they] never resorted to the customary feminine wiles to obtain information."[48] De Bettignies and her "sisters in arms" knew their place in society despite the unusual roles they had assumed during the war; they were not aping men or losing sight of their feminine virtue.[49]

Interestingly enough, most books and articles about Louise de Bettignies focus on her time in prison, her suffering, and her death. After their arrest in 1915, de Bettignies and Vanhoutte were tried and sentenced to death, but their sentences were commuted to hard labor in prison. The two were sent to Siegburg Prison in Germany where they lived side-by-side with the surviving Cavell network women (Marie de Croÿ, Louise Thuliez, and Jeanne de Belleville) and with captured women from many other British, French, and Belgian intelligence networks. Prison conditions were poor, with terrible food and cold cells. De Bettignies is mentioned in a variety of prison memoirs because of her defiance of prison authorities. She led a strike among prisoners to stop the practice of forcing the women to assemble munitions parts, persisting in her position even after suffering through the pain of solitary confinement in frigid conditions. One woman described de Bettignies's role in the prison: "Mlle. De Bettignies is the person that I most admired in the prison. She served as an example of courage and sacrifice for us."[50]

Unlike the other spy-martyrs of the war, de Bettignies was not shot by a firing squad, but died in prison. She contracted a respiratory disease and spent many of her last months ill. Her death came slowly, and she never recovered following an operation in April 1918 to remove a tumor from her chest. She died on September 27, 1918, a portrait of courage through suffering, or so many wrote after the war. As with Cavell, Grandprez, Petit, and others, de Bettignies's body was exhumed after the war and reburied with great pomp in her hometown of St. Amand. The monument to her memory in Lille was dedicated in 1927.[51]

All of the women martyrs of the First World War whose bravery is etched in the stone of national monuments and in the pages of interwar histories were portrayed as good women. They were female spies and resisters who had risen above petty national rivalries to symbolize either motherly goodness (although none were mothers) or virginal and pure patriotism (like Joan of Arc), yet they also stood as powerful symbols of their nations. Women, in the rhetoric of warfare, inhabited the realm of home not front, so their participation in war implied suffering and victimhood. Thus "courage" became gendered in postwar discourse to reflect the fundamental assumption that men fought wars to save women from such victimhood. As Klaus Theweleit notes in his study of postwar male fantasies, "Suffering [of women] is not only taken for granted, it is expressly admired."[52] Their statues emphasize patriotic fervor and selfless sacrifice, reinscribing on a war-torn world the gendered separation of women from warfare. As John Laffin wrote in his study of women warriors, male soldiers have "the intense desire . . . to return home to women and bed. If a man is to have women at war with him, if he is to think of women as comrades-in-arms rather than as mistress-on-mattress, the inducement disappears."[53] The women spy-martyrs of World War I paid a price for their boldness but also made the postwar woman able to retreat to the home and the protection of men, reinforcing gendered notions of warfare as men's work.

CONCLUSION

Of the female intelligence agents of the occupied zones, Edith Cavell, Louise de Bettignies, and Gabrielle Petit garnered most of the fame in the 1920s and 1930s, but today their names are mostly forgotten. Historian Margaret Darrow notes that when she questioned people in Lille about de Bettignies in the 1990s, most did not know who de Bettignies was despite a central square in town being named after her. Even the tourist bureau was not quite sure where her monument was located.[54] Why were spy-martyrs such a fleeting phenomenon? It seems likely that the suffering, torture, and death that were commemorated in the 1920s was eclipsed by the horror of Nazi executions and deportations of the Second World War. More important, these women spy-martyrs were necessarily seen as aberrations in the postwar world. They had been warriors in their own extraordinary time but as the war ended so did their usefulness. In a climate where "back to normalcy" was the fervent hope of many people in Europe, honorable she-soldiers and daring women spies had no place. Joan of Arc had served her purpose and died a martyr, a lasting symbol of the French nation. Likewise, Petit, Cavell, and de Bettignies were more valuable to rebuilding nation-states as martyrs than as heroic resisters.

After the war, governments sought to herd women back into their prewar roles as wives and mothers, unconscious of the sexual freedoms that would have to be harnessed. In occupied territories and at home, women's sexual freedom was seen as both suspect and dangerous to the fabric of the nation-state, and governments took steps to reimpose controls and to encourage women to reassume previous roles in the home. Unfortunately for government officials, there was no way to erase the topsy-turviness of the war period, especially in liberated regions such as Belgium and northern France formerly under the control of Germany. In these areas careful cautionary tales emerged as a harmony line to the melody of the spy-martyr; this counter-narrative included the tales of bad women, collaborators, and spies suspect for their intimate relations with the enemy.

6

Intimate Traffic with the Enemy

All were equally careless in their intercourse with women and at the height of their passion would whisper, into the ear of their companion-in-lust, secrets that were never meant to be thus used. The army did much more to prevent soldiers from becoming infected with venereal diseases than to protect them against the grave evil of espionage.

—Magnus Hirschfeld,
The Sexual History of the World War

DESPITE ABUNDANT EVIDENCE of women as competent and efficient agents and informants, their popular image depicts female spies as seductresses who used their sexuality to glean information from powerful yet susceptible men. "Intercourse with women," as described by Magnus Hirschfeld, captured this double-edged sword—*sexual* intercourse with women opened men up to *verbal* intercourse with their seductress, creating an opportunity in both the official and the popular mind for women to gain the secrets of nations.[1] Historian Margaret Darrow astutely notes in her study of French women during the war that the sexualized female spy tapped into societal fears that accompanied the rise of the bold and independent "New Woman." She argued, "it was not such women's ubiquity and invisibility that made them dangerous, but their femininity. . . . Cleaning lady, governess, and courtesan had collapsed into one phantasm of seduction and betrayal."[2]

This image of the spy-seductress was not confined to the popular imagination of 1914; it has appeared in many histories of espionage as well. Often the histories draw implicit or explicit connections with biblical women "spies" such as Rahab, Delilah, Salome, and even Eve. For example, both Christopher Andrew and Phillip Knightley in their histories of modern intelligence mention biblical harlot-spies to help

define espionage and establish the historical context. Even the title of
Knightley's book, *The Second Oldest Profession,* builds on this link between sexuality and espionage.[3] In J. Bernard Hutton's 1971 sensationalized history of women spies the author warns male agents to "Fear all
women! Eve is efficient as a spy. But as a spy-catcher, she is deadly."[4]
Richard Rowan's study of espionage history examines both Delilah,
who "used her sex to gain intelligence," and Rahab, "the harlot of Jeri-
cho," noting that the latter established the narrative tradition of using
the "siren in secret service" to romanticize the profession.[5]

Other historians have posited a "natural" connection between
women's sexual promiscuity and their role in intelligence. Some writers
have declared that "sex is a woman spy's most deadly weapon. . . ."[6]
Jock Haswell wrote in his 1977 study, "espionage was largely a man's
world in which woman usually played the part of the seductress, employed by a combination of spymaster and pander, to extract information either in unguarded moments or as the price of pleasure."[7] Likewise, former CIA employee Elizabeth McIntosh's 1989 study of women
and intelligence notes,

> The early run-of-the-mill Mata Haridans were not trained as they are
> today. They relied on sex, good sense, and a woman's natural instinct
> to be devious when the situation called for covert action. Over the cen-
> turies theirs was a membership in a haphazard trade, more often than
> not a convenient merging of the first and second oldest professions.[8]

McIntosh's comments regarding women's "natural" propensity for deception and their use of sex to weaken men's resolve reflect the broad
consensus in twentieth-century spy writing that women could be useful in getting hard-to-reach information in private spaces. Men were
suspect in private places, but women—servants, prostitutes, wives,
mothers, hostesses—were masters of that domain. Ironically, women's
autonomy in the private sphere was both valued and feared, as men
were vulnerable to both the spy and the prostitute in the quiet corners
of life. The female spy blurred the distinction of private and public (as
did the prostitute) by performing "public" work in "private" spaces,
making her both effective and dangerous.

Although the *horizontale,* or woman spy-prostitute, is not unknown
in the history of British intelligence, this image owes more to fictional
fantasies of women spies than to historical realities. Reflecting literature

that portrayed the New Woman as sexually voracious and decadent, stories of female spies emphasized their sexuality and their boldness.[9] The women seemed not to recognize the boundaries of appropriate feminine behavior, just as the New Woman sought to transgress societal norms. Julie Wheelwright found in her study of Mata Hari and spy fiction that the myth of the "spy-courtesan" has a strange resonance in fiction, film, and autobiographies, but suggests that these myths reflect male fantasies and fears of betrayal more than they mirror any reality in the secret world of espionage.[10]

Prewar spy fiction depicting mysterious female seductresses who learned state secrets from susceptible men reflected late Victorian art, which often portrayed a predatory female. In *Idols of Perversity*, Bram Dijkstra studies turn of the century art that shows women in "a veritable iconography of misogyny."[11] As sirens, vampires, Pandoras, and sexually destructive sadists (such as Salome and Judith), females depicted in late nineteenth-century and early twentieth-century art are symbolically slain for their sexual curiosity and inherent perversity. Much of this art reflects male anxieties regarding women's real or imagined power, but it also establishes a clear archetype of women as destroyers of both men and civilizations. Likewise, Klaus Theweleit in his work on male fantasies has documented a series of stereotypical views of aggressive women, noting, "women who don't conform to any of the 'good woman' images are automatically seen as prostitutes, as the vehicles of 'urges.' They are evil and out to castrate, and they are treated accordingly."[12] The female spy images of the war that remained in the popular imagination in the twentieth century fit nicely into these expressions of societal fears. The woman spy provided a convenient explanation for the inexplicable nature of the First World War. As Darrow argues, "Against this secret feminine evil, the open, honest combat of soldiers was impotent."[13]

This final chapter explores the most popular fictionalized and sensationalized images of women spy-harlots from World War I before turning to the consequences these images had for the lives of women in wartime. The pervasive image of the woman spy as prostitute and sexual being created innumerable difficulties for women, especially in occupied territories. If, as popular wisdom dictated, women's bodies were necessary to men, then all females in occupied zones were suspect for subversive activities, espionage, and collaboration with the enemy. Media portraits of women as virtuous, martyred heroines or avaricious spy-prostitutes made it difficult for real women to assert patriotism, heroism, resistance to occupation, and constancy without suspicion. Official secret service work for allied governments was one route to validation as "true" patriots, but even then, women's work was suspect and their loyalty to their nations questioned.

MATA HARI: "FEMME FORTE"

No figure better represents the image of the erotic female spy than Mata Hari, perhaps the best-known woman spy in history.[14] Countless "true" histories, novels, films, plays, documentaries, and even a ballet have featured the story of Mata Hari, and her name has served as a synonym for the female spy.[15] Many know that Mata Hari was a female dancer and spy who was executed for her crimes, but few know the circumstances of her death or even the country that executed her. Mata Hari's biographer, Julie Wheelwright, ponders in the preface to her book, "Why had I remembered her name yet nothing of her story?"[16] Wheelwright's question exposes part of the mystique of Mata Hari and of all women spies. Why, indeed, is the Mata Hari story so powerful, yet so illusory?

Mata Hari captured the public imagination precisely because her invented self—a mysterious, "foreign," and erotic being—fit perfectly the sexualized myth of women spies constructed in the years before and during the war. She embodied the fictional female spy that inhabited the imaginations of the populace; she represented the decadence of Salome with her exotic dancing, the hidden female threat with her sexual exploits, and the enemy within through her espionage. In describing the connection between espionage and eroticism, Hirschfeld makes the skills of women spies plain: "we find in the infamous activities of espionage not only all the sordid tricks of crime but also the variants of eroticism and prostitution."[17] Mata Hari died not for her great success as a master spy but because she was a symbol of the contagion of decadence and treason that seemed to be undermining France, especially in 1917, when widespread mutinies infected the French armies at the front. Darrow sums up this connection, writing,

> The story's staying power came from its apparent revelation of a fundamental truth about 'Woman and War.' Embodying the most mon-

strous incarnation of the Emancipated Woman, Mata Hari showed feminine independence and sexuality leading straight to the death of thousands of men and threatening the survival of the nation.[18]

Mata Hari was, in short, the perfect evil foil for the good women who were represented by the patriotic heroine Edith Cavell and the virtuous mothers and wives of soldiers.

Who was Mata Hari? She was born Margaretha Geertruida Zelle in 1876 in Leeuwarden, Netherlands, and she married a much older Colonial Army officer named Rudolph MacLeod in 1895. Part of her married life was spent in the Dutch East Indies, where Rudolph was posted and where she lived with her two young children, born in 1897 and 1898. The MacLeods's marriage was a rocky one, marked by abuse. After the death of her infant son in 1899 and the family's return to the Netherlands, Rudolph and their daughter left Margaretha in 1902. She went to Paris to find her fortune in 1904. The MacLeods's marriage ended formally in divorce in 1906, but by this time, Margaretha had reinvented herself entirely. She launched her erotic dancing career in 1905 soon adopted the name "Mata Hari," a Malay phrase meaning "eye of the day."[19] Wheelwright described the sensation that Mata Hari caused in prewar Paris with her nude performances:

> The audience that flocked to watch Mata Hari stripping off her multicoloured veils and listen to her "Oriental" tales projected their own fantasies onto the stage. Cloaked in her imitation "otherness." . . . Mata Hari had touched a raw, erotic nerve, that fed seamlessly into powerful myths about the sensuality and licentiousness of Asian women. As her fame increased, her past was transformed into a chapter more befitting a sacred Oriental temple dancer; Java and India were merely interchangeable backdrops.[20]

Margaretha herself seemed to get caught up in the Mata Hari mystique, fashioning new forms of herself and refusing to be defined by her background or by the intrigued media. Even as she faced death in a cell in St. Lazare Prison in 1917, she continued to maintain the identity she had created for herself, writing,

> Remember that all my life as a woman, I have lived as Mata Hari, that I think and act as such, that I have lost all notion of travel, distances,

As one of history's most famous women spies, Mata Hari is often depicted as an exotic dancer as she appeared before the war. Most photos focus on her seductive body, and since 1917 they have continued to be the most popular illustrations of her. *Library of Congress.*

dangers, nothing exists for me. . . . I lose—I win—I defend myself when someone attacks me—I take when someone has taken from me. But I beg you to believe that I have never worked as a spy against France. Never. Never.[21]

Indeed, Mata Hari had laid out the philosophy of her life in this statement, together with the things that made her such a danger in the eyes of French authorities. Demonstrating her pragmatic approach to existence, she asserted independence, freedom, and self-definition.

Not only a successful dancer, Mata Hari became involved in a series of affairs with high-profile, older men including politicians and military

officers. These liaisons increased her notoriety and made her more suspect in the eyes of intelligence officials tracking her activities. What male
officials saw in 1916 was an actress nearing forty years old who traveled
widely despite the state of war, was in debt, and pursued sexual liaisons
with officers and public officials from a variety of national backgrounds.
Often short of money, Mata Hari depended on her stage earnings and
the largesse of current lovers for lodging, food, and a lavish lifestyle.

As early as 1916, Mata Hari was being watched in France, and
British authorities had marked her as possibly suspicious in December
of 1915.[22] Accounts disagree about the exact nature of her contribution
to either French or German intelligence, but it is clear that she accepted
money from the French and traveled to Belgium and Spain on missions
for France. Documents also show that Mata Hari was denounced by the
Germans as spy "H-21," and that she repeatedly denied being a German spy when interrogated by French and British authorities in 1915

This last portrait of Mata Hari, courtesan and
spy, taken in prison before her 1917 execution.
Library of Congress.

and 1916. French scholar Leon Schirmann found evidence in German archives that Mata Hari had been recruited by Germany in the autumn of 1915, but she appeared to have passed on virtually no information of importance. His claims are supported by the fact that after her arrest by the French in February of 1917, Mata Hari admitted that she had agreed to spy for Germans but had never really helped them.[23]

Some authors thought Mata Hari received her just desserts because one of her "victims," German military attaché Arnold von Kalle, betrayed her. He forwarded telegrams referring to her work through insecure channels to Berlin, exposing her French and German double life to authorities in both countries. Any success she had as a spy seemed to have been in the service of France, yet it was the French who arrested, tried, and executed her.[24]

Most evidence against her at the trial was circumstantial at best, and French authorities certainly fabricated some of it.[25] The "proof" that sent Mata Hari to her death included a "confession" she gave in prison in which she attempted to explain how she hoped to use Germany and help France. Money she received from a Dutch lover and from Kalle in Madrid became the additional nails in her coffin, although the prosecution also tried to claim (with no evidence) that Mata Hari had sent fifty thousand men to their deaths through her treachery. She was tried in a closed court session in July of 1917, and her short trial ended with her condemnation for giving intelligence to the enemy. Her attempts to appeal were refused and no clemency was forthcoming. She was executed on October 15, 1917 by a French firing squad.[26]

The real drama of Mata Hari began, however, with her death in 1917 when a series of rumors, tales, and outlandish accounts of her life and death began to circulate. From stories of a miraculous escape from the firing squad to increasingly strident denunciations of her treason, Mata Hari appeared on stage, in novels, in newspaper accounts, and in histories of the war. Perhaps she was the "universal anti-hero" who "mimed Salome, the powerful but deadly female, an enduring nightmare of female betrayal," as Wheelwright has claimed. Maybe she was a "witch" and a "demon" that needed to be sacrificed to save France as Darrow has argued. Or maybe Hirschfeld was right when he wrote that Mata Hari "met her fate, not so much because of the damage she had actually inflicted, but because it was expected that by inflicting the death penalty upon this prominent lover of distinguished men of the enemy camp, a beneficial moral effect would be exercised. . . ."[27] Whatever the reason for Mata Hari's long life in the public's imagination, Mata Hari—the spy-seductress and modern Delilah—functions as a powerful warning to women regarding the dangers of espionage and eroticism. The uncertainty regarding Mata Hari's complicity, the conflicting accounts of her death, and the fuzziness of the popular understanding of her life help reinforce the mythic quality of her memory and open the way for other stories to be cast in the Mata Hari mold.

"MATA-HARIDANS"

Other stories of "mata-haridans" surfaced at the time Mata Hari's image was being solidified in the public consciousness. These women became stock characters in the pantheon of World War I female spies and served as archetypes of the spy-prostitute in the later spy "histories" and fictions of the interwar period. Often explicitly compared to Mata Hari, these women, although now largely forgotten, helped reinforce the image of the female spy as sexual predator.

One of the best known of these spy femme-fatales was a self-made star, Marthe Richer (alias Marthe Richard). Born Marthe Betenfeld in Lorraine in 1889, she married and became a licensed pilot in the years before the war. When war broke out in 1914, Richer formed the Patriotic Union of Women Aviators (Aviatrices) and tried without success to offer their services to the French government.[28] She reported in her memoirs that after her husband was killed at the front she became a spy for the French in Madrid. She noted in her story that her patriotism knew no bounds; she understood her role as a woman spy to mean that virtue was no longer important. On a hint from French spy-master Georges Ladoux to "exploit [her] youth and beauty," Richer became the mistress of German naval attaché in Madrid. She later claimed to have served as a double agent out of necessity, passing on information to him for German use as well as to Ladoux for the French.[29]

Though Richer's exploits were widely publicized in the 1930s in her autobiography and Ladoux's biography of her war work, as well as through scores of news and magazine articles and a film featuring Erich von Stroheim and Edwige Feuillere, recent scholars have exposed problems with her tale.[30] Magazine features and various books from the 1970s to the present cast doubt on her claims, noting that many were outright lies and others exaggerations. Richer, who later wrote fiction, tried to make her wartime tale fit into the Mata Hari mold, often drawing connections between herself and the executed dancer. In a 1970 television program Richer described the similarities: "She was exactly what I was myself—thus, she tried to play the role of double agent . . . [however] I was decorated with the Legion of Honor and Mata Hari was executed."[31]

Although Richer's story may have fit the spy-courtesan model, she lived too long to achieve real notoriety. Mata Hari's prewar reputation as an exotic dancer gave her a measure of fame, but her death and the public punishment of her sins also seems to have given her story the impact that many other tales of spies did not have.

Spy writers did catalog the sins of other women spies, often casting them as Mata Hari-type vamps or as victims of their passion for men. For example, seamstress Marguerite Francillard became a model of the intemperate woman for spy writer Emile Massard. She was castigated for entertaining men, getting drunk on champagne, spying for her lover, and betraying what she knew before being executed in 1917.[32] Sometimes stories of spy- courtesans were fabricated, as in the cases of the German spies caught in the United States, Maria Victorica and Despina Davidovitch Storch. An overweight, middle-aged morphine addict, Victorica was described by one writer as "one of the most talented young women in the service of the Kaiser," leaving readers to interpret what "talents" she might possess.[33] Meanwhile, reporters also seized on the young Storch, noting that "it was easy to see how men would fall under the influence of [Storch's] smile and those brilliant black eyes."[34] The *New York Times* noted that she had friendly relations with many men and that "her personality and position had enabled her to gain the confidence of influential Americans who were used by her, frequently without their knowledge. . . ."[35]

The successors to Mata Hari all had one characteristic in common: they were dangerous sexual creatures with an ability to "use" others, sometimes without their knowledge. In an Allied intelligence officers' training manual, prospective agents are warned about German female spies who are given cameras to hide in their blouses to photograph and "establish the identity of their unconscious informants."[36] What might men do in an unguarded moment with a woman spy? Ladoux's comments in his biography of Richer represent this threat to the nation and to masculinity:

She left behind her a perfidious trail of the "Eternal Feminine," the perfume then in vogue and with which "war godmothers" sprinkled their letters to soldiers at the front. So encouraged, the hardened men in the trenches would rush to the attack, irritated and entranced. And at the same time, there was about that perfume something as subtly dangerous as an asphyxiating gas."[37]

These figures illustrate the mixing of fact and fiction that characterizes tales of female spies, but they also suggest the potency of the courtesan-spy image in historical imagination.

While "mata-haridans" continue to appear in various guises in fiction, film, and journalistic accounts today—almost eighty-five years after the war's end—another character also appears: the "Lady Doctor." Mata Hari was the danger destroyed, while the "Lady Doctor" represents the greater threat that remained after the war: the autonomous woman. In the annals of World War I espionage, the story of the female secret service agent known as the "Lady Doctor" pervades British and French accounts of the period, yet the details of the tale remain tantalizingly elusive nearly nine decades after the war. Where the life and death of Mata Hari received both notoriety and publicity, the work of the "Lady Doctor" is shrouded in mystery and gossip. All the major spy writers of the interwar period and many official intelligence reports note her existence, but few can pinpoint either her identity or her role in German espionage. The Fraulein Doktor, Lady Doctor, or Mademoiselle Docteur became a lasting archetype of the twentieth-century female spy, perhaps all the more powerful for the mere outline of her life that has survived in countless conflicting accounts. Who was this woman and how does she function as part of the spy images created by the war?

The basic outline of her career is consistent in most accounts: the Lady Doctor was a German spy-agent responsible for training agents to infiltrate England and France during the war. She worked at the Antwerp bureau of German espionage, but after the war she disappeared from view. Those few details are the only universally agreed on facts about her life, but provide only a backdrop to the real drama of the postwar narratives about her. The nicknames ascribed to her hint at the Lady Doctor's image as a sadistic *femme fatale* in the fantasies of male Allies. Beyond her "doctor" designations, she was also known as the Red Tiger, Tiger Eyes, the Black Cat, the Queen of Spies, the Fair Lady, the Blonde Lady, *La Baronne*, and the Lady with the Cigarette. Her nick-names describe a sexualized, powerful, and dangerous woman and fit with many twentieth-century stereotypes of women spies.

She appears in spy histories, news articles, interwar fiction, and even in a film by G. W. Pabst called *Mademoiselle Docteur* (1934). She is described by one spy writer as a "mistress-spy," while another claims that that she was "formerly a denizen of the underworld."[38] Ladoux reported that Marthe Richer referred to her as "an A1 specimen" and noted that her German lover always saluted when he mentioned the Lady Doctor.[39] Throughout the interwar period, her permeable image appears in vignettes again and again as she slips from prostitute to sadist to professional to drug-addict to mental patient.

The Lady Doctor's real identity appears to have little connection to the tales recounted about her life even though her actual life story is not known. The Lady Doctor's real name may have been either Anne Marie Lesser or Dr. Elsbeth Schragmuller—the two identities most often associated with her by postwar writers. Lesser was purportedly a young woman led into espionage by her lover, while Schragmuller was a scholar who received her doctorate from the University of Freiburg in 1914. She may have begun her war work in the censorship office before moving to the Antwerp bureau by 1917. Both women supposedly had great skill in languages and superior intelligence, and the two were known to use their beauty and sexuality as tools of power. Pinning down the identity of the Lady Doctor seemed to become a race after the war, with newspapers, espionage fiction writers, and historians publishing their theories. For example, in 1934, *Le Soir* published an obituary of Lesser claiming she was the Lady Doctor as if to answer the 1933 *Paris-Midi* account of the lady doctor's activities by Schragmuller.[40] Historians today still do not agree about her identity or even whether she was a real figure at all.[41]

What made the Lady Doctor such a fascinating subject and an enduring stereotype of women spies? Her characteristic behavior ties her to Mata Hari, but also makes her even more dangerous because she was never caught. How was the Lady Doctor described? First, she was depicted in all her guises as intelligent and cosmopolitan—a knowing woman. In 1919, the London *Times* wrote,

> The Frau Doktor, as she was addressed by her colleagues, spoke
> French without a trace of a foreign accent, and showed by her manner

and dress that she had lived for a long time in France, and probably in Paris. She used to address her "tools" [agents] with a French cigarette between her lips, leaning back seductively in a large armchair.[42]

She was educated and canny, with a knack for using people to her advantage. In some ways, she combined the efficient women of the intelligence bureaucracy with the deviousness and deviance of Mata Hari. Although described as seductive and beautiful, accounts often stress her professionalism, her skill at administration, and her efficiency. In fact, MI5 Chief Sir Vernon Kell described her with admiration: "She must have been a woman of some ability from the many accounts received, for she inspired respect, and her identity was concealed for a considerable time, in spite of many attempts to discover it."[43]

The second characteristic usually associated with the Lady Doctor was her ability to intimidate and coerce others, particularly men. These accounts expose clear anxiety about the reversal of gender roles and her "unnatural" power as the head of the Antwerp spy bureau. Some attributed a vicious sadism to her, describing rumors of her use of masks and locked rooms, torture and intimidation. One of the earliest books about German espionage after the war alluded to the power she had over others: "Weird stories were current all over Holland as to the awful oaths she made her agents swear. . . ."[44] A British intelligence officer noted that she was reported to have shot agents who failed in their assignments and betrayed weak agents to the enemy. Other writers spoke of her callousness and her willingness to kill, saying, "she respected human life about as deeply as she respected the conventions."[45]

In addition to her ruthlessness and her efficiency, the final characteristic she embodied in all reports was that of the seductress. This particular trait was emphasized over and over in graphic detail in all accounts of her life. Her physical attractiveness is noted first: she is "buxom" and "good-looking" in more than one account of her, and many accounts described her blonde beauty.[46] Writers also discuss her powers of seduction. In some cases she is listed as a former prostitute fatally addicted to morphine and cocaine, while in others she merely lured men to their downfalls using "her seductive charm, and her way of smiling from under drooping eyelashes. . . ."[47] One would-be biographer writes a completely fabricated account of her death by firing squad, describing her en route as "an exceptionally beautiful creature. Further she was clever and charming. Altogether the type of woman who could fetch a man down like a punch from a boxing glove, with a horse-shoe in it."[48] The sum of the descriptions equals a Mata-Hari type vamp who used sex to control and betray men. Magnus Hirschfeld called her "a woman with nerves of steel, a cold, logical engine for a mind, well-controlled sensuality, a fascinating body, and demoniac eyes."[49] In short, the Lady Doctor embodied all the stereotypes and fears of women: she was sexual and voracious, yet controlled and cold.

Whatever the truth of the Lady Doctor's life story, she clearly symbolizes the power of women over men. Whether using her intelligence, her efficiency, her sadism, or her sexuality, the Lady Doctor was in control of the men and women she directed. Like Salome or Delilah, the Lady Doctor knew her own power and used it effectively in her life and work. As with Mata Hari, she is the secret female evil of the war; unlike Mata Hari, she gets away with her treachery. Never caught and never conclusively identified, the Lady Doctor symbolizes the continuing threat from female spies, and by extension, from women's sexuality. One spy writer ended his account of her life by quoting (he claims) one of her agents: "C'est une créature terrible."[50]

This "terrible creature" has become a romantic legend and a stock character to rival Mata Hari in the public imagination.[51] She was immediately portrayed in interwar spy novels and films, but her characteristics also translated into the fictional spy universe of the Cold War, where the Lady Doctor was reborn as the cold, calculating, sadistic, and often lethal, communist female spy. The Lady Doctor was the original *La Femme Nikita*, and her character appears in various guises in James Bond films as characters such as Helga Brandt in *You Only Live Twice* (1967) and Rosa Klebb in *From Russia with Love* (1962). The evil Lady Doctor, the deviant Mata Hari, and the virtuous Edith Cavell all defined the phenomenon of women in espionage for twentieth-century audiences—and all served as cautionary tales for women. For a postwar population that yearned for "normalcy" and an end to topsy-turvy gender roles, these stories neatly packaged women's war participation into "acceptable" stereotypes.

The problem with these over-simplified descriptions of women spies was that they failed to reflect the reality of female experience of war. These images assumed that women had complete control over their sexual lives and that they had ownership of their bodies. This false assumption, combined with official fear on both sides of the conflict that female sexuality was a danger that undermined soldiers' health and morale meant that women faced a serious dilemma in occupied zones. If female espionage was a hidden evil tied to sexuality, what options did women under foreign occupation have in expressing patriotism and resistance? Where did women who survived the experience of occupation fit if they didn't match one of the acceptable stereotypes of martyred heroine or horizontal collaborator? For instance, how was a female soldier of *La Dame Blanche* categorized?

OCCUPIED TERRITORIES

A good example of the dilemma that women in occupied territories faced is reflected in Marthe Cnockaert McKenna's 1933 memoirs. Born in Westroosebeke, Belgium, McKenna was a young woman trained as a nurse when the Germans invaded her village in 1914. Her home was burned and her family was temporarily separated. McKenna was employed almost immediately by the Germans to work among the wounded, first in her village and then in the town of Roulers after women were evacuated there in January of 1915. She worked at the Roulers German Hospital as a nurse until late 1916, winning the Iron Cross for her service. When she was arrested and charged with espionage in 1916, the Iron Cross and the recommendation of her hospital superiors helped save her from the firing squad.[52] McKenna's dilemma during the war was a simple one: help the Allies with whom she sympathized or help the Germans in order to maintain a livelihood for her family. McKenna chose to do both, walking a careful line between collaboration and resistance. She tried to protect herself from both sides of the conflict, but made herself suspect in the eyes of both.

In establishing the context for her account, McKenna describes the experience of civilians living under foreign occupation. For almost five years, Belgians had to live among the German army, especially in front-line garrison towns like Roulers. As McKenna noted, much of the food produced in the area was earmarked for the German Levying Commission, and civilians were left with only about one-fourth of production capacity and relief food from Herbert Hoover's American effort—the Commission for Relief in Belgium (CRB).[53] The timing of the invasion exacerbated the food problem, leaving many harvests standing in the fields during August and September of 1914. Belgians, who imported most of their grains, were left scrambling to feed themselves. In fact, by early 1915, one-fifth of the Belgian population could not afford to buy bread—a figure that continued to rise over the four years that the CRB functioned.[54]

Beyond food shortages and the disruption of work for tens of thousands of people, the Germans placed demands on those living in occupied Belgium and northern France. German officials restricted travel, established curfews, and instituted a pass system to control local residents in occupied zones. In some cases, mayors were held responsible for illegal activities, harboring of soldiers or spies, or possession of arms, pigeons, or other forbidden items. German military authorities requisitioned products and labor, and families, especially in garrison towns, were forced to billet German soldiers. Those who billeted soldiers or sold them goods and services could expect payment in cash or kind, and German officials pledged (via proclamation) that civilians would be paid for any provisions taken from them for the army's purposes.[55] Civilians under German occupation, then, were faced with a tricky moral dilemma. To survive, a certain level of complicity with their enemies seemed inevitable. Was it collaboration to billet and serve German troops? Should inhabitants feel guilty for working voluntarily for Germans? As Helen McPhail noted in her study of occupied France, "[t]he need for food brought degradation to everyone, no matter their peace-time status: former land-owners could be seen doing the washing-up for the German officers lodged in the Casino, farmer's wives washed and ironed clothing for the soldiers . . . everyone's morals were undermined."[56]

For women, the strain of occupation was particularly apparent because of its sexual overtones. Women have historically been a crucial but invisible part of expeditionary forces, performing "needed support services" as cooks, nurses, prostitutes, laundresses, wives, drivers, and provisioners.[57] The military's need for these services is complicated by the experience of occupation with its explicit power dynamic between invading enemy male and conquered female. Women, especially working-class women, were seen as sexually available by many soldiers, and the combination of desperate civilian conditions and the longevity of the war led many females to prostitute themselves in order to survive and help their families. Many other women, who billeted, provisioned, or worked for Germans, faced accusations of prostitution and the assumptions that their activities were by their own choice. Marie X., a women deported from Lille to work for the Germans, describes her shame at this association:

> One of the most painful aspects of my captivity . . . was to feel weighing on me the scornful gaze of those who not knowing me took me for what I am not . . . [w]hore of the Boches! It was impossible to make them understand, to explain to them. I could only go back to my room and hide.[58]

Likewise, women who bore illegitimate children or who were treated for venereal disease were often treated as "horizontal collaborators." Officials were caught between their pity for women claiming to have been raped and their suspicion that these same women were lying. Hirschfeld, in summing up the experience of occupation, encapsulates many of the preconceptions people had of women. Hirschfeld notes that many women had "overheated imaginations" and explains the difficulty officials faced in finding "real" female victims:

> The conquest of woman and the act of copulation presuppose, on the man's part, a definite joy in attacking. The woman who, in the act of love, is the one that gives herself, reacts to this with passion. The normal woman desires to be conquered by the man, to be forced; and only one step separates her from the female masochist, who wishes, not only to be overwhelmed, but also to be raped and brutalized."[59]

Feminist scholars have echoed Hirschfeld's understanding of rape, noting that heterosexuality is a "forced, penetrative" act, so "rape is indigenous, not exceptional, to women's social condition."[60] How does one distinguish between "normal" sex and rape, these scholars ask? In wartime and under foreign occupation, what constitutes consensual sex for women?

To deal with these questions, German and Allied officials often ascribed guilt to women, holding them responsible for the transmission of venereal diseases and assuming they beguiled men. As Ruth Harris shows in her work on rape and war babies, "men's anxieties and fantasies, much more than the tragedy of women's experience, shaped the discussion [of rape]" and its consequences.[61] During and after the war,

Allied authorities compiled lists of suspected women who had "intimate relations with the enemy," often basing their reports on hearsay and reports from neighbors. Because of the preconceived notion of a tie between espionage and prostitution, many of these women were reported as suspected spies.

Consider excerpts from just one page of such a report from French intelligence to intelligence officers of the American Expeditionary Force as the allied forces moved into formerly occupied territory in the summer of 1918:

The following persons have been signaled by the French authorities as being possibly suspect—

Mme. Bouteiller. . . . was favored by the Germans owing to her having permitted her five daughters to prostitute themselves. Still in invaded territory.

Mme. Aumont. . . . Has had intimate relations with a German railway employee at Troipont, Belgium.

Mme. Delcroix . . . age 28. . . . Signalled as having had intimate relations with German officers, which she denies.

The sisters Mantion, ages 19, 20, and 25, still in invaded territory. Are reported as having had intimate relations with German soldiers.

Mme. Raulin . . . age 30 . . . sent to her cousin M. Quillatre at the school at Annexe de Varzy, Nièvre. Was on very good terms with Corp. Ritter of the Kdtr at Thilay.

Mlle. Coplin . . . age 22 . . . said to have had intimate relations with Germans: procured abortion.

Mlle. Louby . . . age 24: intimate relations.[62]

This excerpt is part of a weekly intelligence update that detailed activities of thousands of civilian suspects in Belgium and northern France and often included women who were *reported to have had* intimate relations" [my emphasis] with the enemy. Any suspected relationship with enemy males was listed in these reports and was signaled as dangerous. Often women who ran boardinghouses or cafes were designated as dangerous for running establishments "much frequented by

Germans with whom [they] had intimate relations." Civilian men in these positions were merely designated "war profiteers" with no "intimate relations" assigned to their activities.[63]

Women's capacity for intimacy was at the heart of the concerns expressed by both occupying and liberating officials. Women could catch men at their most vulnerable and could use sexuality to manipulate men. This gave women an edge in undermining soldiers' morale and in espionage, so officials sought to control female sexuality and contain their threat. Military officials wanted women's sexual services to maintain men's morale, but they also feared the insidious nature of female sexuality and prostitutes' access to soldiers' thoughts and feelings. As political scientist Cynthia Enloe notes of the militarization of women's lives in wartime, armies maintained a contradictory policy of distributing prophylactics to troops and regulating prostitution where possible, while attempting to police women's sexual access to soldiers.[64] Fear of female espionage combines these generalized concerns about women's sexuality with anxieties about men's moral weakness in the face of intimacy.

It was in this climate of suspicion of civilians that Marthe McKenna began her life as a secret agent for British Intelligence. Recruited by Lucelle Deldonck, a family friend serving as a courier, McKenna agreed to gather information and pass it to a local informant who would deliver the message to British General Headquarters. As a nurse at a German hospital during the day and as a waitress in the evening at her parents' café, McKenna had ample opportunity to gather information from German soldiers and officers. Not only did she interact with Germans in her work, but three German officers billeted with her family. She describes her strange existence early in her memoirs, saying that no Belgian forgot the Germans were their conquerors, but she admitted that most Germans were "guardedly friendly" with the Belgians.[65]

When first approached by Deldonck about spying for Britain, McKenna was horrified. "I knew what she must mean, a spy, and for a moment I was filled with horror. I knew that spies existed in Belgium and that they were serving their country, yet somehow I had regarded them as things inhuman and far removed from my own sphere."[66] She overcame her fear, however, and soon embraced the job wholeheartedly. McKenna worked between two other female agents, a vegetable seller nicknamed "Canteen Ma" and a female agent named "No. 63," whom Martha never met face to face. Canteen Ma, deemed harmless because of her advanced age, roamed the countryside with her produce cart and delivered coded messages and instructions to McKenna. No. 63 acted as the letterbox—her window in a secluded alley served as a place for McKenna to deliver her own messages.[67] The information McKenna delivered was often in response to a specific request, but she also passed on unsolicited remarks she overheard in the hospital, enabling allied bombers to target and attack ordnance trains and depots with her information.

McKenna muses often in her memoir about the problems women faced in occupied territory, writing about fighting off the advances of drunken German soldiers or amorous officers. Although she used her attractiveness to manipulate men into giving her information, she never sacrificed her virtue (although she comes close). Despite agreeing to travel to Brussels for several days with a German officer and getting trapped in a house for several hours with two German soldiers, each time she was threatened she used her ingenuity to escape a sexual encounter. McKenna recognized her luck, writing with pity for the not-so-fortunate girls at a Brussels dance club:

> Hounded down, driven to distraction by punishments meted out to their kinsfolk, subject to atrocities and unmentionable acts of outrage, they were caught in a holocaust over which they had no control, until they were literally driven into the arms of their oppressors by sheer want and starvation, utterly bewildered by a world gone mad.[68]

Brussels, as the center of prostitution for German armies behind the western front, had military brothels under formal control, but the women McKenna met were desperate amateurs.[69] A study of Ghent women during the war estimated that four-fifths of "occasional" prostitutes were married mothers with small children.[70]

McKenna also suffered from feelings of guilt when she realized the depth of her betrayal of the German men she often came to like, especially when her information led to their deaths. Eventually she was forced to confront her double life when she was asked (in no uncertain terms) to spy on other Belgians for the Germans. She recorded her anxiety:

> I was in a terrible quandary; against my will I had become a spy for friend *and* foe. But I must bring forward some information for the

Germans which would not hurt my friends or the Allies, but which nevertheless would seem of value to Otto . . . I was frightened of a German firing-party in the cold dawn.[71]

Although her life as a double agent ended quickly with the death of her German lodger Otto, her precarious position was apparent to her. Soon after this escapade, she and another agent performed the dangerous task of dynamiting a supply depot, which led to her arrest and imprisonment on espionage charges in 1916. Although initially sentenced to execution, her sentence was commuted to life imprisonment because of her good work for the German hospital. She spent the remainder of the war in prison at Ghent.[72]

McKenna's experiences capture the difficulties that women faced *as* occupied territory. Their bodies and minds were subject to regulation by the German authorities, and they were suspected for crimes ranging from hiding soldiers to espionage to aiding the enemy. Claire Hénin, a schoolteacher in northern France tried to remind German authorities that they weren't technically prisoners of war: "Monsieur, you forget that we are an occupied country, not a conquered one."[73] But it was often difficult to define the roles of the citizens in the occupied zones.

McKenna tried to control the uncertainties of her existence in occupied Belgium. She made a deal in her own mind that she would serve humanity by nursing, serve her parents by waitressing, and serve herself by spying for the Allies, but the reality of splitting her loyalties created a terrific psychological strain. She became suspect as a spy and a collaborator, and the ambiguity of her wartime work was reflected in her German Iron Cross and her British distinguished service citation; she became, in fact, a woman without a country. In his preface to McKenna's memoir, Winston Churchill reminds readers that McKenna was indeed honorable, not merely out for money, fame, or infamy. He writes, "[T]he heroine of this account, fulfilled in every respect the conditions which make the terrible profession of a spy dignified and honourable." He continues, acknowledging espionage as sordid and deceitful, but writing that McKenna was "a Secret Service agent . . . not actuated by any sordid motive, but inspired by patriotism, and ready to pay the well-known forfeit. . . ."[74]

Because women in occupied Belgium were forced into two categories during and after the war: victims of German aggression or sordid sexual collaborators and spies, the role of women as heroic and active patriots was hard for the postwar public to accept. Just as the women of *La Dame Blanche* faded from view in the rush to publish tales of female spy intrigue, women secret service agents remained a hidden group except for the precious few like Mata Hari and the Lady Doctor who fit the stereotype of sexual collaborator or of war martyr like Edith Cavell and Louise de Bettignies.

CONCLUSION

Karl Marx in explaining the French Revolution, perceptively wrote, "A nation and a woman are not forgiven the unguarded hour in which the first adventurer that came along could violate them."[75] In Marx's words lie the key to the popularity of the female spy-prostitute icon. Violated women, who have ceded their greatest asset—their virtue—are suspect; How can a fallen woman be trusted as a citizen? Furthermore, in an occupied nation such as Belgium, weren't women doubly suspect? Female spy-prostitutes became a convenient image for all that was wrong with the Allied nations during the war. They served as a focus for male anxieties at home: unfaithful wives, women war workers who had taken over men's jobs, and female prostitutes who carried venereal diseases.

Real women spies who actively resisted German occupation could never live up to the image of female spy that Mata Hari embodies. Espionage, defined at the time as foreign and corrupting work, did not fit with the understanding of women's proper roles in society, just as women's participation in war undermined notions of masculine warfare. It was easier to see women as victims, as nurturing nurses, as sweethearts back home, or as spy-prostitutes than to deal with the anxious shift in gender roles that appeared to be taking place. With women supplying sex and bullets behind the lines, the carefully constructed, gendered nation seemed under attack even as men fought in the trenches to defend it. The simple response to these male fears was to vilify the sexualized, improper, unnatural woman spy.

Conclusion

"Perpetual Concubinage to Your King and Country"

> For the women, an affair outside the Service automatically made you a "security risk" and in the last analysis you had a choice of resignation from the Service and a normal life, or of perpetual concubinage to your King and Country. Loelia Ponsonby knew that she had almost reached the time for decision and all her instincts told her to get out. But every day the drama and romance of her Cavell-Nightingale world locked her more securely into the company of the other girls at Headquarters and every day it seemed more difficult to betray by resignation the father-figure which The Service had become.
>
> —Ian Fleming, *Moonraker* (1955)

LIKE LOELIA PONSONBY, women in state intelligence services in the twentieth century face a central paradox in their lives and work. Seen as sexualized beings in popular imagination, women's employment by the state in the secrets community combines the essential invisibility of women's participation with an assumption of their role as mothers or sex workers for the state. As with prostitutes in military brothels whose usefulness for citizen armies was established between 1914 and 1918, women spies and agents gained a similar legacy from World War I—the assumption that their only utility to the state was as Mata Hari-style seductresses or as victims in need of state protection. This book has addressed this erroneous assumption by exposing the actual work of women in intelligence during the Great War, while examining how and why the myths of the spy-seductress have had such power in the modern popular imagination.

Women proved their ability and willingness to serve state intelligence organizations during the First World War, yet they gained no lasting public recognition of their successful work and little approbation for their service and sacrifices. Few people today realize the number of women who helped create the British secrets industry and the "secret state" in the opening years of the twentieth century, and many believe that women's first widespread employment by intelligence operations did not come until the Second World War.[1] Newspaper stories exposing the activities of female spies are often greeted with astonishment at the idea of women in espionage. When Melita Norwood's work as a Soviet spy was exposed in 1999, British newspapers wondered how this "unremarkable little old lady" could have passed British nuclear secrets to the KGB (Komitet Gosudarstvennoi Bezopasnoti; or Soviet State Security Committee) for forty years without detection.[2]

What is truly remarkable about women's presence in intelligence is not their excellent record in the secrets industry but the invisibility of their work, even after almost one hundred years of female employment in permanent, professional, information-gathering agencies. The director of the American Office of Strategic Services (OSS) in World War II, Maj. Gen. William Donovan, described his multitude of female staffers as the "invisible apron strings of an organization which touched every theater of the war."[3] Donovan demonstrates both the gendered nature of women's participation in intelligence and the importance of their silent presence throughout the twentieth century.

When the war demobilization came in 1919, most of the women and men employed by the British as spies, couriers, analysts, and clerks were released from their duties. By 1920, the postal censorship rolls had shrunk from almost five thousand employees to only six, the British espionage networks in occupied territory had been dismantled; only a small postwar cryptography bureau was established to keep British skills and technology from decay.[4] The Directorate of Military Intelligence reduced its employees from more than six thousand to approximately 150 by 1920.[5] Although MI5 considered paying some women a small retaining fee to "register as a reserve class" in case of future conflicts, MI5 abandoned the plan and severely cut back on staff by 1920.[6] As employees were reduced, expenditure from the Secret Service Vote (funds from Parliament) also dropped precipitously in 1920 and 1921 in all areas except home security and Irish operations, reflecting the postwar preoccupation with domestic subversion (especially Bolshevism) and a war with Irish revolutionaries.[7]

Women were still represented in these much smaller interwar intelligence operations as clerks, couriers, and covert operatives. Little has been published about these women besides a few individual but sensational memoirs detailing female employment in British operations between the 1920s and the outbreak of World War II.[8] Because so little has been written about the work of secret offices in this period, there is an erroneous assumption that women were not employed in non-wartime situations. Interwar dialogue about female spies was shaped by fiction, film, and the occasional First World War heroine's account of her experiences.[9] These accounts, along with Second World War memoirs, show that women were indeed present in British intelligence from its formal inception in 1909 throughout the twentieth century.[10]

If the Great War saw the first widespread employment of women in professional intelligence organizations, it was the Second World War that publicized its heavy dependence on women to staff its secrets offices. Once again, women flocked to work in counterespionage, cryptography, overseas stations, resistance and secret service networks, courier services, and censorship. Women, some of them veterans of World War I intelligence jobs, made important contributions to the World War II Allied war effort between 1939 and 1945. Especially important were women cryptographers and interceptors of enemy radio messages such as Joan Clarke Murray and Aileen Morris Clayton. Murray worked on the breaking of the German Enigma machine code at Bletchley Park along with scores of other women, while Clayton went abroad as a WAAF (Women's Auxiliary Air Force) officer assigned to listen to enemy messages with fellow female WAAFs.[11] Women and men of *La Dame Blanche* rejoined the British war effort in the 1940s under the same Belgian network chief, but with the new name of Network *Clarence*.[12] MI5 hired multitudes of female clerks, and the need for female labor in government propaganda, misinformation, censorship, and other intelligence agencies led to major recruitment of educated women. Finally, a few women gained notoriety after World War II for their participation in a daring operation known as the Special Operations Executive (SOE). About fifty women parachuted into enemy territory to organize resistance activities and gather information.[13] Like its British ally, the American government also employed large numbers of women in intelligence occupations, especially through its wartime agency, the Office of Strategic Services (OSS).[14] Despite the highly publicized role of women in Second World War intelligence and a spate of memoirs and films about their activities, individual names have not entered into the public memory, and the most likely name to be mentioned in relationship to women spies is still Mata Hari.

Mata Hari's name appears in such diverse studies as autobiographies, scholarly histories of women in the Vietnam War, and in reviews of former MI5 director Stella Rimington's memoirs. Rimington herself is an example of the professional female intelligence operative, joining MI5 as a "bored diplomatic wife" in 1969 and then rising to head the agency in 1991.[15] Yet, as she notes, women faced serious sex discrimination in intelligence work even in the 1960s and 1970s; they were locked into low-level positions. As Rimington wrote of her entry into MI5 in 1969, "It did not matter that I had a degree, that I had worked for several years already in the public service, at a higher grade than they were offering, or that I was thirty-four years old. The policy was that men were recruited as what were called 'officers' and women had their own career structure. . . ."[16] Rimington herself was the first woman appointed to the position of agent-running officer, and eventually she saw other women rise in the ranks by the 1990s.

By the 1990s, half of all MI5 employees and more than 40 percent of the U.S. Central Intelligence Agency (CIA) staff were women, yet these statistics still have not captured public attention.[17] The lingering cultural stereotypes of women as harlots for the state still shape the discussion of female intelligence work and still plague the women who try to work for intelligence agencies. In a series of well-publicized cases in the mid-1990s, several women in the CIA sued the agency charging gender discrimination and sexual harassment in the workplace. Former CIA station chief Janine Brookner won a four hundred thousand dollar settlement in 1994, and the CIA tried to settle out of court with another group of women employees who claimed the existence of institutionalized discrimination in 1995.[18]

The fundamental gendering of intelligence work has long been recognizable in the writings of male secret service officers who often describe female agents as good "ladies" serving tea and finding files or as dangerous vamps out to seduce them. Nicholas Everitt's 1920 sensational (and mostly fictional) account of his secret service work depicts his disguised forays into a world of spy-actresses and prostitutes. He emphasizes how as a "man of honour" he calls upon his individual strength of will in spurning these women.[19] In a similar vein, intelligence official and fiction author John Buchan described beautiful female spy Hilda von Einem in his 1916 *Greenmantle* as a nightmare for his hero Richard Hannay: "I hated her instinctively, hated her intensely, but I longed to arouse her interest. To be valued coldly by those eyes was an offence to my manhood, and I felt antagonism rising within me."[20]

True men were professionals and women were merely dilettantes, sleeping their way into the spy world. Vernon Kell, first chief of MI5, tried to demythologize female spies in a postwar lecture, saying, "the beautiful vamp who removes Secret Treaties from the pockets of Ambassadors after a couple of cocktails, has, I fear, no counterpart in real life," yet in this same speech he also claimed that "women do not make good . . . agents."[21] Perhaps the clearest statement of the nature of modern intelligence comes from former CIA director Allen Dulles, who wrote: "The intelligence officer . . . cannot permit himself, as do the lucky heros of spy novels, to become entangled with luscious females who approach him in bars or step out of closets, lightly clad, in hotel rooms. . . . Sex and hard-headed intelligence operations rarely mix well."[22] Even Dulles, knowing women worked for him, assumes in his statement that all intelligence officers are male.

Where does that leave the history of female intelligence? Women, historically defined as dependents of fathers, husbands, and states, have yet to shed the protective paternal cloak of the past in order to pick up the dagger. Women might serve loyally in times of war and peace in intelligence or military positions, but their work is still perceived as exceptional, rare, and surprising. Edith Cavell might be a heroic martyr to the war, and Mata Hari might be an example of a woman gone wrong in wartime, but few women are truly expected to fit either of these roles. As long as women in intelligence are perceived to be in "perpetual concubinage" as sexual servants of the state, their professional aspirations will be meaningless and their histories will be marginalized.

Notes

ABBREVIATIONS USED IN NOTES AND BIBLIOGRAPHY

AGR	Archives Générale du Royaume, Brussels
BMD	Bibliothèque Marguerite Durand, Paris
CCAC	Churchill College Archives, Cambridge
CEGES	Centre d'Etudes et de Documentation Guerre at Sociétés contemporaines
CPOHC	Consignia Post Office Heritage Centre, London
IWM	Imperial War Museum, Department of Documents, London
NARA	National Archives and Records Administration, College Park, MD
PRO	Public Record Office, Kew Gardens

NOTES TO THE INTRODUCTION

1. Nicholas Hiley has explored the expansion of the purview of Britain's counter-espionage system in a provocative article, "Counter-Espionage and Security in Great Britain during the First World War," *English Historical Review* 101:400 (July 1986): 635–661.

2. Claire A. Culleton, *Working-Class Culture, Women, and Britain, 1914–1921* (New York: St. Martin's Press, 1999), 135, 140; Gerard De Groot, *Blighty: British Society in the Era of the Great War* (London: Longman, 1996), 141.

3. Many historians since the 1970s have sought to understand the mixed legacy of the First World War for women. Especially helpful have been studies of women workers. See, for example: Gail Braybon, "Women and the War," in *The First World War in British History*, Stephen Constantine, Maurice W. Kirby, and Mary B. Rose, eds. (London: Edward Arnold, 1995); Braybon, *Women Workers in the First World War* (Totowa, NJ: Croom Helm, 1981); Culleton; Ute Daniel, *The War from Within: German Working-Class Women in the First World War*, Margaret Ries, trans. (Oxford: Berg, 1997); Laura Lee Downs, *Manufacturing Inequality: Gender Division in the French and British Metalworking Industries, 1914–1939* (Ithaca: Cornell University Press, 1995); Mathilde Dubesset,

Françoise Thébaud, and Catherine Vincent, "The Female Munition Workers of the Seine," in *The French Home Front 1914–1918*, Patrick Fridenson, ed. (Oxford: Berg, 1992); Deborah Thom, *Nice Girls and Rude Girls: Women Workers in World War I* (London: I. B. Taurus, 1998); Angela Woollacott, *On Her Their Lives Depend: Munitions Workers in the Great War* (Berkeley: University of California Press, 1994); and Susan Zeiger, *In Uncle Sam's Service: Women Workers with the American Expeditionary Force* (Ithaca: Cornell University Press, 2000).

4. Overviews of modern intelligence include Christopher Andrew, *Her Majesty's Secret Service: The Making of the British Intelligence Community* (New York: Viking, 1986); Philip H. J. Davies, *The British Secret Services* (New Brunswick, NJ: Transaction, 1996); and Phillip Knightley, *The Second Oldest Profession: Spies and Spying in the Twentieth Century* (New York: W. W. Norton, 1987). An exception is Michael Occleshaw's *Armour against Fate: British Military Intelligence in the First World War* (London: Columbus Books, 1989), which looks specifically at the intersections of World War I and the newly emerging intelligence establishment.

5. See, for example, René Deruyk, *Louise de Bettignies Résistante Lilloise, 1880–1918* (Lille: La Voix du Nord, 1998); M. H. Mahoney, *Women in Espionage: A Biographical Dictionary* (Santa Barbara: ABC-CLIO, 1993); Rowland Ryder, *Edith Cavell* (New York: Stein and Day, 1975); Janet Wallach, *Desert Queen: the Extraordinary Life of Gertrude Bell: Adventurer, Adviser to Kings, Ally of Lawrence of Arabia* (New York: Nan A. Talese/Doubleday, 1996); and Julie Wheelwright, *The Fatal Lover: Mata Hari and the Myth of Women in Espionage* (London: Collins and Brown, 1992).

6. John Keegan, *The First World War* (New York: Vintage, 1998); Arthur Marwick, *The Deluge: British Society and the First World War* (New York: W. W. Norton, 1965); and Niall Ferguson, *The Pity of War* (New York: Basic Books, 1999). Intelligence is raised in a more sustained way (although again in relationship to strategy) in Hew Strachan, *The First World War.* Vol. I (Oxford: Oxford University Press, 2001).

7. Margaret Darrow, *French Women and the First World War: War Stories of the Home Front* (Oxford: Berg, 2000); Helen McPhail, *The Long Silence: Civilian Life under the German Occupation of Northern France, 1914–1918* (London: I. B. Taurus, 2001); and Wheelwright, *The Fatal Lover*.

8. Such early histories include Sir George Aston, *Secret Service* (New York: Cosmopolitan, 1930); Jean Bardanne, *Mlle. Doktor contre la France* (Paris: Editions Baudinière, 1933); H. R. Berndorff, *Espionage!* (New York: D. Appleton, 1930); Robert Boucard, *Les femmes et l'espionnage* (Paris: Les Editions Documentaires, 1929); E. H. Cookridge, *Sisters of Delilah: Stories of Famous Women Spies* (London: Oldbourne, 1959); Maj. Thomas Coulson, *The Queen of Spies: Louise de Bettignies* (London: Constable, 1935); E.7, *Women Spies I Have Known* (London: Hurst and Blackett, 1939); A. A. Hoehling, *A Whisper of Eternity: The Mystery of Edith Cavell* (New York: Thomas Yoseloff, 1957); Georges Ladoux, *Marthe Richard the Skylark:*

The Foremost Spy of France (London: Cassell, 1932); and Kurt Singer, *The World's Greatest Women Spies* (London: W. H. Allen, 1951).

NOTES TO CHAPTER I

1. Alan Marshall, *Intelligence and Espionage in the Reign of Charles II, 1660–1685* (Cambridge: Cambridge University Press, 1994), 116; and Bernard Porter, *Plots and Paranoia: A History of Political Espionage in Britain, 1790–1988* (London: Routledge, 1992), 20.

2. Thomas G. Fergusson, *British Military Intelligence, 1870–1914: The Development of a Modern Intelligence Organization* (Frederick, MD: University Publications of America, 1984), 237.

3. For a good definition of intelligence and its functions, see John Bruce Lockhart, "Intelligence: A British View," in *British and American Approaches to Intelligence*, K. G. Robertson, ed. (New York: St. Martin's Press, 1987), 37.

4. Fergusson, 8.

5. B. A. H. Parritt, *The Intelligencers: The Story of British Military Intelligence up to 1914* (Ashford, U. K.: Intelligence Corps Association, 1983), 1–2. Parritt notes that the position of the scoutmaster has been documented as far back as the fourteenth century.

6. Some authors point to Elizabeth I's spymaster Sir Francis Walsingham as the definitive beginning of modern intelligence. See, for example, Allison Ind, *A History of Modern Espionage* (London: Hodder & Stoughton, 1965), 30.

7. Richard Deacon, *British Secret Service* (London: Grafton, 1991), 15, 50, and Parritt, 7. Cromwell appointed a young lawyer as official head of intelligence in December 1652, and with Parliamentary funds, John Thurloe established an expensive network of spies and informers. Although his network did not remain after his departure, a precedent had been set for using state funds for the development of a secret service network.

8. Louis XIV apparently used a network of informers within France while diplomatic spies of many nations circulated through Europe. For a general descriptive history of some of these practices, see Richard Wilmer Rowan, *Secret Service: Thirty-Three Centuries of Espionage* (New York: Hawthorn Books, 1967), 93–117.

9. Porter, 16–17; Marshall, 85–87. The Post Office Act of 1711 made it possible for governments to issue warrants for the opening of mail; Fergusson, 10.

10. Marshall, 23, 93–95. Wallis apparently negotiated the perils of the Civil War without political consequences.

11. Marshall, 116.

12. Marshall, 119.

13. Elizabeth Sparrow, *Secret Service: British Agents in France, 1792–1815* (Woodbridge, U. K.: The Boydell Press, 1999), 7–19.

14. Porter, 22.

15. Sparrow, 26–27.

16. Sparrow, 27.

17. Sparrow, 19–23.

18. Stephen J. Lee, *Aspects of British Political History, 1815–1914* (London: Routledge, 1994), 19.

19. See, for example, Rory Muir, *Tactics and the Experience of Battle in the Age of Napoleon* (New Haven: Yale University Press, 1998).

20. Porter, 45.

21. Rowan, 240; Andrew, *Her Majesty's Secret Service,* 6; and Davies, xi–xii. Italian nationalist, Giuseppe Mazzini, discovered that the British were opening and reading his mail, and he was able to convince a Member of Parliament to open an inquiry. This led to the dissolution of mail censorship and deciphering branches in 1844.

22. Sparrow, 412–413.

23. C. A. Bayly, *Empire and Information: Intelligence Gathering and Social Communication in India, 1780–1870* (Cambridge: Cambridge University Press, 1996), 315–316.

24. See Stephen M. Harris, *British Military Intelligence in the Crimean War, 1854–56* (London: Frank Cass, 1999) for an examination of the intelligence that emerged during the Crimean War after officials realized how important such information could be to the war effort.

25. PRO WO 106/6083 Lt. Col. William R. Isaac, "The History of the Development of the Directorate of Military Intelligence, the War Office 1855–1939," 8; Parritt, 88–99, 111. A separate Indian intelligence branch developed in 1878.

26. Porter, 101–103.

27. Andrew, 8–15.

28. Britain's Channel 4 broadcasted a series in 2001 on the history of surveillance that suggested that the nineteenth century marked the age of increased government surveillance and assaults on privacy. However, Edward Higgs argues persuasively in a review that these Victorian changes functioned merely as a precursor to the "modern 'Information State'" developed in the twentieth century. Edward Higgs, "Victorian Spies," *History Workshop Journal* 53 (Spring 2002): 232–235.

29. John Mackenzie, ed. "Introduction," to *Popular Imperialism and the Military* (Manchester: Manchester University Press, 1992), 1; W. J. Reader, *At Duty's Call: A Study in Obsolete Patriotism* (Manchester: Manchester University Press, 1988), 41–42; and John Saville, "Imperialism and the Victorians," in *In Search of Victorian Values*, Eric Sigsworth, ed. (Manchester: Manchester University Press, 1988), 170–171.

30. The classic article on this topic is Olive Anderson, "The Growth of Christian Militarism in Mid-Victorian Britain," *English Historical Review* 86 (January 1971): 46–72. See also Pamela Walker, *Pulling the Devil's Kingdom Down: The Salvation Army in Victorian Britain* (Berkeley: University of California Press, 2001).

31. Edward M. Spiers, *The Late Victorian Army, 1868–1902* (Manchester: Manchester University Press, 1992), 2, 30, 61, 180. Beyond public perceptions of the army, changes were also taking place in army organization and conception. Reform of army procedures and organization took place under Secretary of State for War Edward T. Cardwell in the late 1860s and early 1870s. Under the War Office Act of 1870, military administration was streamlined and reorganized, but as Spiers points out, the legislation was limited both in its scope and effectiveness, and little real reform took place until the Boer War. In fact, the size of the army dropped in the immediate aftermath of the act, only recovering its 1860s numbers by the 1890s.

32. Saville, 170–171. For more information on the volunteers, see Hugh Cunningham, *The Volunteer Force: A Social and Political History, 1859–1908* (London: Croom Helm, 1975).

33. Anne Summers, *Angels and Citizens: British Women as Military Nurses* (London: Routledge and Kegan Paul, 1988), 67.

34. John Rees, "'The Multitude of Women': An Examination of the Numbers of Camp Followers with the Continental Army," *Minerva: Quarterly Report on Women and the Military* 14:2 (30 June 1996); [GenderWatch database].

35. See, for instance: Charles Carlton, ed., *State, Sovereigns and Society in Early Modern England: Essays in Honour of A.J. Slavin* (New York: St. Martin's Press, 1998). Katie Hickman, *Daughters of Britannia: The Lives and Times of Diplomatic Wives* (New York: William Morrow, 1999), 55–56.

36. The literature on women and political power, whether during wartime or peace is vast, but these are some of the most recent works examining the ways that women gathered and brokered information in European history. Theodore Evergates, ed., *Aristocratic Women in Medieval France* (Philadelphia: University of Pennsylvania Press, 1999); Elizabeth Ewan and Maureen M. Meikle, eds., *Women in Scotland: c.1100—c.1750* (East Linton, U. K.: Tuckwell Press, 1999); Barbara Harris, *English Aristocratic Women, 1450–1550: Marriage and Family, Property and Careers* (New York: Oxford University Press, 2002); Sara Mendelson and Patricia Crawford, *Women in Early Modern England 1550–1720* (New York: Oxford University Press, 1998); and Amanda Vickery, ed., *Women, Privilege, and Power: British Politics, 1750 to the Present* (Stanford: Stanford University Press, 2001). Brian Crim goes so far as to claim that, "At no time in European history were so many women engaged in warfare—as spies, foragers, artillery personnel, or soldiers—than between 1500 and 1650." Brian Crim,

"Silent Partners: Women and Warfare in Early Modern Europe," in *A Soldier and A Woman: Sexual Integration in the Military,* Gerard De Groot and Corinna Peniston-Bird, eds. (Essex, U. K.: Pearson, 2000), 27. Another article provides an intriguing look at how women protected their interests in times of civil conflict: Evelyn M. Cherpak, "The Participation of Women in the Wars for Independence in Northern South America, 1810–1824," *Minerva: Quarterly Report on Women and the Military* 11 (31 December 1993); [GenderWatch database].

37. This well-known example of a female spy using her cover as a charwoman to gather intelligence has at its center Marie Bastian, whose discovery of a small note in a German officer's wastebasket led to the investigation of Alfred Dreyfus for treason. For information on the Dreyfus case and Bastian's role in it, see Pascal Krop, *Les Secrets de l'espionnage français de 1870 à nos jours* (France: Éditions Jean-Claude Lattès, 1993), 47–53, and Douglas Porch, *The French Secret Service: From the Dreyfus Affair to the Gulf War* (New York: Farrar, Straus, and Giroux, 1995), 29.

38. Marshall, 215, 222.

39. Marshall, 125.

40. Marshall, 20.

41. Marshall, 19. Susan Kingsley Kent, *Gender and Power in Britain, 1640–1990* (London: Routledge, 1999), 21. These women included scouts, "she-soldiers," and aristocrats who passed information and performed services in the field.

42. Much has been written on Aphra Behn's life and writing; an excellent bibliography is Mary Ann O'Donnell's, *Aphra Behn: An Annotated Bibliography of Primary and Secondary Sources* (New York: Garland, 1986). One of the most recent works to discuss Behn's espionage is Janet Todd, *The Secret Life of Aphra Behn* (New Brunswick, NJ: Rutgers University Press, 1997). Behn was known as "Astrea" and as "Agent 160" according to Todd, 5. Behn may have spied earlier for English Royalists in the 1650s, but evidence is sparse.

43. Marshall, 136–137, 151–152.

44. Sparrow, 198–199.

45. Sparrow, 249.

46. Sparrow, 175–178, 204, 217, 232, 249. Women may have served the British Admiralty as spies during the Napoleonic Wars, according to Richard Deacon in *A History of the British Secret Service* (London: Frederick Muller, 1969), 101.

47. Bayly, 19, 228, 365.

48. Dea Birkett, *Spinsters Abroad: Victorian Lady Explorers* (New York: Dorset Press, 1989), 211–244. Such women included Isabella Bird, Mary Gaunt, Mary Kingsley, and Marianne North, to name a few.

49. Susan Goodman, *Gertrude Bell* (Heidelberg, Germany: Berg, 1985), 3–29, 115, and Wallach, 9–20.

50. H. V. F. Winstone, *The Illicit Adventure* (London: Jonathan Cape, 1982), 41–44, 198.

51. Goodman, 81–2.

52. Spiers, 328–329.

53. Summers, 204, and Reader, 12. For more on the nurses, see Christopher Schmitz, "'We Too Were Soldiers': The Experiences of British Nurses in the Anglo-Boer War, 1899–1902," in De Groot and Peniston, 49–65.

54. Donald Lowry, "Introduction: Not Just a 'Teatime War,'" in *The South African War Reappraised* (Manchester: Manchester University Press, 2000), 2; and Schmitz, 50.

55. Bill Nasson, *The South African War 1899–1902* (New York: Oxford University Press, 1999), 74–75.

56. Parritt, 179–182, 212; Andrew, *Her Majesty's Secret Service*, 29.

57. For an interesting article on the nationalist and political implications of this involvement, see Helen Bradford, "Regendering Afrikanerdom: The 1899–1902 Anglo-Boer War," 207–225, in *Gendered Nations: Nationalism and Gender Order in the Long Nineteenth Century,* Ida Blom, Karen Hagemann, and Catherine Hall, eds. (Oxford: Berg, 2000).

58. Nasson, 221–223. For more on women and the camps, see Paula Krebs, "'Last of the Gentleman's Wars': Women in the Boer War Concentration Camp Controversy," *History Workshop Journal* 33 (1992): 38–56. For a study of civilian involvement in the war, see S. B. Spies, *Methods of Barbarism? Roberts and Kitchener and Civilians in the Boer Republics, June 1900–May 1902* (Cape Town: Human and Rousseau, 1977).

59. Alan Judd, *The Quest for 'C': Sir Mansfield Smith Cumming and the Founding of the British Secret Service* (London: HarperCollins, 1999), 69.

60. PRO WO 106/6083 Isaac, 14. Col. James Edmonds headed a "secret service" branch in 1907, but the 1909 Security Services were really the first permanent creations.

61. Summers, 204, 275, and Reader, 12.

62. Morris, 226, and Reader, 81–89.

63. A. J. A. Morris, *The Scaremongers: The Advocacy of War and Rearmament 1896–1914* (London: Routledge and Kegan Paul, 1984), 226, Reader, 81–89 and Summers, 237–278.

64. Tim Jeal, *The Boy-Man: The Life of Lord Baden-Powell* (New York: William Morrow, 1990), 148–154, 384–386.

65. A well-written account of Edwardian fears of degeneration can be found in Deborah Dwork, *War is Good for Babies and Other Young Children: A History of the Infant and Child Welfare Movement in England, 1898–1918* (London: Tavistock, 1987), 6–22, 123–125, 184. See also Anna Davin, "Imperialism and Motherhood," *History Workshop Journal* 5 (1978): 9–65, and Sally Ledger, "The New Woman and the Crisis of Victorianism," in Sally Ledger and Scott

McCracken, eds., *Cultural Politics at the Fin de Siecle* (Cambridge: Cambridge University Press, 1995).

66. Many historians have documented the fears of the degeneration of society that surfaced at the turn of the century. In particular, see George L. Mosse, *The Image of Man: The Creation of Modern Masculinity* (New York: Oxford University Press, 1996), 80–86, and Dwork, 6–22, 123–125. For a discussion of World War I as a purifier of a degenerate society, see Samuel Hynes, *A War Imagined: The First World War and English Culture* (New York: Atheneum, 1990), 58–60.

67. Nicholas Hiley, "Decoding German Spies: British Spy Fiction 1908–1918," *Intelligence and National Security* 5:4 (October 1990): 55–79. Hiley argues an interesting position that British spy fiction functions as a reflection of the subconscious longings of a group of middle-aged men in a time of radical change. His article catalogs much of the spy fiction and drama of the period while discounting earlier theses that link spy fiction to national decline. See also, David Stafford, "Spies and Gentlemen: The Birth of the British Spy Novel, 1893–1914," *Victorian Studies* 24 (1981): 489–509, and David Trotter, "The Politics of Adventure in the Early British Spy Novel," *Intelligence and National Security* 5:4 (October 1990): 30–54.

68. Hiley, "Decoding German Spies," 55.

69. Cecil Degrotte Eby, *The Road to Armageddon: The Martial Spirit in English Popular Literature, 1870–1914* (Durham and London: Duke University Press, 1987), 11.

70. Trotter, "The Politics of Adventure," 31; Panikos Panayi, *The Enemy in Our Midst: Germans in Britain during the First World War* (Oxford: Berg, 1991), 32.

71. Reader, 52–72, and Morris, 148–163.

72. Among officials who were fascinated by spy fiction are Lt. Col. James Edmonds, Sir Edward Grey, and Captain Vernon Kell. Ferguson, 12–14, and James Hampshire, "Spy Fever in Britain, 1900 to 1914," *The Historian* 72 (Winter 2001), 25–26.

73. Panayi, 27, 32; Susanne Terwey, "Juden sind keine Deutschen! Über antisemitische Stereotpye um Juden und Deutschland in Großbritannien vor und während des Ersten Weltkrieges und die jüdishe Abwehr," *Sachor* 11 (2001): 41–62, and David Feldman, "The Importance of Being English: Jewish Immigration and the Decay of Liberal England," in *Metropolis London: Histories and Representations since 1800*, David Feldman and Gareth Stedman Jones, eds. (London: Routledge, 1989), 56, 76.

74. Andrew, *Her Majesty's Secret Service*, 181.

75. PRO KV 1/2 War Office Memorandum by J. S. Ewart, M.G. D.M.O., 31 December 1908. This file contains several missives between senior officers regarding the need for a Secret Service in Britain.

76. Andrew, *Her Majesty's Secret Service*, 53–54; Knightley, 9.

77. Knightley, 24.

78. PRO KV 1/3 Memorandum re: Foundation of a Secret Service Bureau, August 1909. This meeting followed the work of a subcommittee of the Committee of Imperial Defence, which recommended such a move in April 1909; PRO CAB 16/232.

79. Andrew, *Her Majesty's Secret Service*, 59–60, 73–74. See also, Judd, 1–26, 87–94.

80. PRO KV 1/9 Kell's 6-Month Reports, April–October 1910.

81. PRO KV 1/1 Note prepared for the DMO, "Organisation of Secret Service," 4 October 1908.

82. PRO KV 3/1 Counterespionage Laws in Foreign Countries. Translation of an article by A. Rezanov, "Espionage: the Meaning of the Term as used in the Legislation of Certain European Countries (1810–1911)," *Voenni Sbornik* (Sep/Oct 1911). The classic work on the Official Secrets Acts is David G. T. Williams, *Not in the Public Interest: The Problem of Security in Democracy* (London: Hutchinson, 1965).

83. Andrew, *Her Majesty's Secret Service*, 63–64, and David French, "Spy Fever in Britain, 1900–1915," *The Historical Journal* 21:2 (1978): 361.

84. Andrew, *Her Majesty's Secret Service*, 64–69.

85. Nicholas Hiley, "The Play, the Parody, the Censor, and the Film," *Intelligence and National Security* 6:1 (1991): 222.

86. P. G. Wodehouse, *The Swoop! Or How Clarence Saved England, A Tale of the Great Invasion* (London: Alston Rivers, 1909), 116.

87. Rachael Low, *The History of the British Film 1914–1918* (London: Allen and Unwin, 1973), 178–179.

88. See, for example: Cate Haste, *Keep the Home Fires Burning: Propaganda in the First World War* (London: Allen Lane, 1977), 109–110; and Andrew, *Her Majesty's Secret Service*, 177–182.

89. IWM 87/26/1 Miss R. A. Neal; IWM 78/51/1 Miss M. B. Foote; IWM P355 Daisy Williams Diary.

90. IWM 93/22/1 Miss J. H. Gifford. For other countries and their wartime spy panics, see Elizabeth McIntosh, *The Role of Women in Intelligence* (McLean, VA: Association of Former Intelligence Officers, 1989), 8; and Michael Miller, *Shanghai on the Metro: Spies, Intrigue, and the French between the Wars* (Berkeley: University of California Press, 1994), 4.

91. London *Times* (12 September 1914), 5B.

92. De Groot, 182.

93. London *Times* (18 September 1914), 4D. The two headlines mentioned occurred in the London *Times* (26 August 1914), 5C and (12 September 1914), 5B.

94. PRO HO 45/10756/267450 Spies in England and the Spy Peril.

95. Claire Culleton argues that the British public was "complicit" in its own regulation. Culleton, 140.

96. CCAC, Lt. Col. Adrian Grant-Duff papers; especially 1/4 and 1/5, correspondence regarding War Book.

NOTES TO CHAPTER 2

1. PRO KV 1/44; PRO CRIM 1/176/1 Martha Earle Case. Earle was eventually charged under DRR18, 22A, 24A, and 48.

2. The BNSA was a revision of the Naturalisation Act of 1870—the first law to remove women's British citizenship on marriage. Not until 1948 could women keep their natural citizenship after marriage to a foreigner. M. Page Baldwin, "Subject to Empire: Married Women and the British Nationality and Status of Aliens Act," *Journal of British Studies* 40:4 (October 2001): 522–26, 553.

3. PRO KV 1/37 Section of the Defence of the Realm Regulations affecting MI5.

4. Culleton, 135.

5. De Groot, 140–142.

6. Susan R. Grayzel, "The Enemy Within: The Problem of British Women's Sexuality during the First World War," in *Women and War in the Twentieth Century: Enlisted with or without Consent,* Nicole Dombrowski, ed. (New York: Garland, 1999), 72–89.

7. De Groot, 234–235.

8. French, "Spy Fever in Britain," 361. One historian calls it part of "some of the most illiberal peacetime legislation of the twentieth century." Hampshire, 27.

9. CCAC, Lt. Col. Adrian Grant-Duff papers, 5 Sept. 1911; AGDF 2/1. Grant-Duff was Assistant Secretary of the Committee of Imperial Defence subcommittee on intelligence.

10. Rosamund Thomas, *Espionage and Secrecy: The Official Secrets Acts 1911–1989 of the United Kingdom* (London/New York: Routledge, 1991), 6–9.

11. PRO KV 1/35 F Branch Report MI5, The Prevention of Espionage, Volume I; PRO KV 1/9 Kell's 6-Month Reports, November 1911.

12. De Groot, 195.

13. Panayi, 46–55. The passport system was extended to British citizens after New Year's Day, 1915.

14. De Groot, 158.

15. IWM PP/MCR/120 Sir Vernon Kell papers, Reel I SVK/2; Lecture on "Control of Civil Populations in War," n.d. For more information on male internment, see PRO HO 45/10946/266042, HO 45/10947/266042, and HO 144/1172.

16. Panayi, 99–109, 114. Internee Rudolf Rocker and historian Panikos Panayi both mention that wealthier internees could sometimes purchase comforts—better food and living conditions. Douglas, on the Isle of Man, had three

internee sections: a "privilege camp" for the wealthy, a "Jewish" camp that served kosher food, and an "ordinary" camp for the majority of the prisoners.

17. Panayi, 80.

18. PRO HO 45/10785/291742 Alyesbury—Women Internees, letter from Mr. Dryhurst (Prison Comm.) to Under Secretary of State, 26 June 1917.

19. Rudolf Rocker, *The London Years* (London: Robert Anscombe, 1956), 251–356, 336.

20. Rocker, 358–359. The Rockers fled Germany in 1933 (both because Milly was Jewish and because of their leftist political activities) living the rest of their lives in the United States.

21. Haste, 121.

22. Eby, 206.

23. See, for example, correspondence in the London *Times* between August 22 and 26, 1914.

24. PRO HO 45/10756/267450 Spies in England and the Spy Peril, George Mears (Constitutional Club) to CID, 30 June 1916; Report by Joseph Clarkson, Superintendent CID, 17 July 1916.

25. For information on the organization of British war propaganda, see Gary S. Messinger, *British Propaganda and the State in the First World War* (Manchester: Manchester University Press, 1992).

26. CCAC, Sir James Wycliffe Headlam-Morley papers, HDLM Acc 727/34—Correspondence 1914–1916.

27. PRO HO 45/11005/260251 Treatment of Destitute Aliens; Panayi, 259.

28. IWM MISC 29, Item 522—Anonymous woman's diary 1914.

29. IWM P472, Miss Winifred L. B. Tower's journal (26 July 1914–February 1916).

30. *Punch*, September 2, 1914 and October 21, 1914.

31. PRO HO 45/10787/298199 Mistreatment of German Women.

32. French, "Spy Fever," 365.

33. London *Times* 26 August 1914, 5C.

34. Anti-German sentiment was also high in the United States during the war as was fear of subversion. Kathleen Kennedy examines the women targeted by sedition legislation *in Disloyal Mothers and Scurrilous Citizens: Women and Subversion during World War I* (Bloomington: Indiana University Press, 1999). The opposite of this sentiment—Anglophobia—is explored in a recent work: Matthew Stibbe, *German Anglophobia and the Great War, 1914–1918* (Cambridge: Cambridge University Press, 2001).

35. Linda Colley, *Britons: Forging the Nation, 1707–1837* (New Haven: Yale University Press, 1994). Colley traces the ways that fear of French invasion and the threat of war with France helped create a sense of national identity in the eighteenth and early nineteenth centuries. This Francophobia is replaced with a fear of Germany by the late nineteenth century.

36. PRO HO 45/10756/267450 Spies in England and the Spy Peril. It is useful to note that under British law, women automatically assumed the citizenship of their husbands but not vice versa.

37. London *Times* 15 July 1918, 3A.

38. Rocker, 245.

39. Panayi, 197–254.

40. French, "Spy Fever," 370.

41. Eby, 206.

42. Philip Hoare, *Oscar Wilde's Last Stand: Decadence, Conspiracy, and the First World War* (London: Duckworth, 1997), 57–59.

43. Hoare, 91. See other discussions of the case in Panayi, 178–179 and De Groot, 195.

44. Hoare, 94.

45. London *Times*, 5 June 1918, 7A.

46. Nicholas Hiley, "Decoding German Spies: British Spy Fiction 1908–1918," *Intelligence and National Security* 5:4 (October 1990), 75–76.

47. London *Times*, 31 May 1918, 4.

48. Hoare, 96, 113–120, 180.

49. Jodie Medd, "'The Cult of the Clitoris:' Anatomy of a National Scandal," *Modernism/Modernity* 9:1 (2002): 44.

50. Ibid.

51. The phrase "ruling passion" comes from a description of Eva de Bournonville (one of the female spies captured in Britain) in Aston, 153.

52. PRO KV 1/7 List of Persons Arrested since Outbreak of War.

53. PRO KV 1/44 MI5 G Branch Report.

54. PRO KV 1/42 MI5 G Branch Report.

55. Darrow, 6, 15–16.

56. For an excellent study exploring women's roles in the wartime state, see Susan R. Grayzel, *Women's Identities at War: Gender, Motherhood, and Politics in Britain and France during the First World War* (Chapel Hill: University of North Carolina Press, 1999).

57. E.7, 7–8.

58. Ferdinand Tuohy, "Women as Secret Service Agents," *The Statesman* (17 January 1926), 21. Thanks to Françoise Labrique Walusius for this reference.

59. For further discussion of women spy icons, see chapters 5 and 6. An interesting discussion of the iconic female spy appears in an article by Julie Wheelwright, "Poisoned Honey: The Myth of Women in Espionage," *Queen's Quarterly* 100:2 (Summer 1993): 291–309.

60. Robert Baden-Powell, *Aids to Scouting for N.C.O.s and Men* (London: Gale & Polden, 1914), 141; and Nicholas Everitt, *British Secret Service during the Great War* (London: Hutchinson, 1920), xvii. A scholarly study of the impact of women motorists is Virginia Scharff's *Taking the Wheel: Women and the Coming of*

the Motor Age (New York: The Free Press, 1991). Chapter 6 is especially useful because it examines women drivers in the First World War, noting that they "unhinged conventional understandings of masculinity and femininity" (109).

61. IWM PP/MCR/120 Sir Vernon Kell papers—SVK/2 Reel I Col. Edmonds, lecture notes p. 12; SVK/1 Reel I Constance Kell, "Secret Well Kept," TS, 135.

62. Hamil Grant, *Spies and Secret Service: The Story of Espionage, its Main Systems and Chief Exponents* (New York: Frederick A. Stokes, 1915), 24–25.

63. PRO KV 1/39 MI5 G Branch Report.

64. PRO KV 1/44 MI5 G Branch Report.

65. David French, "Sir John French's Secret Service on the Western Front, 1914–1915," *The Journal of Strategic Studies* 7:4 (1984): 430.

66. Officials were especially alarmed to find that she had applied to work in British Postal Censorship. PRO KV 1/43 MI5 G Branch Report.

67. PRO KV 1/39 MI5 G Branch Report.

68. Aston, 153.

69. Sir Basil Thomson, "The Tragedy of the Woman Spy," *The Statesman* (22 January 1933): 23.

70. PRO KV 1/43 MI5 G Branch Report.

71. PRO DPP 1/28 Maud Gould Case.

72. PRO WO 141/3/1 Case of Lizzie Wertheim and Reginald Rowland, 207.

73. PRO KV 1/43 MI5 G Branch Report.

74. PRO KV 1/39 MI5 G Branch Report.

75. Rocker, 320–336.

76. Sidney T. Felstead, *German Spies at Bay* (London: Hutchinson, 1920), 198–199.

77. PRO HO 45/267603 Aliens and Prisons: "Prison Commission to Sir E. Troup," 22 February 1916.

78. Felstead, 195.

79. PRO HO 45/10785/291742 Aylesbury—Women Internees: "S. F. Fox (Governor, Aylesbury) to Prison Commission," 11 June 1917.

80. PRO KV 1/41 MI5 G Branch Report.

81. PRO DPP 1/32 *REX v. A Female Spy*: trial transcript 18–19 January 1916.

82. PRO CRIM 1/176/1 Martha Earle Case; PRO KV 1/44 MI5 G Branch Report.

83. Wheelwright, *The Fatal Lover*, 106.

84. London *Times*, 21 October 1915, 5F.

85. Wheelwright, *The Fatal Lover*, 106.

86. PRO KV 1/40 MI5 G Branch Report.

87. PRO KV 1/42 MI5 G Branch Report.

88. Tuohy, "Women as Secret Service Agents," 21.

89. Hoehling, *Women Who Spied,* vii.

90. For an interesting article on racial difference in the 1920s, see Laura Tabili, "The Construction of Racial Difference in Twentieth-Century Britain: The Special Restriction (Coloured Alien Seamen) Order, 1925," *Journal of British Studies* 33 (January 1994): 54–98. The argument could be made that intolerance was a pervasive part of British society long before the war, and that wartime legislation just contributed to solidifying official prejudice. See, for example, Paul R. Deslandes, "'The Foreign Element': Newcomers and the Rhetoric of Race, Nation, and Empire in 'Oxbridge' Undergraduate Culture, 1850–1920," *Journal of British Studies* 37 (January 1998): 54–90.

91. Cannon Schmitt, *Alien Nation: Nineteenth-Century Gothic Fictions and English Nationality* (Philadelphia: University of Pennsylvania Press, 1997), 161.

92. Sandra M. Gilbert, "Soldier's Heart: Literary Men, Literary Women, and the Great War," in *Behind the Lines: Gender and the Two World Wars,* Margaret Higonnet et al., ed. (New Haven: Yale University Press, 1987), 198–199.

93. Andrew, *Her Majesty's Secret Service,* 241, and Panayi, 183.

NOTES TO CHAPTER 3

1. MI5 and its precursor MO5 had been located in a variety of smaller buildings but spent much of the last years of the war in Haymarket. MI5 moved to the six-floor Waterloo House in August 1916, but by 1918 the branch expanded again and took over Greener House next door. The two buildings were modified and linked with doors. There was also a small annex in a bungalow at 14a Charles Street. This complex remained MI5's headquarters until demobilization precipitated a move to smaller premises in December of 1919. PRO KV 1/49, MI5 "H" Branch Report (71–76).

2. For studies of the development of work and of the gendered workplace see Arthur J. MacIvor, *A History of Work in Britain, 1880–1950* (New York: Palgrave, 2001); and Deborah Simonton, *A History of European Women's Work, 1700 to the Present* (London: Routledge, 1998).

3. Keith Jeffery, "British Military Intelligence Following World War I," in *British and American Approaches to Intelligence,* K. G. Robertson, ed. (New York: St. Martin's, 1987), 55.

4. PRO WO 106/6083 Lt. Col. William R. V. Isaac, "The History of the Development of the Directorate of Military Intelligence, the War Office 1855–1939," 23.

5. PRO WO 32/10776 Maj. Gen. W. Thwaites (DMI), "Historical Sketch of the Directorate of Military Intelligence during the Great War, 1914–1919," 6 May 1921, 20.

6. Hilda Martindale, *Women Servants of the State, 1870–1938* (London: Allen & Unwin, 1938), 17.

7. Martindale, 75.

8. There were different kinds of mail censors during the war including army field censors and naval censors, but the bulk of civil mail went through the War Office's Postal Censorship Branch (MI9).

9. Martindale, 76.

10. CPOHC, POST 56/57 Lt. Col. A. S. L. Farquharson, "Report on Postal Censorship during the Great War (1914–1919)," (31 March 1920), 321.

11. Patrick Beesley, *Room 40: British Naval Intelligence 1914–1918* (London: Hamish Hamilton, 1982), 174.

12. Francis Toye, *For What We Have Received: An Autobiography* (New York: Alfred A. Knopf, 1948), 18.

13. PRO HW 3/6 W. F. Clarke papers. See also: R. A. Denniston, "The Professional Career of A. G. Denniston," in *British and American Approaches to Intelligence*, K. G. Robertson, ed. (New York: St. Martin's Press, 1987), 105–106; Penelope Fitzgerald, *The Knox Brothers* (New York: Coward, McCann and Geoghegan, 1977), 145, 169: and Viscount Mersey (2nd Viscount), *A Picture of Life, 1872–1940* (London: John Murray, 1941), 275–276.

14. PRO KV 1/59 MI5 Staff List, December 1919.

15. PRO KV 1/49 "H" Branch Report, Organisation and Administration.

16. Compton Mackenzie, *Greek Memories* (Frederick, MD: University Publications of America, 1987), 376–377.

17. PRO KV 1/49 and KV 1/50.

18. Farquharson, 319.

19. PRO KV 1/54 "H" Branch Report, Annexure #23 "Duties of 'H' Branch."

20. IWM 96/32/1 Papers of Mrs. B. de Quidt. M. S. Aslin, "An Essay on the Girl Guide," *The Nameless Magazine* (March 1920): 6.

21. CCAC, MISC 20; Professor W. H. Bruford to Penelope Fitzgerald, 2 January 1975.

22. PRO KV 1/22 "E" Branch Report. The searchers' work, as the historical report notes, was "arduous and disagreeable and necessarily irregular." Kell worried about corruption of searchers, saying "it was no good to lock up a venal charwoman and a plutocratic spy without a watch-dog to see that they did not collude." The Women's Army Auxiliary Corps (WAACs) was founded in 1917 to help provide labor for the armed services in a variety of non-combat roles. See Jenny Gould, "Women's Military Services in First World War Britain," in *Behind the Lines: Gender and the Two World Wars,* Margaret Higonnet et al., eds. (New Haven: Yale University Press, 1987), 114–125.

23. PRO KV 1/50 "H" Branch Report (Supplement on Women's Work).

24. These five women, Venetia Cooper, Lucy Farrer, Mary Shaw, Mabel Maynard, and Evelyn Hatch, were linguists, authors, and historians—trained scholars in fact. PRO KV 1/53 "H" Branch Report, Annexure #22.

25. PRO KV 1/50 "H" Branch Report (Supplement on Women's Work).

26. PRO KV 1/50 "H" Branch Report (Supplement on Women's Work).

27. PRO KV 1/49 "H" Branch Report.

28. CCAC, MISC 20; Professor W. H. Bruford to Penelope Fitzgerald, 2 January 1975; W. Lionel Fraser, *All to the Good* (London: Heinemann, 1963), 62.

29. Farquharson, 314, 325.

30. Fisher's job in Paris was to extract detailed information from German soldiers' paybooks taken from prisoners of war. Intelligence Corps Museum, Chicksands, "Report by Charlotte E. Bosworth Fisher, 1970," Bosworth Papers 343. My gratitude goes to Jim Beach for this reference.

31. The MBE (Member of the British Empire) is part of a series of awards created on June 4, 1917 by King George V to honor the vast numbers of people involved in the war effort. Women and foreigners were eligible for these awards, marking the first state recognition of the role of "unconventional" soldiers in the conflict. In 1918, a military division was added to the civil division. For more information, see Alec Purves, *The Medals, Decorations, and Orders of the Great War, 1914–1918*, 2d ed. (Polstead, U. K.: J. B. Hayward & Son, 1989). Thank you to the members of H-ALBION for information on the British honors system, and in particular Don Creiger, Ed Haynes, Susan Hoyle, Andrea Tanner, and Angus Trumble.

32. IWM 79/50/1 Sir Ivone Kirkpatrick, "The War 1914–1918," unpub. TS, 114, 149; PRO WO 106/6192 Nominal Rolls of Allied and Neutral Secret Service Agents Appointed CBE, OBE, MBE, and BEM for 1914–1918 (Western Front).

33. The British Mission was officially part of an office called the Bureau Centrale Interallie, which had missions from all the Allied governments. May Wedderburn Cannan, *Grey Ghosts and Voices* (Kineton, U. K.: Roundwood Press, 1976), 126–131.

34. Mersey, 279.

35. Meta Zimmeck, "Strategies and Stratagems for the Employment of Women in the British Civil Service, 1919–1939," *Historical Journal* 27:4 (1984): 902.

36. PRO HW 3/6 W. F. Clarke papers.

37. CCAC, DENN 1/3 Alastair G. Denniston, Manuscript of chapter on development of staff.

38. Dorothy Evans, *Women and the Civil Service* (London: Sir Isaac Pitman & Sons, 1934), 24.

39. Farquharson, 326, 345.

40. Farquharson, 318, 345.

41. Graham Mark, *British Censorship of the Civil Mails during World War I, 1914–1919* (Bristol, U. K.: Stuart Rossiter Trust Fund, 2000), 26.

42. Farquharson, 326.

43. Woollacott, 115. Men made an average of £4 6s. 6d, while women only averaged wages of £2 2s. 4d.

44. Lucy Moorehead, ed. *Freya Stark Letters: The Furnace and the Cup, 1914–1930.* vol. 1 (Salisbury, U. K.: Compton Russell, 1974), 20, 22.

45. Freya Stark, *Traveller's Prelude* (London: John Murray, 1950), 169–170.

46. CPOHC Archives 7/10a. *The London Censorship, 1914–1919 by Members of the Staff, Past and Present,* printed for private circulation 1919, 35.

47. PRO KV 1/53 "H" Branch Report, Annexure #9 Notes on the Registry by Miss Cribb.

48. PRO KV 1/69 and KV 1/70, Analysis of Accounts.

49. IWM 92/22/1 Mrs. D. B. G. Line (née Dimmock), "Reminiscences of World War I," TS, n.d.

50. IWM 96/32/1 Papers of Mrs. B. de Quidt, "The 'K' Club," *The Nameless Magazine* (March 1920): 4.

51. PRO KV 1/50 "H" Branch Report (Supplement on Women's Work).

52. IWM 95/14/1 Miss Florence Rees papers, Memo from Col. G. S. H. Pearson to Postal Censorship Examiners, 1 January 1918.

53. Barbara Bagilhole, *Women, Work, and Equal Opportunity: Underachievement in the Civil Service* (Aldershot, U. K.: Avebury, 1994), 60, Martindale, 75, and Zimmeck, 912. See also PRO NATS 1/1267 Woman Power in the United Kingdom—Policy File.

54. Stella Rimington, *Open Secret: The Autobiography of the Former Director-General of MI5* (London: Hutchinson, 2001), 90.

55. Cannan, 123.

56. Moorehead, 13.

57. PRO KV 1/54 "H" Branch Report, Annexure #23 "Duties of 'H' Branch"; KV 1/50; KV 1/49.

58. IWM 92/22/1, Line, "Reminiscences of World War I."

59. Ibid.

60. Martindale, 79.

61. CCAC, MISC 20; Professor W. H. Bruford, "History of Room 40," TS, (23 Feb 1977); HW 3/6 Clarke papers.

62. Fitzgerald, 145, 169; Beesley, 175.

63. IWM 96/32/1 Papers of Mrs. B. de Quidt, "Editor's Note," *The Nameless Magazine* (1921), 7.

64. IWM 96/32/1 Papers of Mrs. B. De Quidt, *The Nameless Magazine* (1921).

65. The Oxford African Survey was a two-thousand-page project. Michael Carney, *Stoker: The Life of Hilda Matheson, OBE 1888–1940* (Published by author, 1999), 11–17, 90–91, 109; [Mrs. Donald Matheson], *Hilda Matheson* (Letchworth, U. K.: Hogarth Press, 1941), 10–13.

66. PRO HW 3/6 Papers of W. C. Clarke.

67. Stark, 169–171 and Goodman, 68–82.

68. PRO KV 1/53 "H" Branch Report, Annexure #9 Notes on the Registry by Miss Cribb.

69. Farquharson, 66–68.

70. CPOHC; *The London Censorship*, 64–68.

71. PRO RECO 1/885 Ministry of Reconstruction, *Report of the Women's Employment Committee* (London: HMSO, 1919), 33, 51.

72. Zimmeck, 910–911.

73. De Groot, 262–263.

74. Zimmeck, 912–913, 924. Women in private clerical work—another postwar outlet for women demobilized in 1919—also suffered from sex discrimination in wages and promotion; see Susanne Dohrn, "Pioneers in a Dead-End Profession: The First Women Clerks in Banks and Insurance Companies," in *The White-Blouse Revolution,* Anderson, ed., 51–59. For an overview of the gradual feminization of clerical work, see Jane Lewis's chapter in the same work, "Women Clerical Workers in the Late Nighteenth and Early Twentieth Centuries," 28–43. For more on post–World War II civil service opportunities for women, see Elizabeth Brimelow, "Women in the Civil Service," *Public Administration* LIX (1981), 313–335.

75. IWM PP/MCR/120 SVK/1 Constance Kell, "Secret Well Kept," TS, 173.

76. IWM 96/32/1 Papers of Mrs. B. de Quidt, "Editor's Note," *The Nameless Magazine* (March 1920): 1.

77. PRO KV 1/53 "H" Branch Report Annexure #19 Proposals as to the future of the Service of Security Bureau.

78. PRO KV 1/53 "H" Branch Report Annexure #20 Proposal for Distribution of Duties under Re-Organisation May 1920.

79. PRO KV 1/50 "H" Branch Report (Supplement on Women's Work), V. G. W. Kell to Miss E. A. Lomax (Controller of Women's Staff), 18 August 1919.

80. PRO KV 1/50 "H" Branch Report (Supplement on Women's Work), Appendix.

81. For discussions of government replacement practices, see Thom, 9, and Braybon, *Women Workers,* 51–61.

82. PRO CO/850/212/4 Marriage Bar in the Civil Service: Report of the Civil Service National Whitley Council Committee, August 1946. Bagilhole (p. 62) notes that a 1971 report found the marriage gratuity still at work in some departments as an incentive to get women to resign on marriage.

83. Martindale, 175.

NOTES TO CHAPTER 4

1. Quoted in P. Decock, "La Dame Blanche: un réseau de renseignements de la grande guerre 1916–1918," (Ph.D. thesis, Histoire Contemporaire, Université Libre de Bruxelles, 1981), 141. [TH 183, Centre d'Etudes et de Documentation Guerre at Sociétés contemporaines, CEGES, Brussels].

2. McPhail, 137.

3. Occleshaw, 147–157.

4. Work on *La Dame Blanche* has been sparse, even among historians of intelligence networks. The most detailed study is the Decock thesis from 1981. Other works that include information on *La Dame Blanche* and its wartime work are: Christopher Andrew, *Secret Service: The Making of the British Intelligence Community* (London: Heinemann, 1985), Henri Bernard, *Un géant de la résistance: Walthère Déwe* (Belgium: La Renaissance du Livre, 1971), and Occleshaw. Another source on *La Dame Blanche* is a book banned in Britain but published in the United States by the British officer assigned to manage *La Dame Blanche* from 1917 to 1919: Henry Landau, *Secrets of the White Lady* (New York: G. P. Putnam's Sons, 1935).

5. The "White Lady" (*die Weisse Frau* or *la Dame Blanche*) supposedly appeared just before the deaths of the Hohenzollern kings or other important members of the family. Her most famous appearances came before the assassination of King Friedrich Wilhelm and before the death of Wilhelm I. The legend appeared in plays and operas as well as in popular folklore. Andre Leveque, "Le 'Spectre en Femme Voilee' dans le Dom Juan de Moliere," *Modern Language Notes* 76:8 (December 1961): 746; and "The White Lady of the Hohenzollerns," *The Living Age* 26:324 (3 August 1850): 201.

6. PRO WO 106/45 Lt. Col. R. J. Drake, "History of Intelligence (B), B. E. F., France, from January 1917–April 1919," (5 May 1919), 1.

7. Archives Générale du Royaume (AGR)/P-212, Historical Notices; W. Dewe, "Notice sur le Corps d'Observation Allié Attaché à l'armée anglaise," 1919, 1. The French offer was declined, the Belgian affiliation broke down almost immediately, and the British Army GHQ service was abandoned when sloppiness led to the arrest of some members of the network.

8. Occleshaw, 189. Landau was on a recuperative leave from the front after contracting German measles.

9. In wartime, the lines between prostitution (especially for women needing to make enough money to feed their families) and rape are blurry. See Andrea Dworkin's discussion of sexual intercourse as an occupation of women's bodies and as a form of surrender (collaboration, complicity) in *Intercourse* (New York: Free Press, 1987), 122–143.

10. Decock, 86.

11. An examination of this imagery and its implications for the history of Belgium during the war is Sophie de Schaepdrijver's, "Deux Patries: La Belgique entre exaltation et rejet, 1914–1918," *Cahiers d'Histoire du Temps Présent* 7 (mai 2000): 17–49.

12. An excellent recent book addresses both the myths and realities of German atrocities in Belgium: John Horne and Alan Kramer, *German Atrocities 1914: A History of Denial* (New Haven: Yale University Press, 2001).

13. This historical amnesia is discussed in Aurore François and Frédéric Vesentini, "Essai sur l'origine des massacres du mois d'août 1914 à Tamines et à Dinant," *Cahiers d'Histoire du Temps Présent* 7 (mai 2000): 51–82. For coverage of this issue in occupied France, see McPhail and Annette Becker, *Oubliés de la grande guerre* (Paris: Éditions Noêsis, 1998). It is interesting to note that many World War I resistance networks were resurrected in the Second World War. Emmanuel Debruyne is currently examining the social aspects of the networks in both wars and charting connections between them.

14. Horne and Kramer, 178–180.

15. These archives are used by some Belgian scholars, but they appear to have been largely ignored by historians outside of Belgium.

16. Decock, 129.

17. PRO WO 106/45 E. A. Wallinger to R. J. Drake 1 June 1918.

18. PRO WO 106/6192 Names of French and Belgian Secret Service Agents—Awards.

19. Parritt, 224–230. Thanks to Jim Beach for providing information regarding this issue.

20. AGR/P-224, Battalion III service records. Louise Thuliez, *Condemned to Death,* Marie Poett-Velitchko, trans. (London: Methuen, 1934), 81.

21. AGR/P-224 Battalion III service records.

22. Decock, 49.

23. Landau, *Secrets of the White Lady,* 113.

24. Bernard, 25; Landau, *Secrets of the White Lady,* 110.

25. AGR/P-224 Battalion III service records. AGR/P-207, AGR/P-208, and AGR/P-209 have many records of financial transactions between Landau and the leaders in Liège.

26. Other networks operating in Belgium deliberately hired people living outside the realm of "respectability" in order to gain different kinds of information. These intelligence groups included prostitutes, thieves, and con men, and the agents were paid in cash or drugs for their services.

27. AGR/P-224 Battalion III service records.

28. AGR/P-222 Reports on the Organization of Battalion III.

29. IWM La Dame Blanche Box 2, Folder 13—Paul Chautard, "La Dame Blanche des Hohenzollern," *La Liberté* (24 février 1922): 1.

30. Landau, *Secrets of the White Lady*, 73.

31. Landau, *Secrets of the White Lady*, 78.

32. AGR/P-223, Reports on the COA.

33. IWM La Dame Blanche Box 2, Folder 13—Paul Chautard, "La Dame Blanche des Hohenzollern," *La Liberté* (22 février 1922): 1–2.

34. AGR/P-207, Correspondence.

35. Landau, *Secrets of the White Lady*, 142–145; IWM La Dame Blanche Box 1, Folder 4 (a/b).

36. IWM La Dame Blanche Box 1, Folder 4 (a/b).

37. IWM La Dame Blanche Box 2, Folder 11, "Service de Passage Organise par la Vicomtesse Gabrielle de Monge de Franeau (Nov 1914–April 1916). Landau, *Secrets of the White Lady*, 242.

38. Bernard, 53–55.

39. AGR/P-212, Historical Notices. "Serment."

40. AGR/P-212, Historical Notices.

41. Landau, *Secrets of the White Lady*, 61–62.

42. AGR/P-212, "Circulaire No. 3."

43. In his work on postwar veterans, Antoine Prost suggests that fraternity validated the war experience when patriotism could not. Prost, *In the Wake of War: "Les Anciens Combattants" and French Society*, Helen McPhail, trans. (Oxford: Berg, 1992). Belgian men were afraid of being thought of as shirkers or collaborators and soldier status gave them hope of postwar legitimacy. For a discussion of the rupture between frontline soldiers and civilians see Stéphane Audoin-Rouzeau, *Men at War 1914–1918: National Sentiment and Trench Journalism in France during the First World War*, Helen McPhail, trans. (Oxford: Berg, 1992), 92–111.

44. L'Abbe Philippot and Herman Chauvin, as quoted in Decock, 103.

45. AGR/P-207, Correspondence of COA (Belg.) and SA (War Office) in Holland.

46. IWM La Dame Blanche Box 2, Folder 12a/b; Henry Landau to Capt. Vigors, Sect 4a MI1C, 24 February 1919.

47. AGR/P-222, Report on 8th Company; L. L. Blanjean, "Rapport du Commandant concernant l'action de la Compagnie au cours de la guerre 1914–1918," 16 janvier 1919, 18.

48. IWM La Dame Blanche Box 1, Folder 4 (a/b).

49. See Gilbert, 197–226.

50. Gilbert, 200. Many scholars have begun to examine the gender anxieties created by the war and its aftermath. See, for example, works by Deirdre Beddoe, *Back to Home and Duty: Women Between the Wars, 1918–1939* (New York: HarperCollins, 1998); Joanna Bourke, *Dismembering the Male: Men's Bodies, Britain, and the Great War* (Chicago: University of Chicago Press, 1996); Atina

Grossman, *Reforming Sex: The German Movement for Birth Control and Abortion Reform, 1920–1950* (Oxford: Oxford University Press, 1995); Susan Kingsley Kent, *Making Peace: The Reconstruction of Gender in Interwar Britain* (Princeton: Princeton University Press, 1993); and Mary Louise Roberts, *Civilization without Sexes: Reconstructing Gender in Postwar France, 1917–1927* (Chicago: University of Chicago Press, 1994).

51. IWM La Dame Blanche Box 1, folder 8; T. de Radigues, "Notice sur le Poste 49," 27 janvier 1919.

52. Inscribed on Gabrielle Petit monument in Place St. Jean, Brussels.

53. Thuliez, 216.

54. Thuliez, 207–209.

55. Quoted in Ben Macintyre's *The Englishman's Daughter: A True Story of Love and Betrayal in World War I* (New York: Farrar, Straus and Giroux, 2001), 168.

56. Marie de Croÿ, *Souvenirs de la Princesse Marie de Croÿ 1914–1918* (Paris: Librairie Plon, 1933), 191.

57. René Deruyk, *Louise de Bettignies*, 214; and de Croÿ, 193.

58. Thuliez, 190–191, and De Croÿ, 172.

59. Thuliez, 192; and De Croÿ, 169.

60. Deruyk, *Louise de Bettignies*, 207–208; and Thuliez, 197–198.

61. AGR/P-222, folder 7 Jeanne Delwaide report, 10 janvier 1919; Landau, *Secrets of the White Lady*, 126; Bernard, 60–61.

62. IWM La Dame Blanche Box 1, Folders 4 (a/b)—reports by Jeanne Goeseels, Paul Istas, and Ferdnand Van Berg.

63. Salle Ulysse Capitaine, Central Library, Liège, Madame Jeanne Goeseels, *La Dame Blanche: Organe mensuel de la fraternelle Walthère Dewé* 2:17 (October 1948).

64. AGR/P-212. Former women prisoners formed postwar associations and social clubs to retain ties with each other and to legitimize their wartime activities.

65. IWM La Dame Blanche Box 2, folder 13, news clipping from *Moniteur*, 31 janvier 1919.

66. AGR/P-212, Historical Notices; "Attestation Donnée le 16 mars 1919, signé H. Landau, Captain."

67. Decock, 7; IWM 79/50/1, Sir Ivone Kirkpatrick, "The War 1914–1918," unpublished typescript, 163–169; Marthe McKenna noted in her memoirs that when she tried to claim additional reimbursement from the British for her time as an agent she was turned away and told to seek restitution from the Germans, which seemed a laughable suggestion to her. Marthe McKenna, *I Was a Spy* (London: Jarrolds, 1932).

68. Landau, *Secrets of the White Lady*, 252.

69. Darrow, 4.

70. See, for example, Grayzel, *Women's Identities at War*, 11–13, and Joanna Bourke, *An Intimate History of Killing: Face- to-Face Killing in Twentieth-Century Warfare* (New York: Basic Books, 1999), 328.

71. Bourke, *An Intimate History of Killing*, 326–337.

NOTES TO CHAPTER 5

1. Ryder, 1–3, 12–15, 20, 39–44, 61–83.

2. Ryder, 136; Thuliez, 71–89, 97. See also, de Croÿ.

3. Thuliez, 108–112; Ryder, 174–176. Ryder notes that Baucq's thirteen-year-old daughter, Yvonne, tried to hide the illegal newspapers on a ledge outside an upstairs window, but the papers fell down on the German officials below.

4. Darrow, 281; Ryder, 249–250.

5. Ryder, 194–209; Helen Judson, *Edith Cavell* (New York: Macmillan, 1941), 259, 277; Wheelwright, *The Fatal Lover*, 120.

6. IWM 93/22/1 Miss J. H. Gifford Diary, "Experiences in Brussels, 1914–1919," 10, 40.

7. Poster reprinted in *Scraps of Paper: German Proclamations in Belgium and France* (London: Hodder and Stoughton, 1916), 31. Ironically, this book gathered together German proclamations and provided Allied commentary for a powerful pro-Ally propaganda document.

8. The *Christchurch Press* was quoted in Katie Pickles, "Edith Cavell—Heroine, No Hatred or Bitterness for Anyone?" *History Now* 3:2 (1997): 1.

9. *New York Times*, 22 October 1915 and 28 October 1915.

10. "Miss Cavell's Death Inflames England," *New York Times* (22 October 1915): 2.

11. Wheelwright (120) notes that a French souvenir medal was minted in her memory, while Darrow (280) discusses the renaming of schools and hospitals in her honor in France.

12. Ryder, 251–252.

13. "10,000 Led to Enlist by Miss Cavell's Fate," *New York Times* (25 October 1915): 1.

14. "London Contrasts the Execution of Edith Cavell with Mild Treatment of Woman Spy in England," *New York Times* (22 October 1915): 1.

15. In particular, the Germans questioned the cases of Ottilie Voss and Marguerite Schmitt. See, for example, coverage in the *New York Times*, 22 October 1915. Later the Germans used Mata Hari's execution as proof of French atrocity.

16. "Belgian Court Martial Gives Death Sentence to Belgian Woman Accused of Spying, an Exposure of Ally Hypocrisy," facsimile copy of English

translation of article and document published in the *North German Gazette*, 2 December 1915; Public Library of Cincinnati.

17. Horne and Kramer write that "her tale particularized the surrogate relationship of British opinion with the invasion of Belgium by providing a direct victim." Horne and Kramer, 311.

18. Darrow, 276.

19. Alison Blunt, "Embodying War: British Women and Domestic Defilement in the Indian 'Mutiny,' 1857–1858," *Journal of Historical Geography* 26:3 (2000), 408.

20. Schmitt, 162. This imagery of the victimized woman is particularly strong in accounts of the Indian Mutiny-Rebellion of 1857.

21. Robert Underwood Johnson, "Edith Cavell," *New York Times* (24 October 1915).

22. Darrow, 280, and Wheelwright, 122–123.

23. Quoted in Karen Chase and Michael Levenson, *The Spectacle of Intimacy: A Public Life for the Victorian Family* (Princeton: Princeton University Press, 2000), 132.

24. An interesting work on images of Florence Nightingale is Mary Poovey, *Uneven Developments: The Ideological Work of Gender in Mid-Victorian England* (Chicago: University of Chicago Press, 1988), 164–198.

25. Darrow, 44.

26. For an interesting study of the *fusillés* (in particular, French soldier mutineers) and their memorialization in France, see Nicholas Offenstadt, *Les Fusillés de la Grande Guerre et la Memoire Collective, 1914–1999* (Paris: Éditions Odile Jacob, 1999).

27. Many authors—both journalists and scholars—describe many of these tales. For an example, see Ryder, 222.

28. For an excellent study of French war memorials and their imagery, see Annette Becker, *Les Monuments aux Morts: Patrimoine et Memoire de la Grande Guerre* (Paris: Éditions Errance, 1988).

29. Antoine Redier, *The Story of Louise de Bettignies,* Olive Hall, trans. (London: Hutchinson, 1926), 30–31.

30. Hubert P. Van Tuyll van Serooskerken, *The Netherlands and World War I: Espionage, Diplomacy, and Survival* (Boston: Brill, 2001), 162.

31. Ibid., 132.

32. IWM La Dame Blanche Box 1, Folder 2—"Etudes des Services de Passages."

33. Landau, *Secrets of the White Lady,* 256–257; Antoine Redier, *La Guerre des Femmes: Histoire de Louise de Bettignies et de ses Compagnes* (Paris: Éditions de la Vraie France, 1924), 75; Coulson, 200; and IWM La Dame Blanche Box 2, Folder 13, Paul Chautard "La Dame Blanche des Hohenzollern," *La Liberte* (7 March 1922): 1–2, in clippings file.

34. Adolphe Hardy, *L'Ardenne heroique* (Bruxelles: Association des Ecrivains Belges, 1920), 10–48. See also, Landau, 252–255.

35. *New York Times* (5 July 1917): 5; and the London *Times* (5 July 1917): 6B.

36. Real del Sarte was a sculptor known for his monuments to the dead of the Great War. He was often commissioned by a community to memorialize those slain for the cause. Having lost an arm in the war, Real del Sarte was a celebrated war artist who was known for his ability to capture the "death sacrifice" of the war. In addition to his Stavelot monument mentioned here, Real del Sarte also sculpted the Louise de Bettignies monument in Lille. Becker, *Les Monuments aux Morts*, 24–25.

37. BMD Dossier Gabrielle Petit; Memorial program with quotation from Monseigneur Keesen at the Belgian Senate on 2 July 1919. Hélène d'Argoeuves, "Louise de Bettignies, la 'Jeanne d'Arc du Nord,'" *Les Annales Politiques et Littéraires* (10 January 1938): 10.

38. IWM 82/28/1 Lt. Col. W. Kirke diaries, 7 October 1915.

39. Annette Becker, *War and Faith: The Religious Imagination in France, 1914–1930*, Helen McPhail, trans. (Oxford: Berg, 1998), 60–61. Joan of Arc was canonized in 1920 and her image was invoked by both rightist and leftist politicians in the postwar period.

40. IWM 82/28/1 Lt. Col. W. Kirke diaries, 1 January 1916.

41. Isabelle Gérard, *Sept Dames de Qualité: De Mémoire de Femmes Belges* (Bruxelles: Editions J. M. Collet, 1982), 99–104, and Arthur Deloge, *Gabrielle Petit: Sa Vie et Son Oeuvre* (Bruxelles: Vve Ferdinand Larcier, 1922), 1–34, 60, 79–80, 115–176.

42. Deloge, 94.

43. "Honour for a Belgian Heroine," London *Times* (31 May 1919): 11B.

44. Gem Moriaud, *Louise de Bettignies: Une Heroine Française* (Paris: Jules Tallandier, 1928), 243. Moriaud compares the statues of three national heroines here: Edith Cavell, Louise de Bettignies, and Gabrielle Petit.

45. Annette Becker, "Tortured and Exalted by War: French Catholic Women, 1914–1918," in *Women and War in the Twentieth Century: Enlisted with or without Consent*, Nicole Dombrowski, trans., ed. (New York: Garland, 1999), 50.

46. René Deruyk, *1914–1918, Lille Dans Les Serres Allemandes* (Lille: La Voix du Nord, 1992), 169; Coulson, 30–37; and McPhail, 147.

47. IWM 82/28/1 Lt. Col. W. Kirke diaries, 13 September 1915 and 29 November 1915; Military Intelligence minute quoted in McPhail, 154.

48. Coulson, 72.

49. "Sisters in Arms" is a translation of the title of a film made in the interwar period about Louise de Bettignies and her female companions in espionage. Léon Poirier directed the film *Soeurs d'Armes*.

50. Deruyk, *Louise de Bettignies*, 175, 207–215.

51. Deruyk, *Louise de Bettignies*, 231–237.

52. Klaus Theweleit, *Male Fantasies, Volume I: Women Floods Bodies History,* Stephen Conway, trans. (Minneapolis: University of Minnesota Press, 1987), 104. An example of the emphasis on women's role as sufferers in war is the Girl Guide organization's commemoration of Edith Cavell with a special badge in her honor. Called the "Badge of Fortitude" by the 1920s, it was only available from 1926 on to physically handicapped Guides—a curious twist on the Cavell legacy. For more information, see Tammy Proctor, "Gender, Generation, and the Politics of Guiding and Scouting in Interwar Britain," Ph.D. diss. Rutgers University, 1995, 43–44.

53. From John Laffin, *Women in Battle,* quoted in Bourke, *Intimate History of Killing,* 326.

54. Darrow, 283.

NOTES TO CHAPTER 6

1. Magnus Hirschfeld, *The Sexual History of the World War* (New York: Panurge Press, 1934), 248.

2. Darrow, 272.

3. Andrew, *Her Majesty's Secret Service,* 1; and Knightley, 3.

4. J. Bernard Hutton, *Women Spies* (London: W. H. Allen, 1971), 188.

5. Rowan, 8, 10.

6. Hutton, 8.

7. Jock Haswell, *Spies and Spymasters: A Concise History of Intelligence* (London: Thames and Hudson, 1977), 126.

8. McIntosh, 1.

9. For a contextualized history of the New Woman, see Ledger, 22–44.

10. Wheelwright, "Poisoned Honey," 308–309. See also: Wheelwright, *The Fatal Lover.*

11. Bram Dijkstra, *Idols of Perversity: Fantasies of Feminine Evil in Fin-de-Siècle Culture* (New York: Oxford University Press, 1986), viii.

12. Theweleit, 171.

13. Darrow, 270.

14. PRO KV 2/2 Mata Hari MI5(G) Records; H. A. Pakenham to Maj. Waterhouse, 28 November 1917. Pakenham, in sorting Mata Hari's file at the British Mission in Paris, had sent items of interest to London, adding a note saying "She was a 'femme forte' and she worked alone."

15. Some of the best known performance works that use the Mata Hari story include films starring Marlene Dietrich (1931), Greta Garbo (1932), and Jeanne Moreau (1964); David Gordon's ballet, *Murder*; and a musical, *Little Mary Sunshine.* Numerous biographical accounts exist, although the most noted are the studies by Wheelwright, Sam Waagenaar, Russell Howe, and Leon Schirmann.

16. Wheelwright, *The Fatal Lover*, vi.

17. Hirschfeld, 268.

18. Darrow, 294.

19. Wheelwright, *The Fatal Lover*, 1–14.

20. Wheelwright, *The Fatal Lover*, 15.

21. Mata Hari to Captain Bouchardon 5 June 1917, Margaret Higonnet, ed. *Lines of Fire: Women Writers of World War I* (New York: Plume Books, 1999), 275–276.

22. PRO KV 2/1 Mata Hari (P.F.), MI5(E) records—various correspondence; Wheelwright, *The Fatal Lover*, 48–50.

23. Leon Schirmann, *L'Affaire Mata Hari: Enquête sur une Machination* (Paris: Tallandier, 1994), 10–11, 28. Schirmann is so sure of Mata Hari's incompetence as a German spy that he has undertaken a campaign to persuade the French Justice Ministry to reopen her case; "Mata Hari Case Is Revisited," *Kansas City Star* (21 October 2001): A23.

24. Schirmann, 11–12, and Krop, 240–241.

25. Wheelwright, *The Fatal Lover*, 66–84; C. David Coveny, "Intrigue," *Military History* 16:1 (April 1999): 22–24; Darrow, 290. Wheelwright notes on 68 that "Ladoux was adroit at shaping the evidence to fit the crime."

26. Wheelwright, *The Fatal Lover*, 80–99. After Mata Hari's execution her body went unclaimed by relatives and was used for dissection by medical students. Her severed head and other remains were taken to the Museum of Anatomy in Paris in 1918. Her head remained there as part of a collection of criminal celebrities—viewed by scores of medical students over the years—until it was reported missing in July 2000. For an account of her head, see Adam Sage, "Mystery of How Mata Hari Lost Her Head," London *Times* (13 July 2000).

27. Wheelwright, *The Fatal Lover*, 101; Darrow, 290; Hirschfeld, 265.

28. Ladoux, *Marthe Richard The Skylark*, 37. See also Darrow, 240–241.

29. Marthe Richer, *I Spied for France*, Gerald Griffin, trans. (London: John Long, 1935), 42, 51, 96–98.

30. Articles questioning her story appeared in *Le Monde* in 1974 and 1977, and in *Paris Villages* in 1985 after her death. BMD dossier Marthe Richard. See also the discussion in Darrow, 294. Ironically, Richer is perhaps best known today for her contribution to closing down all the brothels in France in 1946.

31. Quoted in Schirmann, 185.

32. Emile Massard, *Les Espionnes à Paris* (Paris: Albin Michel, 1922), 105–110. Krop (p. 231) notes that Francillard was a courier for her lover, who was executed by the French. The manner of her death (she refused a blindfold) also belies the story Massard tells of a stupid, drunken girl.

33. Wheelwright, *The Fatal Lover*, 115–116. Even modern scholars have picked up these stories, with Nathan Miller calling Victorica "one of the few

spies who measures up to Hollywood's standards." Miller, *Spying for America: The Hidden History of U.S. Intelligence* (New York: Paragon House, 1989), 191.

34. Quoted in Wheelwright, *The Fatal Lover,* 113.

35. "Mme. Storch Dead; Was Held As Spy," *New York Times* (31 March 1918): 16.

36. NARA "German Espionage Methods and Notes on Passports," I.P. Book #3 (10687-105-1) 1917, RG 165 Entry 65, MID Correspondence.

37. Ladoux, 93.

38. Winfried Ludecke, *Behind the Scenes of Espionage: Tales of the Secret Service* (London: George G. Harrap, 1929), 239, and Baroness Carla Jenssen, *I Spy: Sensational Disclosures of a British Secret Service Agent* (London: Jarrolds, 1930), 197.

39. Ladoux, 93.

40. BMD dossier espionne, *Le Soir* 28 September 1934, *Paris-Midi* 19 November 1933 and 24 November 1933.

41. Early spy writers seemed to be equally split on the question of her identity, but Darrow notes that among recent French historians, Leon Schirmann maintains that there was a lady Doctor, while Pascal Krop claims that she was legendary. Several historians, including Bernard Newman and Richard Rowan, had to change positions after having acknowledged that they had previously published inaccuracies about the Lady Doctor.

42. "The Blond Lady. Keeping Watch on a German Spy," London *Times* 18 December 1919: 11e.

43. IWM PP/MCR/120 Sir Vernon Kell, Reel I SVK/2, "Security Intelligence in War," 28.

44. Felstead, 286. See also Haswell, 128–129.

45. Jenssen, 197, and Henry Landau, *All's Fair: The Story of the British Secret Service behind the German Lines* (New York: G. P. Putnam's Sons, 1934), 165.

46. Landau, *All's Fair,* 165; Felstead, 286; Aston, 157; and Massard, 136.

47. Berndorff, 131–132.

48. Edwin Woodhall, *Spies of the Great War* (London: Mellifont Press, 1939), 58. Herbert Yardley also spun a fictional tale out of the Lady Doctor story in *The Blond Countess,* as described in Wheelwright, "Poisoned Honey."

49. Hirschfeld, 252.

50. Massard, 136.

51. Perhaps playing on the success of Greta Garbo's *Mata Hari* (1932), films about the Lady Doctor began appearing in the 1930s as well. Hollywood's version, *Stamboul Quest* (1934), starring Myrna Loy, was followed by German director G. W. Pabst's *Mademoiselle Docteur* in 1936 for French audiences and a 1937 British version. Again, perhaps inspired by the 1964 Jeanne Moreau *Mata Hari,* Dino de Laurentis directed a new version, *Fraulein Doktor,* in 1968. For information on the films, see John W. Williams, "The Films of 'Fraulein Doktor,'"

first published in *Foreign Intelligence Literary Scene*, accessed via Principia College website (www.prin.edu/users/els/departments/poli_sci/film_politics/fraudoc.html).

52. McKenna, *I Was a Spy!* (New York: Robert M. McBride, 1933), 30, 33–34, 273.

53. McKenna, *I Was a Spy!*, 36–37.

54. McPhail, 55–88.

55. For reproductions of many German proclamations to occupied populations, see *Scraps of Paper*. See also Macintyre, 65–67.

56. McPhail, 44.

57. Cynthia Enloe, *Maneuvers: The International Politics of Militarizing Women's Lives* (Berkeley: University of California Press, 2000), 40–45.

58. From Henriette Celarié, *En Esclavage: Journal de Deux Déportées* (Paris: Bloud et Gay, 1917), 127–131, in Higonnet, ed., *Lines of Fire*, 128.

59. Hirschfeld, 321–322.

60. Catharine MacKinnon, *Toward a Feminist Theory of the State* (Cambridge: Harvard University Press, 1989), 172–174. See also Susan Brownmiller, *Against Our Will: Men, Women, and Rape* (New York: Simon and Schuster, 1975).

61. Ruth Harris, "The 'Child of the Barabarian': Rape, Race, and Nationalism in France during the First World War," *Past and Present* 141 (November 1993): 175. Another useful discussion of the issue of rape and war babies is Stéphane Audoin-Rouzeau, *L'Enfant de l'Ennemi, 1914–1918* (Paris: Aubier, 1995).

62. NARA G-2-B Counterespionage Reports, Entry 195; Records of the AEF (WWI), Record Group 120; "Suspects" Memorandum from Lieutenant E. D. Curtis, I.O., Evian, to GHQ, I(b), 2 July 1918.

63. NARA G-2-B Counterespionage Reports, Entry 195; Records of the AEF (WWI), Record Group 120; "Suspects" Memorandum from Lieutenant E. D. Curtis, I.O., Evian, to GHQ, I(b), 23 June 1918.

64. Enloe, 38.

65. McKenna, *I Was a Spy!*, 37–39.

66. McKenna, *I Was a Spy!*, 39.

67. McKenna, *I Was a Spy!*, 43, 155.

68. McKenna, *I Was a Spy!*, 135.

69. Daniel, 140–143. Daniel notes that the German military tried to find other work for Belgian women (even getting them a contract for making underclothes!) and regulate the sex lives of the civilian population under their control.

70. Hirschfeld, 160.

71. McKenna, *I Was a Spy!*, 158–160.

72. McKenna, *I Was a Spy!*, 273–277.

73. Quoted in Macintyre, 108. For her patriotic defiance, Hénin was arrested and imprisoned in Siegburg prison in Germany.

74. Winston Churchill, "Foreword," in McKenna, *I Was a Spy!*, 5.

75. Karl Marx, "The Eighteenth Brumaire of Louis Bonaparte," in *The Marx-Engels Reader*, 2nd ed., Robert C. Tucker, ed. (New York: W. W. Norton, 1978), 599.

NOTES TO THE CONCLUSION

1. Andrew Lownie, "MI5 women use their intelligence," *Sunday Telegraph* (22 December 1991), 3.

2. Sarah Hall, "Little Old Lady's 'Ordinariness' Put Her above Suspicion," *The Guardian* (13 September 1999), 8.

3. Quoted in Elizabeth P. McIntosh, *Sisterhood of Spies: The Women of the OSS* (New York: Dell Publishing, 1998), 13.

4. PRO WO 32/10776 Maj. Gen. W. Thwaites, "Historical Sketch of the DMI during the Great War, 1914–1919," May 1921.

5. Jeffery, 55–56.

6. PRO KV 1/53 Memo, "Proposals as to the future of the Service of the Security Bureau." By 1921, only thirty-five were still employed in MI5. IWM 96/32/1 Papers of Mrs. B. de Quidt, *The Nameless Magazine*, March 1921, 10.

7. PRO T 165/445 Secret Service Blue Notes. Jeffery, 69–71, and Eunan O'Halpin "Financing British Intelligence: the Evidence up to 1945," in Robertson, 195.

8. One such example includes Jenssen.

9. Personal stories of the work of women spies and resisters in the First World War have not been adequately studied. Beyond the scores of biographical books and films published about dead female spies such as Louise de Bettignies, Edith Cavell, and Mata Hari, there were survivors who spoke at commemoration ceremonies and who told their stories to local reporters. One example of the importance of this informal network is the story of Lydie Bastien who was inspired to do covert work in World War II by a speech she heard as an adolescent. Lydie embraced "the secret attraction of a clandestine life" a few years after hearing Leonie Vanhoutte describe her World War I courier work for the British and her subsequent imprisonment in Siegburg. See Pierre Péan, *La diabolique de Caluire* (Paris: Fayard, 1999), 71–72.

10. An interesting examination of some of these memoirs is Deborah Van Seters, "'Hardly Hollywood's Ideal': Female Autobiographies of Secret Service Work, 1914–45," *Intelligence and National Security* 7:4 (1992): 403–424. Other short biographies of women agents are available in Mahoney.

11. "In Memoriam," *Intelligence and National Security* 13:2 (Summer 1998): 213–214, and Aileen Clayton, *The Enemy is Listening* (London: Hutchinson, 1980).

12. For information on the Clarence network, see Henri Bernard. See also Emmanuel Debruyne's work on the social composition of another of the Secret Service groups in occupied territory, Tégal: "Services de Renseignements et Société: Le Cas du Réseau Tégal, 1940–1944," *Cahiers d'Histoire du Temps Présent* 9 (novembre 2001): 105–152.

13. There have been scores of individual and group studies of the SOE and its female agents. See, for example, Beryl E. Escott, *Mission Improbable: A Salute to the RAF Women of SOE in Wartime France* (Wellingborough, U. K.: Stephens, 1991); James Gleeson, *They Feared No Evil: The Woman Agents of Britain's Secret Armies 1939–45* (London: Corgi, 1976); Patrick Howarth, *Undercover: The Men and Women of the Special Operations Executive* (London: Routledge, 1980); Liane Jones, *A Quiet Courage* (London: Bantam, 1990); and Rita Kramer, *Flames in the Field: The Story of Four SOE Agents in Occupied France* (London: Michael Joseph, 1995).

14. McIntosh discusses the role of women in the OSS, an organization that eventually employed more than 21,000 people during the Second World War.

15. "Her Secret's Out—She's Got Precious Little to Say," *The Sunday Times* (9 September 2001). For more information, see Rimington.

16. Rimington, 90–91.

17. "Women Spies Come in from the Cold," *The Independent* (30 October 1994), and McIntosh, 310. In 2002, 47 percent of MI5's 1832 employees were women, according to the MI5 Security Service website.

18. Douglas Stanglin, "Old Boys and Women Spies," *U.S. News & World Report* 117:11 (19 September 1994), 33, and "The Angry Women of the CIA," *U.S. News & World Report* 118:14 (10 April 1995), 47; Hugh Davies, "CIA Women Wage Secret War on Jobs for the Boys," *The Daily Telegraph* (6 June 1995), 15; Peter Hillmore, "The Women Spies Who Have What It Takes to Tease out the Secrets," *The Observer* (12 October 1997), 19; and Tim Weiner, "Woman Who Was CIA Chief Requests Criminal Investigation," *New York Times* (18 July 1995), A10.

19. Everitt.

20. John Buchan, *Greenmantle* (London: Thomas Nelson & Sons, 1916), 235.

21. IWM PP/MCR/120 Sir Vernon Kell, lecture notes on "Security Intelligence in War," SVK/2, Reel I.

22. Allen Dulles, *The Craft of Intelligence* (New York: Harper & Row, 1965), 187.

Bibliography

ARCHIVES

Archives Générale du Royaume (AGR), Brussels

Records of the Service Patriotique (1914–1918), Corps d'Observation Anglais; P207-P224

Bibliothèque Marguerite Durand (BMD), Paris

Dossiers:
espionnes
Louise de Bettignies
Gabrielle Petit
Marthe Richard

Churchill College Archives, Cambridge (CCAC)

Collections:
Penelope Fitzgerald and Professor W. H. Bruford (MISC 20)
Lt. Col. Adrian Grant-Duff (AGDF)
Sir James Wycliffe Headlam-Morley (HDLM)
Alastair G. Denniston (DENN)

Consignia Post Office Heritage Centre (CPOHC), London

POST 56/57 Lt. Col. A. S. L. Farquharson. "Report on Postal Censorship during the Great War (1914–1919)." (31 March 1920).
The London Censorship, 1914–1919 by Members of the Staff, Past and Present. Printed for private circulation 1919. 7/10a.

Imperial War Museum (IWM), Department of Documents, London

Collections:
IWM 78/51/1 Miss M. B. Foote
IWM 79/50/1 Sir Ivone Kirkpatrick

IWM 87/26/1 Miss R. A. Neal
IWM 92/22/1 Mrs. D. B. G. Line (née Dimmock)
IWM 93/22/1 Miss J. H. Gifford Diary
IWM 95/14/1 Miss Florence Rees
IWM 96/32/1 Mrs. B. de Quidt
IWM MISC 29, Item 522 Anonymous woman's diary 1914
IWM P355 Daisy Williams Diary
IWM P472, Miss Winifred L. B. Tower's journal
IWM PP/MCR/120 Sir Vernon Kell Papers
IWM La Dame Blanche papers (2 boxes)

Intelligence Corps Museum, Chicksands

Bosworth Papers 343 [photocopied by Jim Beach]

Salle Ulysse Capitaine, Central Library, Lège

Madame Jeanne Goeseels, *La Dame Blanche: Organe mensuel de la fraternelle Walthère Dewé* 2:17 (October 1948).

National Archives and Records Administration (NARA), College Park, MD

G-2-B Counterespionage Reports, Entry 195; Records of the AEF (WWI), Record Group 120

Public Record Office (PRO), Kew Gardens, NY

CAB 16/232
CO/850/212/4 Marriage Bar in the Civil Service Reports
CRIM 1/176/1 Martha Earle Case
DPP 1/28 Maud Gould Case
DPP 1/32 *REX v. A Female Spy*, 18–19 January 1916
HO 45/10756/267450 Spies in England and the Spy Peril
HO 45/10785/291742 Aylesbury—Women Internees
HO 45/10787/298199 Mistreatment of German Women
HO 45/10946/266042
HO 45/10947/266042
HO 45/11005/260251 Treatment of Destitute Aliens
HO 45/267603 Aliens and Prisons
HO 144/1172
HW 3/6, W. F. Clarke papers
KV 1/1–1/70, MI5 Historical Reports

KV 2/2 Mata Hari MI5(G) Records
NATS 1/1267 Woman Power in the United Kingdom—Policy File
RECO 1/885 Ministry of Reconstruction. *Report of the Women's Employment Committee.* London: HMSO, 1919.
WO 32/10776 Maj. Gen. W. Thwaites (DMI). "Historical Sketch of the Directorate of Military Intelligence during the Great War, 1914–1919."
WO 106/45 Lt. Col. R. J. Drake. "History of Intelligence (B), B. E. F., France, from January 1917–April 1919."
WO 106/6083 Lt. Col. William R. V. Isaac. "The History of the Development of the Directorate of Military Intelligence, the War Office 1855–1939."
WO 106/6192
WO 141/3/1 Case of Lizzie Wertheim and Reginald Rowland

NEWSPAPERS AND PERIODICALS

Les Annales Politiques et Litteraires (France)
The Daily Telegraph (U. K.)
The Guardian (U. K.)
The Independent (U. K.)
The Kansas City Star (U.S.)
La Liberté (Belgium)
The Living Age (U.S.)
Le Monde (France)
Moniteur (Belgium)
The New York Times
The Observer (U. K.)
Paris-Midi (France)
Punch (U. K.)
Le Soir (France)
The Statesman (India)
Sunday Telegraph (U. K.)
Sunday Times (U. K.)
Times (U. K.)
U.S. News & World Report

PUBLISHED BOOKS AND ARTICLES

Anderson, Gregory, ed. *The White Blouse Revolution: Female Office Workers since 1870.* Manchester: Manchester University Press, 1988.
Anderson, Olive. "The Growth of Christian Militarism in Mid- Victorian Britain," *English Historical Review* 86 (January 1971): 46–72.

Andrew, Christopher. *Her Majesty's Secret Service: The Making of the British Intelligence Community.* New York: Viking, 1986.

———. *Secret Service: The Making of the British Intelligence Community.* London: Heinemann, 1985.

Aston, Sir George. *Secret Service.* New York: Cosmopolitan, 1930.

Audoin-Rouzeau, Stéphane. *L'Enfant de l'ennemi, 1914–1918.* Paris: Aubier, 1995.

———. *Men at War 1914–1918: National Sentiment and Trench in France during the First World War.* Helen McPhail, trans. Oxford: Berg, 1992.

Baden-Powell, Robert. *Aids to Scouting for N.C.O.s and Men* London: Gale & Polden, 1914.

Bagilhole, Barbara. *Women, Work, and Equal Opportunity: Underachievement in the Civil Service.* Aldershot: Avebury, 1994.

Baldwin, M. Page. "Subject to Empire: Married Women and the British Nationality and Status of Aliens Act," *Journal of British Studies* 40 (October 2001): 522–556.

Bardanne, Jean. *Mlle. Doktor contre la France.* Paris: Éditions Baudinière, 1933.

Bayly, C. A. *Empire and Information: Intelligence Gathering and Social Communication in India, 1780–1870.* Cambridge: Cambridge University Press, 1996.

Becker, Annette. *Les Monuments aux Morts: Patrimoine et Memoire de la Grande Guerre.* Paris: Éditions Errance, 1988.

———. *Oubliés de la grande guerre.* Paris: Éditions Noêsis, 1998.

———. "Tortured and Exalted by War: French Catholic Women, 1914–1918." In *Women and War in the Twentieth Century: Enlisted with or without Consent.* Nicole Dombrowski, trans., ed. New York: Garland, 1999.

———. *War and Faith: The Religious Imagination in France, 1914–1930.* Helen McPhail, trans. Oxford: Berg, 1998.

Beddoe, Deirdre. *Back to Home and Duty: Women between the Wars 1918–1939.* New York: HarperCollins, 1998.

Beesley, Patrick. *Room 40: British Naval Intelligence 1914–1918.* London: Hamish Hamilton, 1982.

Bernard, Henri. *Un géant de la résistance: Walthère Déwe.* Belgium: La Renaissance du Livre, 1971.

Berndorff, H. R. *Espionage!* New York: D. Appleton, 1930.

Birkett, Dea. *Spinsters Abroad: Victorian Lady Explorers.* New York: Dorset Press, 1989.

Blom, Ida, Karen Hagemann, and Catherine Hall, eds. *Gendered Nations: Nationalism and Gender Order in the Long Nineteenth Century.* Oxford: Berg, 2000.

Blunt, Alison. "Embodying War: British Women and Domestic Defilement in the Indian 'Mutiny', 1857–1858," *Journal of Historical Geography* 26:3 (2000): 403–428.

Boucard, Robert. *Les femmes et l'espionnage*. Paris: Les Editions Documentaires, 1929.

Bourke, Joanna. *Dismembering the Male: Men's Bodies, Britain, and the Great War*. Chicago: University of Chicago Press, 1996.

———. *An Intimate History of Killing: Face-to-face Killing in Twentieth-Century Warfare*. New York: Basic Books, 1999.

Bradford, Helen. "Regendering Afrikanerdom: The 1899–1902 Anglo- Boer War." In *Gendered Nations: Nationalism and Gender Order in the Long Nineteenth Century*. Ida Blom, Karen Hagemann, and Catherine Hall, eds. Oxford: Berg, 2000.

Braybon, Gail. "Women and the War." In *The First World War in British History*. Stephen Constantine, Maurice W. Kirby, and Mary B. Rose, eds. London: Edward Arnold, 1995.

———. *Women Workers in the First World War*. Totowa, NJ: Croom Helm, 1981.

Brimelow, Elizabeth. "Women in the Civil Service." *Public Administration* LIX (1981): 313–335.

Brownmiller, Susan. *Against Our Will: Men, Women, and Rape*. New York: Simon & Schuster, 1975.

Buchan, John. *Greenmantle*. London: Thomas Nelson & Sons, 1916.

Cannan, May Wedderburn. *Grey Ghosts and Voices*. Kineton, U. K.: Roundwood Press, 1976.

Carlton, Charles, ed. *State, Sovereigns, and Society in Early Modern England: Essays in Honour of A. J. Slavin*. New York: St. Martin's Press, 1998.

Carney, Michael. *Stoker: The Life of Hilda Matheson, OBE 1888–1940*. Published by author, 1999.

Celarié, Henriette. *En Esclavage: Journal de Deux Déportées*. Paris: Bloud et Gay, 1917. In *Lines of Fire: Women Writers of World War I*. Margaret Higonnet, ed. New York: Plume Books, 1999.

Chase, Karen, and Michael Levenson. *The Spectacle of Intimacy: A Public Life for the Victorian Family*. Princeton: Princeton University Press, 2000.

Cherpak, Evelyn M. "The Participation of Women in the Wars for Independence in Northern South America, 1810–1824." *Minerva: Quarterly Report on Women and the Military* 11 (31 December 1993); [GenderWatch database].

Clayton, Aileen. *The Enemy Is Listening*. London, Hutchinson, 1980.

Colley, Linda. *Britons: Forging the Nation, 1707–1837*. New Haven: Yale University Press, 1994.

Constantine, Stephen, Maurice W. Kirby, and Mary B. Rose, eds. *The First World War in British History*. London: Edward Arnold, 1995.

Cookridge, E. H. *Sisters of Delilah: Stories of Famous Women Spies*. London: Oldbourne, 1959.

Coulson, Maj. Thomas. *The Queen of Spies: Louise de Bettignies*. London: Constable, 1935.

Coveny, C. David. "Intrigue." *Military History* 16:1 (April 1999), 22–24.

Crim, Brian. "Silent Partners: Women and Warfare in Early Modern Europe." In *A Soldier and a Woman: Sexual Integration in the Military*. Gerard De Groot and Corinna Peniston-Bird, eds. Essex, U. K.: Pearson, 2000.

Culleton, Claire A. *Working-Class Culture, Women, and Britain, 1914–1921*. New York: St. Martin's Press, 1999.

Cunningham, Hugh. *The Volunteer Force: A Social and Political History, 1859–1908*. London: Croom Helm, 1975.

Daniel, Ute. *The War from Within: German Working-Class Women in the First World War*. Margaret Ries, trans. Oxford: Berg, 1997.

Darrow, Margaret. *French Women and the First World War: War Stories of the Home Front*. Oxford: Berg, 2000.

Davies, Philip H. J. *The British Secret Services*. New Brunswick, NJ: Transaction, 1996.

Davin, Anna. "Imperialism and Motherhood." *History Workshop Journal* 5 (1978): 9–65.

Deacon, Richard. *British Secret Service*. London: Grafton, 1991.

———. *A History of the British Secret Service*. London: Frederick Muller, 1969.

Debruyne, Emmanuel. "Services de Reseignements et Société: Le Cas du Réseau Tégal, 1940–1944," *Cahiers d'Histoir du Temps Present* 9 (novembre 2001): 105–152.

Decock, P. "La Dame Blanche: un réseau de renseignements de la grande guerre 1916–1918." Ph.D. thesis, Histoire Contemporaire, Université Libre de Bruxelles, 1981. [CEGES, TH 183 Brussels]

de Cröy, Marie. *Souvenirs de la Princesse Marie de Cröy 1914–1918*. Paris: Librairie Plon, 1933.

De Groot, Gerard J. *Blighty: British Society in the Era of the Great War*. London: Longman, 1996.

De Groot, Gerard J., and Corinna Peniston-Bird, eds. *A Soldier and a Woman: Sexual Integration in the Military*. Essex, U. K.: Pearson, 2000.

Deloge, Arthur. *Gabrielle Petit: sa vie et son oeuvre*. Bruxelles: Vve Ferdinand Larcier, 1922.

Denniston, R. A. "The Professional Career of A. G. Denniston." In *British and American Approaches to Intelligence*. K. G. Robertson, ed. New York: St. Martin's Press, 1987.

Deruyk, René. *1914–1918, Lille Dans les Serres Allemandes*. Lille: La Voix du Nord, 1992.

———. *Louise de Bettignies résistante lilloise, 1880–1918*. Lille: La Voix du Nord, 1998.

de Schaepdrijver, Sophie. "Deux Patries: La Belgique entre exaltation et rejet, 1914–1918," *Cahiers d'Histoire du Temps Présent* 7 (mai 2000): 17–49.

Deslandes, Paul R. "'The Foreign Element': Newcomers and the Rhetoric of Race, Nation, and Empire in 'Oxbridge' Undergraduate Culture, 1850–1920." *Journal of British Studies* 37 (January 1998): 54–90.

Dijkstra, Bram. *Idols of Perversity: Fantasies of Feminine Evil in Fin-de-Siècle Culture.* New York: Oxford University Press, 1986.

Dohrn, Susanne. "Pioneers in a Dead-End Profession: The First Women Clerks in Banks and Insurance Companies." In *The White-Blouse Revolution: Female Office Workers since 1870.* Gregory Anderson, ed. Manchester: Manchester University Press, 1988.

Dombrowski, Nicole, ed. *Women and War in the Twentieth Century: Enlisted With or Without Consent.* New York: Garland, 1999.

Downs, Laura Lee. *Manufacturing Inequality: Gender Division in the French and British Metalworking Industries, 1914–1939.* Ithaca: Cornell University Press, 1995.

Dubesset, Mathilde, Françoise Thébaud, and Catherine Vincent, "The Female Munition Workers of the Seine." In *The French Home Front 1914–1918.* Patrick Fridenson, ed. Oxford: Berg, 1992.

Dulles, Allen. *The Craft of Intelligence.* New York: Harper & Row, 1965.

Dwork, Deborah. *War Is Good for Babies and Other Young Children: A History of the Infant and Child Welfare Movement in England, 1898–1918.* London: Tavistock, 1987.

Dworkin, Andrea. *Intercourse.* New York: Free Press, 1987.

E.7. *Women Spies I Have Known.* London: Hurst & Blackett, 1939.

Eby, Cecil Degrotte. *The Road to Armageddon: The Martial Spirit in English Popular Literature, 1870–1914.* Durham: Duke University Press, 1987.

Enloe, Cynthia. *Maneuvers: The International Politics of Militarizing Women's Lives.* Berkeley: University of California Press, 2000.

Escott, Beryl E. *Mission Improbable: A Salute to the RAF Women of SOE in Wartime France.* Wellingborough, U. K.: Stephens, 1991.

Evans, Dorothy. *Women and the Civil Service.* London: Sir Isaac Pitman & Sons, 1934.

Evergates, Theodore, ed. *Aristocratic Women in Medieval France.* Philadelphia: University of Pennsylvania Press, 1999.

Everitt, Nicholas. *British Secret Service during the Great War.* London: Hutchinson, 1920.

Ewan, Elizabeth, and Maureen M. Meikle, eds. *Women in Scotland: c.1100–c.1750.* East Linton, U. K.: Tuckwell Press, 1999.

Feldman, David. "The Importance of Being English: Jewish Immigration and the Decay of Liberal England." In *Metropolis London: Histories and Representations since 1800.* David Feldman and Gareth Stedman Jones, eds. London: Routledge, 1989.

Felstead, Sidney T. *German Spies at Bay*. London: Hutchinson, 1920.

Ferguson, Niall. *The Pity of War*. New York: Basic Books, 1999.

Fergusson, Thomas G. *British Military Intelligence, 1870–1914: The Development of a Modern Intelligence Organization*. Frederick, MD: University Publications of America, 1984.

Fitzgerald, Penelope. *The Knox Brothers*. New York: Coward, McCann & Geoghegan, 1977.

François, Aurore, and Frédéric Vesentini, "Essai sur l'origine des massacres du mois d'août 1914 à Tamines et à Dinant," *Cahiers d'Histoire du Temps Présent* 7 (mai 2000): 51–82.

Fraser, W. Lionel. *All to the Good*. London: Heinemann, 1963.

French, David. "Sir John French's Secret Service on the Western Front, 1914–1915," *The Journal of Strategic Studies* 7:4 (1984): 423–440.

———. "Spy Fever in Britain, 1900–1915," *The Historical Journal* 21:2 (1978): 355–370.

Fridenson, Patrick. *The French Home Front 1914–1918*. Oxford: Berg, 1992.

Gérard, Isabelle. *Sept Dames de Qualité: De Mémoire de Femmes Belges*. Bruxelles: J. M. Collet, 1982.

Gilbert, Sandra M. "Soldier's Heart: Literary Men, Literary Women, and the Great War." In *Behind the Lines: Gender and the Two World Wars*. Margaret Higonnet et al, eds. New Haven: Yale University Press, 1987.

Gleeson, James. *They Feared No Evil: The Women Agents of Britain's Secret Armies, 1939–1945*. London: Corgi, 1976.

Goodman, Susan. *Gertrude Bell*. Heidelberg, Germany: Berg, 1985.

Gould, Jenny. "Women's Military Services in First World War Britain." In *Behind the Lines: Gender and the Two World Wars*. Margaret Higonnet et al., eds. New Haven: Yale University Press, 1987.

Grant, Hamil. *Spies and Secret Service: The Story of Espionage, its Main Systems and Chief Exponents*. New York: Frederick A. Stokes, 1915.

Grayzel, Susan R. "The Enemy Within: The Problem of British Women's Sexuality during the First World War." In *Women and War in the Twentieth Century: Enlisted with or without Consent*. Nicole Dombrowski, ed. New York: Garland, 1999.

———. *Women's Identities at War: Gender, Motherhood, and Politics in Britain and France during the First World War*. Chapel Hill: University of North Carolina Press, 1999.

Grossman, Atina. *Reforming Sex: The German Movement for Birth Control and Abortion Reform, 1920–1950*. Oxford: Oxford University Press, 1995.

Hampshire, James. "Spy Fever in Britain, 1900–1914," *The Historian* 72 (Winter 2001): 22–27.

Hardy, Adolphe. *L'Ardenne heroique*. Bruxelles: Association des Ecrivains Belges, 1920.

Harris, Barbara. *English Aristocratic Women, 1450–1550: Marriage and Family, Property and Careers*. New York: Oxford University Press, 2002.

Harris, Ruth. "The 'Child of the Barbarian': Rape, Race, and Nationalism in France during the First World War," *Past and Present* 141 (November 1993): 170–206.

Harris, Stephen M. *British Military Intelligence in the Crimean War, 1854–1856*. London: Frank Cass, 1999.

Haste, Cate. *Keep the Home Fires Burning: Propaganda in the First World War*. London: Allen Lane, 1977.

Haswell, Jock. *Spies and Spymasters: A Concise History of Intelligence*. London: Thames & Hudson, 1977.

Hickman, Katie. *Daughters of Britannia: The Lives and Times of Diplomatic Wives*. New York: William Morrow, 1999.

Higgs, Edward. "Victorian Spies," *History Workshop Journal* 53 (Spring 2002): 232–235.

Higonnet, Margaret R., ed. *Lines of Fire: Women Writers of World War I*. New York: Plume Books, 1999.

Higonnet, Margaret et al., eds. *Behind the Lines: Gender and the Two World Wars*. New Haven: Yale University Press, 1987.

Hiley, Nicholas. "Counter-Espionage and Security in Great Britain during the First World War," *English Historical Review* 101:400 (July 1986): 635–661.

———. "Decoding German Spies: British Spy Fiction 1908–1918," *Intelligence and National Security* 5:4 (October 1990): 55–79.

———. "The Play, the Parody, the Censor, and the Film," *Intelligence and National Security* 6:1 (1991): 222.

Hirschfeld, Magnus. *The Sexual History of the World War*. New York: Panurge Press, 1934.

Hoare, Philip. *Oscar Wilde's Last Stand: Decadence, Conspiracy, and the First World War*. London: Duckworth, 1997.

Hoehling, A. A. *A Whisper of Eternity: The Mystery of Edith Cavell*. New York: Thomas Yoseloff, 1957.

———. *Women Who Spied*. Lanham, MD: Madison Books, 1993.

Horne, John, and Alan Kramer. *German Atrocities 1914: A History of Denial*. New Haven: Yale University Press, 2001.

Howarth, Patrick. *Undercover: The Men and Women of the Special Operations Executive*. London: Routledge, 1980.

Hutton, J. Bernard. *Women Spies*. London: W. H. Allen, 1971.

Hynes, Samuel. *A War Imagined: The First World War and English Culture*. New York: Atheneum, 1990.

"In Memoriam." *Intelligence and National Security* 13:2 (summer 1998): 213–214.

Ind, Allison. *A History of Modern Espionage*. London: Hodder & Stoughton, 1965.

Jeal, Tim. *The Boy-Man: The Life of Lord Baden-Powell.* New York: William Morrow, 1990.

Jeffery, Keith. "British Military Intelligence Following World War I." In *British and American Approaches to Intelligence.* K. G. Robertson, ed. New York: St. Martin's Press, 1987.

Jenssen, Baroness Carla. *I Spy: Sensational Disclosures of a British Secret Service Agent.* London: Jarrolds, 1930.

Jones, Liane. *A Quiet Courage.* London: Bantam, 1990.

Judd, Alan. *The Quest for 'C': Sir Mansfield Smith Cumming and the Founding of the British Secret Service.* London: HarperCollins, 1999.

Judson, Helen. *Edith Cavell.* New York: Macmillan, 1941.

Keegan, John. *The First World War.* New York: Vintage, 1998.

Kennedy, Kathleen. *Disloyal Mothers and Scurrilous Citizens: Women and Subversion during World War I.* Bloomington: Indiana University Press, 1999.

Kent, Susan Kingsley. *Gender and Power in Britain, 1640–1990.* London: Routledge, 1999.

———. *Making Peace: The Reconstruction of Gender in Interwar Britain.* Princeton: Princeton University Press, 1993.

Knightley, Phillip. *The Second Oldest Profession: Spies and Spying in the Twentieth Century.* New York: W. W. Norton, 1987.

Kramer, Rita. *Flames in the Field: The Story of Four SOE Agents in Occupied France.* London: Michael Joseph, 1995.

Krebs, Paula. "'Last of the Gentleman's Wars': Women in the Boer War Concentration Camp Controversy," *History Workshop Journal* 33 (1992): 38–56.

Krop, Pascal. *Les Secrets de l'espionnage français de 1870 à nos jours.* France: Éditions Jean-Claude Lattès, 1993.

Ladoux, Georges. *Marthe Richard the Skylark: The Foremost Woman Spy of France.* Warrington Dawson, trans., ed. London: Cassell, 1932.

Landau, Henry. *All's Fair: The Story of the British Secret Service behind the German Lines.* New York: G. P. Putnam's Sons, 1934.

———. *Secrets of the White Lady.* New York: G. P. Putnam's Sons, 1935.

Ledger, Sally. "The New Woman and the Crisis of Victorianism." In *Cultural Politics at the Fin de Siècle.* Sally Ledger and Scott McCracken, eds. Cambridge: Cambridge University Press, 1995.

Lee, Stephen J. *Aspects of British Political History, 1815–1914.* London: Routledge, 1994.

Leveque, Andre. "Le 'Spectre en Femme Voilee' dans le Dom Juan de Moliere," *Modern Language Notes* 76:8 (December 1961): 746.

Lewis, Jane. "Women Clerical Workers in the Late Nighteenth and Early Twentieth Centuries." In *The White-Blouse Revolution: Female Office Workers since 1870.* Gregory Anderson, ed. Manchester: Manchester University Press, 1988.

Lockhart, John Bruce. "Intelligence: A British View." In *British and American Approaches to Intelligence*, K. G. Robertson, ed. New York: St. Martin's Press, 1987.

Low, Rachael. *The History of the British Film 1914–1918*. London: Allen & Unwin, 1973.

Lowry, Donald. "Introduction: Not Just a 'Teatime War.'" In *The South African War Reappraised*. Donald Lowry, ed. Manchester: Manchester University Press, 2000.

Ludecke, Winfried. *Behind the Scenes of Espionage: Tales of the Secret Service*. London: George G. Harrap, 1929.

Macintyre, Ben. *The Englishman's Daughter: A True Story of Love and Betrayal in World War I*. New York: Farrar, Straus and Giroux, 2001.

MacIvor, Arthur J. *A History of Work in Britain, 1880–1950*. New York: Palgrave, 2001.

Mackenzie, Compton. *Greek Memories*. Frederick, MD: University Publications of America, 1987.

Mackenzie, John, ed. *Popular Imperialism and the Military*. Manchester: Manchester University Press, 1992.

MacKinnon, Catharine. *Toward a Feminist Theory of the State*. Cambridge: Harvard University Press, 1989.

Mahoney, M. H. *Women in Espionage: A Biographical Dictionary*. Santa Barbara: ABC-CLIO, 1993.

Mark, Graham. *British Censorship of the Civil Mails during World War I, 1914–1919*. Bristol, U. K.: Stuart Rossiter Trust Fund, 2000.

Marshall, Alan. *Intelligence and Espionage in the Reign of Charles II, 1660–1685*. Cambridge: Cambridge University Press, 1994.

Martindale, Hilda. *Women Servants of the State, 1870–1938*. London: Allen & Unwin, 1938.

Marwick, Arthur. *The Deluge: British Society and the First World War*. New York: W. W. Norton, 1965.

Marx, Karl. "The Eighteenth Brumaire of Louis Bonaparte." In *The Marx-Engels Reader*. Robert C. Tucker, ed. 2nd ed. New York: W. W. Norton, 1978.

Massard, Emile. *Les Espionnes à Paris*. Paris: Albin Michel, 1922.

Matheson, Mrs. Donald. *Hilda Matheson*. Letchworth, U. K.: Hogarth Press, 1941.

McIntosh, Elizabeth. *The Role of Women in Intelligence*. McLean, VA: Association of Former Intelligence Officers, 1989.

McKenna, Marthe. *I Was a Spy!* New York: Robert M. McBride, 1933.

McPhail, Helen. *The Long Silence: Civilian Life under the German Occupation of Northern France, 1914–1918*. London: I. B. Taurus, 2001.

Medd, Jodie. "'The Cult of the Clitoris': Anatomy of a National Scandal," *Modernism/Modernity* 9:1 (2002): 21–49.

Mendelson, Sara, and Patricia Crawford. *Women in Early Modern England 1550–1720*. New York: Oxford University Press, 1998.

Mersey (2nd Viscount), Viscount. *A Picture of Life, 1872–1940*. London: John Murray, 1941.

Messinger, Gary S. *British Propaganda and the State in the First World War*. Manchester: Manchester University Press, 1992.

Miller, Michael. *Shanghai on the Metro: Spies, Intrigue, and the French between the Wars*. Berkeley: University of California Press, 1994.

Miller, Nathan. *Spying for America: The Hidden History of U.S. Intelligence*. New York: Paragon House, 1989.

Moorehead, Lucy, ed. *Freya Stark Letters: The Furnace and the Cup, 1914–1930*. Vol. 1. Salisbury, U. K.: Compton Russell, 1974.

Moriaud, Gem. *Louise de Bettignies: Une heroine Française*. Paris: Jules Tallandier, 1928.

Morris, A. J. A. *The Scaremongers: The Advocacy of War and Rearmament 1896–1914*. London: Routledge and Kegan Paul, 1984.

Mosse, George L. *The Image of Man: The Creation of Modern Masculinity*. New York: Oxford University Press, 1996.

Muir, Rory. *Tactics and the Experience of Battle in the Age of Napoleon*. New Haven: Yale University Press, 1998.

Nasson, Bill. *The South African War 1899–1902*. New York: Oxford University Press, 1999.

Occleshaw, Michael. *Armour against Fate: British Military Intelligence in the First World War*. London: Columbus Books, 1989.

O'Donnell, Mary Ann. *Aphra Behn: An Annotated Bibliography of Primary and Secondary Sources*. New York: Garland, 1986.

Offenstadt, Nicholas. *Les Fusillés de la Grande Guerre et la Memoire Collective, 1914–1999*. Paris: Éditions Odile Jacob, 1999.

Panayi, Panikos. *The Enemy in Our Midst: Germans in Britain during the First World War*. Oxford: Berg, 1991.

Parritt, B. A. H. *The Intelligencers: The Story of British Military Intelligence up to 1914*. Ashford, U. K.: Intelligence Corps Association, 1983.

Péan, Pierre. *La diabolique Caluire*. Paris: Fayard, 1999.

Pickles, Katie. "Edith Cavell—Heroine, No Hatred or Bitterness for Anyone?" *History Now* 3:2 (1997): 1–8.

Poovey, Mary. *Uneven Developments: The Ideological Work of Gender in Mid-Victorian England*. Chicago: University of Chicago Press, 1988.

Porch, Douglas. *The French Secret Service: From the Dreyfus Affair to the Gulf War*. New York: Farrar, Straus, and Giroux, 1995.

Porter, Bernard. *Plots and Paranoia: A History of Political Espionage in Britain, 1790–1988*. London: Routledge, 1992.

Proctor, Tammy. "Gender, Generation, and the Politics of Guiding and Scouting in Interwar Britain." Ph.D. diss. Rutgers University, 1995.

Prost, Antoine. *In the Wake of War: "Les anciens combattants" and French Society.* Helen McPhail, trans. Oxford: Berg, 1992.

Purves, Alec. *The Medals, Decorations, and Orders of the Great War, 1914–1918.* 2d ed. Polstead, Suffolk, U. K.: J. B. Hayward & Son, 1989.

Reader, W. J. *At Duty's Call: A Study in Obsolete Patriotism.* Manchester: Manchester University Press, 1988.

Redier, Antoine. *La Guerre des Femmes: Histoire de Louise de Bettignies et de ses Compagnes.* Paris: Éditions de la Vraie France, 1924.

——. *The Story of Louise de Bettignies.* Olive Hall, trans. London: Hutchinson, 1926.

Rees, John. "'The Multitude of Women': An Examination of the Numbers of Camp Followers with the Continental Army." *Minerva: Quarterly Report on Women and the Military* 14:2 (30 June 1996); [GenderWatch database].

Richer, Marthe. *I Spied for France.* Gerald Griffin, trans. London: John Long, 1935.

Rimington, Stella. *Open Secret: The Autobiography of the Former Director-General of MI5.* London: Hutchinson, 2001.

Roberts, Mary Louise. *Civilization without Sexes: Reconstructing Gender in Postwar France, 1917–1927.* Chicago: University of Chicago Press, 1994.

Robertson, K. G., ed. *British and American Approaches to Intelligence.* New York: St. Martin's Press, 1987.

Rocker, Rudolf. *The London Years.* London: Robert Anscombe, 1956.

Rowan, Richard Wilmer. *Secret Service: Thirty-Three Centuries of Espionage.* New York: Hawthorn Books, 1967.

Ryder, Rowland. *Edith Cavell.* New York: Stein and Day, 1975.

Saville, John. "Imperialism and the Victorians." In *In Search of Victorian Values.* Eric Sigsworth, ed. Manchester: Manchester University Press, 1988.

Scharff, Virginia. *Taking the Wheel: Women and the Coming of the Motor Age.* New York: The Free Press, 1991.

Schirmann, Leon. *L'Affaire Mata Hari: Enquête sur une Machination.* Paris: Tallandier, 1994.

Schmitt, Cannon. *Alien Nation: Nineteenth-Century Gothic Fictions and English Nationality.* Philadelphia: University of Pennsylvania Press, 1997.

Schmitz, Christopher. "'We Too Were Soldiers': The Experiences of British Nurses in the Anglo-Boer War, 1899–1902." In De Groot and Peniston-Bird, eds., Essex, U.K: Pearson, 2000.

Scraps of Paper: German Proclamations in Belgium and France. London: Hodder & Stoughton, 1916.

Sigsworth, Eric, ed. *In Search of Victorian Values.* Manchester: Manchester University Press, 1988.

Simonton, Deborah. *A History of European Women's Work, 1700 to the Present.* London: Routledge, 1998.

Singer, Kurt. *The World's Greatest Women Spies.* London: W. H. Allen, 1951.

Sparrow, Elizabeth. *Secret Service: British Agents in France, 1792–1815.* Woodbridge, U. K.: The Boydell Press, 1999.

Spiers, Edward M. *The Late Victorian Army, 1868–1902.* Manchester: Manchester University Press, 1992.

Spies, S. B. *Methods of Barbarism? Roberts and Kitchener and Civilians in the Boer Republics, June 1900–May 1902.* Cape Town: Human & Rousseau, 1977.

Stafford, David. "Spies and Gentlemen: The Birth of the British Spy Novel, 1893–1914." *Victorian Studies* 24 (1981): 489–509.

Stark, Freya. *Traveller's Prelude.* London: John Murray, 1950.

Stibbe, Matthew. *German Anglophobia and the Great War, 1914–1918.* Cambridge: Cambridge University Press, 2001.

Strachan, Hew. *The First World War.* Vol. I. Oxford: Oxford University Press, 2001.

Summers, Anne. *Angels and Citizens: British Women as Military Nurses.* London: Routledge and Kegan Paul, 1988.

Tabili, Laura. "The Construction of Racial Difference in Twentieth-Century Britain: The Special Restriction (Coloured Alien Seamen) Order, 1925." *Journal of British Studies* 33 (January 1994): 54–98.

Terwey, Susanne. "Juden sind keine Deutschen! Über antisemitische Stereotpye um Juden und Deutschland in Großbritannien vor und während des Ersten Weltkrieges und die jüdishe Abwehr." *Sachor* 11 (2001): 41–62.

Theweleit, Klaus. *Male Fantasies, Volume 1: Women Floods Bodies History.* Stephen Conway, trans. Minneapolis: University of Minnesota Press, 1987.

Thom, Deborah. *Nice Girls and Rude Girls: Women Workers in World War I.* London: I. B. Taurus, 1998.

Thomas, Rosamund. *Espionage and Secrecy: The Official Secrets Acts 1911–1989 of the United Kingdom.* London: Routledge, 1991.

Thuliez, Louise. *Condemned to Death.* Marie Poett-Velitchko, trans. London: Methuen, 1934.

Todd, Janet. *The Secret Life of Aphra Behn.* New Brunswick, NJ: Rutgers University Press, 1997.

Toye, Francis. *For What We Have Received: An Autobiography.* New York: Alfred A. Knopf, 1948.

Trotter, David. "The Politics of Adventure in the Early British Spy Novel," *Intelligence and National Security* 5:4 (October 1990): 30–54.

Tucker, Robert C., ed. *The Marx-Engels Reader.* 2nd ed. New York: W. W. Norton, 1978.

Van Seters, Deborah. "'Hardly Hollywood's Ideal': Feamle Autobiographies of Secret Service Work," *Intelligence and National Security* 7:4 (1992): 403–424.

Van Tuyll van Serooskerken, Hubert P. *The Netherlands and World War I: Espionage, Diplomacy, and Survival.* Boston: Brill, 2001.

Vickery, Amanda, ed. *Women, Privilege, and Power: British Politics, 1750 to the Present.* Stanford: Stanford University Press, 2001.

Walker, Pamela. *Pulling the Devil's Kingdom Down: The Salvation Army in Victorian Britain.* Berkeley: University of California Press, 2001.

Wallach, Janet. *Desert Queen: The Extraordinary Life of Gertrude Bell: Adventurer, Advisor to Kings, Ally of Lawrence of Arabia.* New York: Nan A. Talese/Doubleday, 1996.

Wheelwright, Julie. *The Fatal Lover: Mata Hari and the Myth of Women in Espionage.* London: Collins & Brown, 1992.

———. "Poisoned Honey: The Myth of Women in Espionage," *Queen's Quarterly* 100:2 (Summer 1993): 291–309.

Williams, David G. T. *Not in the Public Interest: The Problem of Security in Democracy.* London: Hutchinson, 1965.

Williams, John W. "The Films of 'Fraulein Doktor.'" First published in *Foreign Intelligence Literary Scene*, accessed via Principia College website.

Winstone, H. V. F. *The Illicit Adventure.* London: Jonathan Cape, 1982.

Wodehouse, P. G. *The Swoop! Or How Clarence Saved England, A Tale of the Great Invasion.* London: Alston Rivers, 1909.

Woodhall, Edwin. *Spies of the Great War.* London: Mellifont Press, 1939.

Woollacott, Angela. *On Her Their Lives Depend: Munitions Workers in the Great War.* Berkeley: University of California Press, 1994.

Zeiger, Susan. *In Uncle Sam's Service: Women Workers with the American Expeditionary Force.* Ithaca: Cornell University Press, 2000.

Zimmeck, Meta. "Strategies and Stratagems for the Employment of Women in the British Civil Service, 1919–1939," *Historical Journal* 27:4 (1984): 901–924.

Index

Admiralty, 13, 23, 27, 54 56, 62; Foreign Intelligence Committee (FIC), 13; Naval Intelligence Department (NID), 13
Alien Act (1793), 11–12
aliens: alien registration, 32–33, 51; anti-alien riots, 39; anti-alien sentiment, 30, 32, 34–42, 51–52; Destitute Aliens Committee, 36; naturalization, 33; repatriation, 33
Aliens Act (1905), 22
Aliens Restriction Act (1914), 23, 32–33, 47, 51
Allan, Maud, 40–42
American Expeditionary Force, 140
American Revolution, 10, 14
Anglicized names, 33, 35, 39
Anglo-Boer War, 8, 14, 18–21, 27, 104; Field Intelligence Department, 19
anti-German sentiment, 22–23, 26, 36–39, 49–50, 161n. 34; British Empire Union (formerly anti-German Union), 38; German invasion fears, 21–22
Arab Bureau, 18
Ardagh, Sir John, 19
Army General Headquarters (GHQ), 61, 75–76, 141

Arnold family, 85 86
Aslin, M. S., 59
Asquith, Margot, 35, 41
Aston, George, 46
Astor, Lady Nancy, 69
Aylesbury Inebriate Reformatory, 33–34, 47–50

Baden-Powell, Robert, 7, 21
Balfour, Arthur, 20
Barnich family, 86
Bastin, Irene, 92
Battle of Dorking, 22
Baucq, Philippe, 101–102, 112–113, 173n. 3
Bayard, Louis, 16–17
Behn, Aphra, 9, 15–16, 156n. 42
Bell, Gertrude, 17–18, 69
Billing, Noel Pemberton, 39–42
black chambers, 9
Blanjean, Leopold, 91
Blankaert, Marguerite, 93
Bosworth, Charlotte, 61
Boy Scouts, 21, 25, 58
Bradley, Jane, 15
British Expeditionary Force (BEF), 79
British Mission in Paris, 57, 59, 61, 66, 166n. 33

British Nationality and Status of Aliens Act (BNSA)(1914), 29, 160n. 2

British Secret Service: Civil War, 9; French Revolution and Napoleonic Wars, 10–12, 16–17, 156n. 46; Intelligence Branch (IB), 12; Intelligence Division (ID), 12; Restoration, 10; Topographical and Statistical Department (T&S), 12; Tudor, 8; Victorian, 8, 12–13, 17–18, 154n. 28

Brookner, Janine, 148

Buchan, John, 149

Buckfast Abbey, 35

Cadet Corps, 21

Callow, S., 53

Cameron, Cecil, 75–76

camp followers, 14, 138

Cannan, May Wedderburn, 66

Canteen Ma, 141–142

Capiau, Hermann, 101

Cavell, Edith, 44, 110, 115, 119–121, 127, 144–145, 149; arrest and imprisonment, 102; execution, 102–105, 107–109, 112–113; illegal activities, 100–102; memorials, 108–109, 173n. 11, 176n. 52; propaganda, 102–107, 119–121

censorship, 30; cable, 2; postal, 3, 12, 45–46, 52, 55–56, 58, 61–64, 66, 69–70, 146, 154n. 21, 165n. 8; press, 2; Secret Office, 9, 11

Central Intelligence Agency (CIA), 148

Chauvin, Herman, 90

Chesney, George, 22

Childers, Erskine, 22

Churchill, Winston, 143

civil service in WWI, 53–73, 146–147; demobilization, 69–73, 146–147; marriage bar, 73, 168n. 82; numbers, 65, 70–71; qualifications, 65–68; working conditions and wages, 55–56, 61–65, 72–73

Clarence, 96, 147

Clayton, Aileen Morris, 147

Cold War, 2, 4

Collard family, 87

commemoration, 96–98, 107, 113–116, 118, 120

Commission for Relief in Belgium (CRB), 137–138

Committee of Imperial Defence, 20, 23, 27

Congress of Vienna (1815), 12

conscription, 54, 81, 104

Constant, J., 68

Contagious Diseases Acts, 31

Cribb, Hilda, 64, 69

Crimean War, 12–13, 154n. 24

Criminal Investigation Department (CID), 12, 35

Cromwell, Oliver, 9, 153n. 7

cryptography, 3, 147; Bletchley Park, 147; Room 40, 56–57, 59, 61–62, 67–69

Cumming, Mansfield Smith, 24

Dame Blanche, La, 76–98, 147, 169n. 5; Battalion III, 79, 81–85; families, 81, 84–89; leadership, 76–79, 81, 94, 147; letterboxes, 84, 87; militarization, 76, 79–80, 89–92, 94, 98; Platoon 49, 87–89, 92; postwar claims, 95–96; trainwatching, 76, 79–80, 83, 85–89; women, 75–98, 137, 144

de Belleville, Jeanne, 101–102, 119

de Bettignies, Louise (pseud. Alice Dubois), 5, 93, 110, 115, 117, 119–121, 144, 175n. 36

de Bournonville, Eva, 45–46, 48–49

de Croÿ, Marie, 101, 119

de Croÿ, Reginald, 101

Defence of the Realm Act (DORA) (1914), 2, 29–34, 42, 44, 47, 49, 51–52

Defoe, Daniel, 9

degeneration, 20–21, 23, 30–32, 39–42, 51–52

Deldonck, Lucelle, 141
de l'Epine, Clemie, 88
Delilah, 123, 131, 136
Delrualle, Juliette, 82
Delwaide, Jeanne, 75, 94–95
de Monge, Gabrielle, 87–88
deportation, 33–34
de Radiguès family, 87–89, 92
De Villermont family, 88
Dewé, Walthère, 90, 94, 96
Director of Military Intelligence
    (DMI), 12, 19, 52, 54, 146
Director of Military Operations
    (DMO), 20, 23, 54
Doctor, Lady (pseud. Fraulein Dok-
    tor, Mlle. Docteur), 44, 133,
    136, 144, 178n. 41
Donovan, William, 146
Douglas, Lord Alfred, 41
Dreyfus, Alfred, 15, 156n. 37
Dulles, Allen, 149

Earle, Martha, 29, 45, 48–49
Edmonds, James, 23, 44
Elizabeth I, 8–9, 153n. 6
Empire Day, 21
Eve, 123–124
Evelin, Gertrude, 47
Ewart, J. S., 23

Farquharson, A. S. L., 62, 66
female spies: in Belgium during
    WWI, 75–98, 107–118, 121; in
    Britain during WWI, 29, 30, 33,
    40–52, 146; as couriers, 16–17, 76,
    81, 84–85, 87, 111–113, 146–147,
    180n. 9; as horizontales/seduc-
    tresses, 44, 123, 146; as informants,
    14–17, 146–147; as martyrs,
    99–121, 125, 137, 144; popular im-
    ages, 3, 123–137; as travelers,
    17–18, 156n. 48
First Aid Nursing Yeomanry (FANY),
    21
Fisher, Charlotte. See Bosworth,
    Charlotte

Fleming, Ian, 145
Fox, S. F., 48
Francillard, Marguerite, 132, 177n.
    32
French Revolution, 10–11, 16–17
fusillées, 107–110

George V, 35, 104, 166n. 31
Girl Guides, vii, 1, 21, 25, 58–60,
    176n. 52
Glauer, Heddy, 45–47
Goeseels, Jeanne, 94–95
Gould, Maud, 46
Gracey, L., 68
Grandprez, Constant, 112–115
Grandprez, Elise, 112–115, 120
Grandprez, François, 112–113
Grandprez, Marie, 112–113
Grant, Hamil, 44
Greenmantle, 149
Gregoire, Andre, 113, 115
Grey, Sir Edward, 111

habeas corpus, 10–11
Haldane, R. B., 23, 41
Hall, William Reginald "Blinker,"
    56
Hambro, Lady Sybil, 61
Harmsworth, Alfred (Lord North-
    cliffe), 22
Harris, Mary, 61
Harrison, Elsie L., 60, 72
Harvey, Joan, 59
Headlam-Morley, James, 35
Heine, Lina, 45, 48
Hénin, Claire, 143, 179n. 73
Hentschel, Patricia Riley, 49–50
Herbert, Louise, 49, 104
Higgs, May, 50
Hill, Gladys, 68
Hirschfeld, Magnus, 123, 126, 130,
    136
Hogarth, David, 18
Hollings, Margery, 67
Holloway Prison, 29, 33
Hoover, Herbert, 137

I.D. 25. *See* cryptography, Room 40
Indian Mutiny-Rebellion, 12–13,
    105–106, 174n. 20
Intelligence Corps, 79
internment: Anglo-Boer War, 19–20,
    104; WWI, 33–34, 36, 38–39,
    44–45, 47–50, 160–161n. 16
Invasion of 1910, The, 22

Jenkin, May, 69
Jenkins, Elinor, 67
Joan of Arc, 99, 110, 115–116, 120–121,
    175n. 39
Judith, 125

Kalle, Arnold von, 130
Kell, Constance, 44
Kell, Vernon G. W., 24–25, 32, 42, 57, 59,
    71–72, 135, 149
Kesseler family, 84–85
King, Joseph, 34
Kipling, Rudyard, 39, 53
Knox, A. D. (Dilly), 68
Kronauer, Marie, 45

Ladoux, Georges, 131–134
Lambert, Dieudonné, 113
Landau, Henry, 76, 84–85, 91, 96, 169n. 8
Lansbury, George, 34, 47
Latouche family, 85
Lawrence, D. H., 34–35
Lawrence, T. E., 18
Lefebvre, Eglantine, 95
Le Queux, William, 21–22
Lesser, Anne Marie. *See* Doctor, Lady
    (pseud. Fraulein Doktor, Mlle. Doc-
    teur)
Libre Belgique, La, 102
Line, Mrs. D. B. G., 66–67
Lomax, Edith A., 60, 64, 72
Louis XVI, 10
Luddites, 12
Lusitania, 39

Mackenzie, Compton, 57
MacLeod, Margaretha Geertruida

Zelle (pseud. Mata Hari), 3, 107,
    125–132, 135–136, 144–145,
    148–149, 176n. 14, 176n. 15, 177n.
    23, 177n. 26
MacLeod, Rudolph, 127
Marriott, J. A., 38
Mata Hari. *See* MacLeod, Margaretha
    Geertruida Zelle
mata-haridans, 123, 131, 133
Matheson, Hilda, 68–69
McKenna, Marthe (née Cnockaert), 1,
    137–144, 172n. 67
McNeill, Eileen, 61
Mersey, Viscount, 61
MI1B, 57
MI1C, 24
MI5, vii, 24, 30, 32, 42, 44, 46–47,
    49–50, 52, 57, 164n. 1; female staff,
    53–54, 57–61, 64–72, 146–148,
    181n. 17; The Nameless Club and
    The Nameless Magazine, 53, 55,
    58–59, 71; Registry, 57–58, 64–66,
    68
MI9. *See* censorship, postal
Military Intelligence. *See* MI1C; MI5
Military Press Control, 57
Milne, Lady Claire, 61
Moonraker, 145
Morrison, Carrie, 68
Mot du Soldat, Le, 81
Murray, Joan Clarke, 147

Napoleonic Wars, 10–12, 16–17, 32
Naturalisation Act (1870), 29, 160n. 2
Neujean, Alexandre, 82
New Woman, 123, 125
Nightingale, Florence, 13, 14, 106, 145
Norwood, Melita, 146
No. 63 (female agent), 141–142

occupation: atrocity stories, 77–78,
    104–107; of Belgium and Northern
    France in WWI, 75–78, 96–98,
    100–121, 137–144; civilian resist-
    ance, 77–78, 84, 100–102, 107–121,
    137–144; women's experiences of,

76–77, 125–126, 138–144, 169n. 9,
179n. 69
Office of Strategic Services (OSS),
146–148, 181n. 14
Officer Training Corps (OTC), 21
Official Secrets Act: of 1889, 24; of
1911, 25, 32, 42

passports, 2, 33, 160n. 13
Peninsular Wars, 11
Pepys, Samuel, 9
Petit, Gabrielle, 5, 92, 99, 110, 115–118,
120–121
pigeons, 33, 138
Pitt, William, 10
Police Act, of 1792, 10
Political Intelligence Department, 35
Polkinghorne, Eleanor, 45
port controls, 2, 33
Post Office, 55–56, 69
propaganda, 78, 100, 102–107, 173n. 7
Propaganda Department, 35, 57
prostitution, 31, 51, 123–145, 148–149,
169n. 9

Quiller-Couch, Arthur, 66

Rahab, 123
Raleigh, Lucie, 66
Rameloo, Leonie, 111–112
rape, 138–140, 169n. 9
Real del Sarte, Maxime, 114, 175n. 36
Rees, Florence, 65
Richer, Marthe Betenfeld (pseud.
Martha Richard), 131–134, 177n.
30
Riddle of the Sands, The, 22
Rimington, Stella, 148
Roberts, Lord Frederick, 19, 49
Rocker, Milly, 34, 47, 161n. 20
Rocker, Rudolf, 34, 39, 161n. 20
Roddam, Olive, 68

Sablonnière, La, 17
St. Gilles prison, 102, 116
St. Lazare prison, 127

Salome, 40–42, 123, 125–126, 136
Schattemann, Emilie, 111–112
Schragmuller, Elsbeth. See Doctor,
Lady (pseud. Fraulein Doktor,
Mlle Docteur)
Scot, William, 16
Scotland Yard, 23–24, 46
secret ink, 45–46
Secret Service Bureau (1909), 1, 8,
23–25, 30, 54
Seditious Meetings Bill (1795), 11
Severin, Louis, 102
sexuality: as collaboration, 139–141;
and espionage, 39–43, 50–52,
123–137, 139–141, 148–149; homo-
sexuality, 40–41; regulation of fe-
male, 31, 33, 40–42, 179n. 69
Siegburg prison, 81, 92–95, 119–120,
179n. 73, 180n. 9
Slager, Pauline, 46
Smith, Louise von Zastrow, 45
Society for Constitutional Informa-
tion, 10
Special Branch (London Metropolitan Police), 12–13
Special Operations Executive (SOE),
147
Spies for the Kaiser, 22
spy fiction, 21–22, 25–26, 124–126,
131–132, 158n. 67
spy films, 25, 126, 131; The Crimson
Triangle (1915), 25; La Femme
Nikita (1990), 136; Fraulein Doktor
(1968), 178n. 51; From Russia With
Love (1962), 136; The German Spy
Peril (1914), 25; Guarding Britain's
Secrets (1914), 25; The Kaiser's
Spies (1914), 25; Mademoiselle Docteur (1934), 134; Mata Hari (1932),
176n. 15; Mata Hari (1964), 178n.
51; Soeur d'Armes (1937), 175n.
50; Stamboul Quest (1934), 178n.
51; You Only Live Twice (1967),
136
spy panics, 26, 30, 36–38
Stanaway, Albertine, 45–47

Stark, Freya, 63–64, 66, 69
Stewart, Jane Shaw, 13
Storch, Despina Davidovitch, 132
subversion, 12, 30, 32, 39–42, 51–52, 161n. 34
surveillance, 30, 33, 42, 51–53, 72
Swoop! The, Or How Clarence Saved England, A Tale of the Great Invasion, 25

Tandel, Laure, 81, 85
Tandel, Louise, 81
Territorial Force, 21
Thomson, Basil, 46
Thuliez, Louise, 93, 101–102, 112, 119
Tinsley, Richard Bolton, 76
Tuohy, Ferdinand, 50

Vanhoutte, Leonie (pseud. Charlotte), 117, 119, 180n. 9
Van Vlaanderen, Isidore, 112
venereal disease, 31, 33, 111, 139
Victorica, Maria, 132, 177–178n. 33

Villiers-Stuart, Eileen, 41
Volunteer Aid Detachment (VAD), 21

Wallinger, Ernest, 76, 79
Wallis, John, 9, 153n. 10
Walsingham, Sir Francis, 9, 153n. 6
War Book, 27
War Office, vii, 18–20, 23, 27, 53–55, 57, 59, 66, 71–72, 76, 78
Weimerskirch family, 87
Wellington, Duke of (Arthur Wellesley), 11
Wertheim, Louise "Lizzie," 45–46
White Lady. See *Dame Blanche, La*
Whitlock, Brand, 103–104
Wilde, Oscar, 40–41
Williams, Arabella, 16
Wodehouse, P. G., 25
Women's Army Auxiliary Corps (WAAC), 59, 91, 165n. 22
Women's Auxiliary Air Force (WAAF), 147
World War II, 2, 5, 71, 77–78, 96, 121, 146–148, 180n. 9, 181n. 14

About the Author

Tammy M. Proctor is Associate Professor and Chair of the Department of History at Wittenberg University in Springfield, Ohio. She is the author of *On My Honour: Guides and Scouts in Interwar Britain.*